EMPOWERING ASIAN YOUTH THROUGH VOLUNTEERING

This book describes the origin, development and current state of volunteerism in Asia and Hong Kong. It also presents a field-tested model of empowering through volunteerism (namely, the CYEP at City University of Hong Kong), that involves youth, non-governmental agencies, and their clients in a rapidly changing society. Volunteerism is then described as a "win-win" situation for all stakeholders/actors. Volunteerism converges the needs, the struggles, the personal motives, and the aspirations of the volunteers, together with the dreams and the difficulties of the clients, the expertise of the professionals and the (lack of) resources of the agencies, the new values emerging in society, the effects of globalization, and the new policies. This book presents actual Asian case examples with the voices of the people involved on the CYEP (volunteers, officers, service recipients) who explain how volunteering changed their lives, their values, their attitudes toward social, civic and community participation, their ethics, and sense of individual responsibility. These stories from the frontlines can be adopted and/or adapted for use by other institutions, but it is also the chance for understanding the emergence of volunteering in Asia overall, and its future direction.

Elaine Suk Ching Liu is the Associate Head and Associate Professor of Department of Social and Behavioural Sciences, City University of Hong Kong.

ROUTLEDGE STUDIES IN ASIAN BEHAVIOURAL SCIENCES

Series Editor: T. Wing Lo, City University of Hong Kong

Psychoanalysis in Hong Kong
The Absent, the Present, and the Reinvented
Diego Busiol

Psycho-Criminological Perspective of Criminal Justice in Asia
Research and Practices in Hong Kong, Singapore, and Beyond
Edited by Heng Choon (Oliver) Chan and Samuel M.Y. Ho

Humour and Chinese Culture
A Psychological Perspective
Yue Xiao Dong

Idol Worship in Chinese Society
A Psychological Approach
Xiaodong Yue and Chau-kiu Cheung

A Comparison of Eastern and Western Parenting
Programmes, Policies and Approaches
Low Yiu Tsang Andrew

Empowering Asian Youth through Volunteering
Examples of Theory into Practice
Elaine S. C. Liu

Understanding Crime in Villages-in-the-City in China
A Social and Behavioural Approach
Zhanguo Liu and T. Wing Lo

Creativity in Chinese Contexts
Sociocultural and Dispositional Analyses
Chau-kiu Cheung and Xiaodong Yue

For the full list of titles in the series visit : https://www.routledge.com/Routledge-Studies-in-Asian-Behavioural-Sciences/book-series/RABS

EMPOWERING ASIAN YOUTH THROUGH VOLUNTEERING

Examples of Theory into Practice

Elaine Suk Ching Liu

Routledge
Taylor & Francis Group
LONDON AND NEW YORK

First published 2020
by Routledge
2 Park Square, Milton Park, Abingdon, Oxon OX14 4RN

and by Routledge
52 Vanderbilt Avenue, New York, NY 10017

Routledge is an imprint of the Taylor & Francis Group, an informa business

British Library Cataloguing-in-Publication Data
A catalogue record for this book is available from the British Library

Library of Congress Cataloging-in-Publication Data
Names: Liu, Elaine S. C., author.
Title: Empowering Asian youth through volunteering : examples of theory into practice / Elaine S. C. Liu.
Description: First edition. | Abingdon, Oxon ;
New York, NY : Routledge, 2020. |
Series: Routledge studies in Asian behavioural sciences |
Includes bibliographical references and index.
Identifiers: LCCN 2019014927| ISBN 9781138106437 (hbk) |
ISBN 9781138106444 (pbk) | ISBN 9781315101613 (ebk)
Subjects: LCSH: Voluntarism--China--Hong Kong. |
Youth--China--Hong Kong.
Classification: LCC HN755.2.V64 L58 2020 | DDC 302/.14--dc23
LC record available at https://lccn.loc.gov/2019014927

ISBN: 978-1-138-10643-7 (hbk)
ISBN: 978-1-138-10644-4 (pbk)
ISBN: 978-1-315-10161-3 (ebk)

Typeset in Bembo
by Taylor & Francis Books

CONTENTS

ILLUSTRATIONS

Figures

Tables

ACKNOWLEDGEMENTS

This book is all about youth volunteerism, and how youth volunteerism can empower young people. An ongoing local youth volunteering project, the City-Youth Empowerment Project (CYEP), created for students of City University of Hong Kong in 2005 is used as a case study demonstrating how to implement youth volunteering. In the last thirteen years of implementation, CYEP has evolved, matured and sustained because of many people's generous help and genuine trust. First, I would like to thank the Vice-President (Undergraduate Education) in City University of Hong Kong in 2004 for endorsing and funding the project with the first sum of seeding money. Thanks go also to other subsequent senior colleagues from City University of Hong Kong who continued to fund the project up to 2017. Different heads of Department of Social and Behavioural Sciences have also kindly accommodated the project under the structure of the department's co-curricular activities and supported the delivery of the project for all university students. Whenever we call for help, many colleagues from our department have unselfishly given us their biggest hand. Special thanks have to go to many colleagues from other administrative offices in City University of Hong Kong for networking us with donors, arranging venues and facilities, and presenting themselves so often at CYEP functions. To all colleagues from City University of Hong Kong who have helped, what you have done means so much to students! To the donors we thus connected, thanks so much for your generous support and trust! Your donations have empowered students as well the community!

The core success of the project comes from a big group of our CYEP staff who are passionate, enthusiastic, energetic, and devoted to the project. To all staff, you have made CYEP more than just a physical presence, but a spiritual hub for yourselves to grow, and for you to grow the volunteers. My sincere and personal thanks to each of you! The next group has to be our big group of volunteers. You are the foundation of the CYEP building, fuel for its machineries, energy for all levels of meaningful relationships, and an endless source for our laughs and fun.

What you have done has given us hope for a better future world! Thanks very much and keep it up! The next has to be a long list of NGOs, their staff, and service recipients. I feel proud to have worked with you and known you! You have added colour and healthy air to our campus! Hurrah to our friendships!

In the process of writing this book, I received tremendous support and understanding from many project staff, research staff, and other professional consultants and editors. All interviewees involved in the book, including members of the Sub-committee on Promotion of Student and Youth Volunteering of Social Welfare Department, Council Chair, and other senior members from the Agency for Volunteer Service, CYEP project staff and CYEP volunteers have unselfishly contributed their time and wisdom for me to finish the book. Without your support, in no way could this book have been actualized!

Last but not least, I have to thank my family members who have supported me for my volunteer endeavour and have given me love for work!

Elaine S. C. Liu

PREFACE

From a social worker to a faculty member in the Department of Social and Behavioural Sciences of City University of Hong Kong since 1990, my research and teaching interests have circled around children and youth, their relationships with families, and finally their engagement with the community. As both a social worker and an academia, my vision is to create and discover innovative ways to practice what I believe in about children and youth and their rights for positive development. In both classroom teaching and co-curricular teaching and learning activities, my teaching philosophy is guided by the Humanistic-Empowerment Approach (see Chapter 11 for the model). In co-curricular projects, I first launched a series of cross-cultural learning programs for our students within our department from 2001 to 2004, ending with the launch of The 1st International Conference on Youth Empowerment (ICOYE): Cross-cultural Learning in 2004. Subsequently, the City-Youth Empowerment Project (CYEP) was created in 2005 for all students in our university. Another academic conference, The 2nd ICOYE: Empowering Youth through Volunteerism, was organized in 2006 for all students and staff to be exposed to the conference's core concepts on youth volunteering and youth empowerment. The conference had hosted nine academics to present plenary speeches and 45 youth groups from twelve different countries and 48 institutions/agencies to exchange on their volunteer projects in the conference's concurrent symposium sessions. The manuscripts we thus collected from the conference presentations were edited into a booked called Youth Empowerment and Volunteerism: Principles, Policies and Practices in 2008. The book has formulated many conceptual models and useful concepts which have been facilitating CYEP to further develop, mature, and sustain till today. Ten years after the first book on youth volunteering was published, and thirteen years after CYEP was implemented, it is about the right time for me to draw a preliminary conclusion on what CYEP has achieved so far for youth volunteering and youth empowerment. It is hoped that this book will inspire all those who are in position of launching and implementing similar projects for young people to strive to empower young people through volunteering.

This text is organized into three parts. In Part I, besides defining and conceptualizing volunteerism, and introducing the Asian and Hong Kong experiences in volunteerism, this part has also unveiled the complex relationships among the three essential processes for volunteerism: the Personal Process, the Organizational Process, and the Community Process. The main characters in this book are young university students. The organization we refer to in this book is CYEP as a case study showing how to create and sustain a volunteer project. Finally, the community we serve is a platform facilitating the reciprocal development of both young volunteers and the service recipients in the community. Part II has seven chapters, including a discussion on different input of concepts and values and important milestones which are facilitative in building and sustaining CYEP; the rationale for CYEP anchoring on a Reciprocal Volunteer Process Model (RVPM) for its implementation; and finally how RVPM is implemented in five different services for different target groups. From conceptual to practice, macro to micro, and finally abstract to concrete, this part demonstrates how and what concepts and values are important for developing a volunteer project, with CYEP as an example. Last but not least, in Part III, a conclusion is drawn on how these youth volunteering reciprocal processes have impacted youth development and youth empowerment, based on the retrospective reflections of a group of youth who have participated in CYEP. To conclude, a unique Humanistic-Empowerment model linking youth volunteering with youth empowerment, and connecting youth's past, present and future, is developed to guide future work.

Elaine S. C. Liu

PART I

Theories and concepts of volunteerism and the brief historical background of volunteering in Asia and Hong Kong

1

DEFINING AND CONCEPTUALIZING VOLUNTEERISM

Origins of volunteering

According to Harris and colleagues (2016), non-organized volunteering can be traced back to the origins of humankind, where formal or organized volunteering in associations date back to about 10,000 years. A group of international researchers led by Harris found evidence of various forms of associations in the majority of ancient societies across the world, which suggest that mutual help is an inherent characteristic of humans. Formal volunteering in 19th and 20th century increased considerably in Europe, particularly due to population growth, improvements in transportation and communication, the Industrial Revolution, and two World Wars. For example, there was a remarkable increase in the number of members of societies of mutual aid in both France and Italy, between the end of 19th century and the beginning of 20th century. Further, it was deemed that by the end of the 20th century about half of the U.K. population was involved with some type of voluntary association (i.e., recreational, educational, or social).

In the U.S. however, voluntary activities became a prominent element in the history of the American political landscape, when associations were formed for combating slavery across the country, and for anti-British activities during colonial times. However, after World War II and the Korean war from 1958 onwards, voluntarism emerged prolifically in the U.S. This was due to many factors, including the number of post-war veterans, changes in socio-demographics, governments contracting social services and then creating new markets, better education and employment opportunities for women, increased civil rights awareness, and veteran's organizations, among others. It was during these final years of the 20th century (in the U.S.), that volunteer service programs and the so-called voluntary sector truly emerged in the non-profit, or third sector. The concept of "third sector" was created by Cornuelle (1965), and Levitt (1973) who were the first to use this term to explain this evolution.

Volunteering and social work

Historically, social work *became* a profession around the turn of the 19th century, and in Europe, the first professional school of social work was established in Amsterdam, in 1899 (Healy, 2008). Prior to that, volunteers did not normally receive any formal training. An important European figure in the development of social work education was Octavia Hill (1838–1912), a teacher from London who spent most of her life helping the poor. She was particularly concerned with the crowded and unsanitary local housing, as she believed that living in a clean and well-maintained environment was one of the essential needs of life that afforded people with minimal dignity. However, she was also aware that simply solving the local London housing issue was not enough to overcome its social issues, but this was only a first step toward the nation's social welfare development.

On the one hand, she believed that only intervention by the state (e.g., providing more adequate public housing) was not sufficient, without the combined voluntary participation of its citizens. Conversely, she also believed that in most cases, philanthropy and charity fostered dependency, so she advocated for a new approach to such help. She founded the Charity Organization Society in 1869, with its aim being not only to eradicate local urban poverty, but also to train community volunteers to improve their intervention effectiveness. She firmly believed in the role of active citizen community participation, and her cutting edge work was deemed as also essential to the establishment of the social work profession as we know it today (Kendall, 2000). Presently, volunteering is still an integral part of global social work education and training, and most universities require (social work) students to complete one or more volunteering experiences in education, health, or human service agencies during their studies. Recently in Hong Kong, social work students' self-reported gains in their perception of social work education were positively associated to the number of hours they spent volunteering, suggesting that the experiences and processes of volunteering were similar to those of social work (Cheung & Tang, 2010).

Today, volunteer activities play an increasingly important role in many societies. Particularly in times of budget cuts and growing social problems, the contribution of volunteers is deemed essential (Feit & Holosko, 2013; Stebbins, 2009). Volunteering was initially considered as a form of leisure, or at best, a non-essential kind of community service (Chapman, 2008). However, it has grown over time and across the world, as it represents a model of re-distribution of social capital, and an effective way for communities to quickly mobilize resources to respond to emergency situations. Currently, volunteering is a tool for responding to both immediate and long-term needs, for creating awareness, and for gathering citizens in groups to effectively conduct lobbying activities and advocate for the needs of various poor and marginalized sub-groups. Many studies have reported on the positive impacts of volunteering on community and social development, as well as on individual mental and physical health (Degli Antoni, 2009; Fraser, Clayton, Sickler, & Taylor, 2009; Hong & Morrow-Howell, 2010). Today, volunteering has evolved from being simply an act of kindness between a few individuals, to a global social phenomenon which involves professional bodies, governmental organizations, entire communities, societies, and the whole world. As such, it is now at the intersection of various social, cultural, and political agendas (Liu, Ching, & Wu, 2017).

Defining the elusive concept of volunteering

It is difficult to find published works on the historical background of the term "volunteer". If we turn to online dictionaries for a suggestion of the origin of the term, one says that it originated in a military context around 1600, to indicate how "one who offers himself for military service"; and, the non-military connotation was first recorded in the 1630s (Online Etymology Dictionary). Similarly, the term "volunteerism" can be traced back to 1844, with reference to the armed forces, whereas its use in reference to altruistic volunteer participation to community activities is far more recent (1977) (Online Etymology Dictionary). Volunteering describes an altruistic voluntary act, without coercion, and/or monetary rewards. The etymology of the term derives from the Latin *voluntas*, meaning will. The concept of will is central to both European and American philosophies, and Christian theology. In philosophy, (free) "will" is considered an autonomous feature, one who is free to do what s/he wants to do. However, in Christianity will is understood as the will of the Lord, meaning that one is free to show concern to others and to volunteer, because this typically means responding to a calling from God (Haers & von Essen, 2015).

Even though volunteering is commonly understood as a provision of free services, a consensually accepted definition of volunteering is still missing (Cnaan, Handy, & Wadsworth, 1996). Additional confusion is generated by the fact that the term volunteering today is frequently adopted for indicating activities that are not necessarily voluntary. For example, these may include activities that are part of judicial mandates, or that are required as part of classes/courses in schools (Liu et al., 2017).

According to Cnaan and colleagues (1996), volunteerism is best described along four intersecting dimensions: 1) free will (it is voluntary by nature); 2) type of rewards (remuneration); 3) formal organization; and, 4) identity of (or proximity to) beneficiaries. Additionally, in order to further clarify volunteering and distinguish it from other pro-social behaviours, some have posited that it should be deliberately planned, and prolonged over time within an organized context (Penner, 2004). A well-regarded definition of volunteering was provided by Snyder and Omoto (2008): "freely chosen and deliberate helping activities that extend over time, which are engaged in without expectation of reward or other compensation and often through formal organizations, and that are performed on behalf of causes or individuals who desire assistance" (p. 3). However, this definition has some limitations and remains rather generic, so that it does not really help to operationalize the concept. Second, it may be culturally biased. Third, it does not capture the most recent forms of occasional engagement in today's volunteering (Liu et al., 2017).

The United Nations General Assembly with Resolution 56/38 of 5 December 2001, defined volunteering as "*an activity undertaken out of free will, for the general public good, and where monetary reward is not the principal motivating factor*" (United Nations, 2014). The U.N. further describes volunteerism as a basic expression of human relationships that reciprocally transforms both volunteers and stakeholders, helps to eliminate poverty, improves basic health and education, addresses environmental issues and social exclusion, and prevents potential violence. As volunteerism across the world grows, and becomes an essential component of social, economic, and environmental sustainable development, in December 2015, the United Nations General Assembly ratified Resolution 70/129 and named it "*Integrating volunteering into peace and development: The plan of action for the next decade and beyond*". They identified three strategic objectives (for 2016–2030): "1) to strengthen people's ownership of the development agenda through enhanced civic engagement and enabling environments for citizen action; 2) to integrate volunteerism into national and global implementation strategies for the post-2015 development agenda; and, 3) to measure volunteerism to contribute to a comprehensive understanding of the engagement of people and their well-being and be part of the monitoring of the Sustainable Development Goals." (United Nations Volunteers, 2016, p.30).

Another well-cited best practice reference for defining volunteerism was presented in the *ILO Manual on the Measurement of Volunteer Work*, developed by the Johns Hopkins Center for Civil Society Studies, partnered with the International Labour Organization (ILO) (International Labour Organization, 2011). The ILO manual defines volunteer work as: "*Unpaid non-compulsory work; that is, time individuals give without pay to activities performed either through an organization or directly for others outside their own household*" (International Labour Organization, 2011, p.13). The manual clearly specifies that volunteering: involves *work*; it is unpaid (although reimbursement of travel costs or costs of equipment, symbolic gifts, and/or stipends that are not contingent on market value, quality or quantity of the work, do not necessarily violates this definition); is non-compulsory or non-obligatory; and, does not limit the scope of volunteer work to a particular beneficiary; and, embraces both "direct" and "organization-based" volunteering.

As noted in the literature, the term volunteerism globally spans a broad range of activities. As cross-cultural research has developed over time, the precise criteria for defining volunteerism has become broader in scope. For example, initially some regarded only the long-term delivery of services within an organizational context, with clear roles, regular attendance, and supervision as "formal" volunteering. Conversely, individual help offered to non-relatives, out of any organizational context was referred to as "informal" volunteering. This longstanding distinction between "formal" and "informal" volunteering seems to implicitly describe what form of volunteering is more legitimate, and/or valuable (Carson, 1999). However, because formal volunteering is very common in many Western societies but not as much in Asian societies, it is now generally accepted that volunteering can be either performed through an organized association, or offered directly by individuals to recipients. Similarly, earlier definitions of volunteering normally included a temporal variable; as all volunteers generally required some sort of long-term commitment, and only those helping activities that were carried out for extended periods of time (e.g., three or six months) were deemed as volunteering. However today, pre-determined lengths of time no longer define what is, or is not volunteering, and many volunteering activities (e.g., environmental protection), are ones that typically involve a large number of persons for a single day or event, or are for the purpose of arousing public awareness and advocating for some social issues. Basic features that describe contemporary volunteering include: 1) non-obligatory activities; 2) being unpaid; and, 3) are targeted for the benefit of others. However, these criteria still leave a few issues rather unclear. For instance, any activity that is non-obligatory can likely be deemed as voluntary; however, this does not necessarily qualify it as volunteering. In some cases, an individual may feel that s/he can hardly refuse (gentle coercion) to volunteer, e.g., if volunteering provides students some additional credits for their studies, or is perceived as a necessary step prior to formal job-hunting, or is an alternative to incarceration. As such, the issue of it being "non-obligatory" and alone, does not imply that such an activity is developed out of one's own altruistic will, and/or for some vocation.

Second, it is very difficult to assess one's true motivational reasons for volunteering. Ideally, both service recipients and volunteers gain from their interactions. It would be naïve to contend that all people volunteer altruistically, just to do good for others. Indeed, volunteering does not connote or promote the notion of "sacrifice". Instead, it is important that volunteer motives and expectations should be tabled, recognized, and elaborated collaboratively (i.e., with their supervisor in the agency, or some other professional), so as to improve the whole volunteering experience, for all volunteers, the agency, and other community stakeholders. Additional benefits of volunteering may include: making new friends, learning about other people/societies, gaining new experiences, learning new skills, finding meaning/purpose in life, travelling to new places, and/or sharing experiences that one would not be able to have otherwise. Some critics of volunteerism have pointed out that volunteers may "need" vulnerable, and/or poor persons to help, more so than they themselves need to volunteer (Lupton, 2011). For example, some people who have experienced distress in their own personal lives (e.g., divorce, abandonment, death of loved ones), may unconsciously aspire to overcome their own personal issues by helping others who are (perceived as) weak, thus dependent, and then unlikely to abandon those who chose to help them. Further, in examining the phenomenon of charitable organizations in the third world, Zizek (1997) suggested that making any kinds of financial contributions offer wealthier people a type of substitute-redemption, and in turn, makes them feel good. At the same time, historically, charity keeps poor people in their condition of need, preventing them from actually questioning the causes of their conditions. The existence of such "selfish" motives for volunteering is not new to researchers. For example, the Volunteer Functions Inventory (VFI) (Clary et al., 1998) – a tool for assessing volunteers' motives – includes among its six factors a subscale for assessing so-called "protective motives", described as a way of protecting the ego from the difficulties of life (e.g., volunteering as a means for escaping negative feelings, reducing sense of guilt, etc.).

Volunteering across various countries

Volunteering is normally described by psychologists, anthropologists, and sociologists as a universally motivated human behaviour, as it was historically observed among many societies (Butcher & Einolf, 2017), implying that volunteering is not a learned behaviour, nor specific only to some cultures. However, as volunteering is expressed in different forms and under different circumstances in various societies, cross-cultural measurement and comparison of volunteering participation is difficult, if not impossible. Today, a few initiatives have compared the rates of volunteerism across nations. One is the Johns Hopkins Comparative Non-profit Sector project, which bi-annually compares formal volunteering in 45 countries of all regions of the world. Comparing developed and developing countries, their researchers found that in the former, an average of 15 % of the adult population volunteered, whereas in the latter, only about 6 % did (Salamon, Sokolowski, & List, 2003). When these data were further broken down by country, the results were even more surprising. For example, it was reported that 52% of the adult population volunteers in Norway, 30% in the UK, whereas only 0.1% in Mexico and 0.2% in Pakistan volunteered. Using studies about Pakistan as an example, however, according to other statistics, Pakistan is reported to have a very high rate of citizens participating in volunteering (Baqir, 2014; Pakistan Centre for Philanthropy, 2016).

How does one explain such discrepancies? One explanation for this finding is that some surveys may focus on formal/organized volunteering only, and do not consider informal forms of volunteering. In some (mainly Western) countries, formal participation in volunteering is more common than in others (e.g., Asian) (Lee & Brudney, 2012). However, this does not mean that in Asian societies, voluntary help is not offered (Busiol, 2016a), or that the levels of participation to community life are less than in Western societies. A second reason may be the current definition of volunteering. For example, in another very large cross-national survey, *The World Giving Index* (WGI), which annually compares data from more than 140 countries globally, only one item is used to assess the prevalence of volunteering – simply by asking respondents if they "did any volunteering in the previous month". Their results showed that rates varied significantly across various continents, from the highest of 37% in North America, to 24.2% in Europe, to 20.4% in Asia, and to a low of 11.2% in the Middle East (Charities Aid Foundation, 2010). Again, is it really that these volunteer rates vary so widely among various societies, or is it that people from different cultures have different understandings of what volunteering is, impacting their responses to this survey? For example, helping or serving someone in some cultures may be understood as a voluntary act of "free will", whereas in other cultures it may be explained in terms of an "obligation" or something that is "natural", or necessary. Similarly, it may be that in some societies (e.g., North America) there is a much clearer divide between what is voluntary, and what is not, than in others (e.g., Asia). If this is true, then differences noted in these volunteering participation rates as assessed by all of these well-cited international surveys reflect a deeper nuanced social and cultural understanding of volunteering.

Volunteerism in Chinese contexts

Most of the empirical and theoretical research on volunteering has been conducted in Western contexts. However some cross-cultural research has shown that Chinese culture is significantly different from Western cultures, i.e., the former emphasizes collectivism, whereas the latter individualism (Cheung, Tang, & Yan, 2006). In turn, one may perceive that this may also reflect on how volunteering is understood and practiced in different cultures. Nevertheless, literature on how volunteerism is defined in Chinese contexts is still rather limited (Liu, Wu, Lo, & Hui, 2012; Wong, Chui, & Kwok, 2011). Historically, Chinese culture has always favoured the collective interests and development (e.g., the family, or the extended family, the clan, the group, etc.), over interests and development of the individuals (Busiol, 2012; Lo, Su, & Jiang, 2009). Interestingly however, in terms of culture alignment, Chinese culture greatly values the development of a harmonious society, which is also the main goal of volunteerism (Liu et al., 2017).

A recent empirical study in Hong Kong provided some insights about the perceptual similarities and differences between Chinese and American students about who is, or is not, a volunteer (Liu et al., 2017). These researchers presented data on a number of variables or items describing people who engaged in various helping situations, and asked survey participants to rank them from the situation that "best described" a volunteering activity, to "the least". Results were then compared to previous findings from studies in the U.S. Interestingly, in both samples, the top five and the bottom ranked five items were very similar, suggesting that both cultures similarly dichotomized who is, or is not, a volunteer. However, the remaining items were ranked quite differently, indicating that perceived significant cultural and contextual differences were apparent. These authors also posited that these different understandings of volunteering could be due to the longer history that volunteering has in the U.S., rather than in Hong Kong, or other Chinese cultural contexts. However, follow-up interviews with their participants revealed different understandings of volunteering were also attributed to a more family-centric, and interdependent Hong Kong Chinese culture, versus a more dominant and independent American culture. Their results clearly indicated that both organizational and cultural contexts must be taken into consideration when defining volunteering. For example, working overtime without pay was ranked as sixth (on a higher end to volunteer work) among the U.S. sample, whereas in the busier context of Hong Kong, where long working hours are the norm, this was ranked only as fourteenth (on a lower end to volunteer work), suggesting that it is not perceived as something occasional, and/ or voluntary, but almost as an obligation (Liu et al., 2017, p.7).

Volunteering versus other types of community service: internship, charity, and service-learning

Volunteering and internship are both normally non-paid activities, however, they are not considered as being equal. An internship is normally defined as "the position of a student or trainee who works in an organization, sometimes without pay, in order to gain work experience or satisfy requirements for a qualification" (www.oxforddictionaries.com). As Holmes (2006) noted, an internship is normally limited in time, and focuses on building a career in a specific human service sector. This is not the case with volunteering, as it also may require a period of training. Further, most people in an internship are typically youth in school, who intend to eventually enter the job market. Conversely, other volunteers may be people from different walks of life including retirees, who desire to remaining active in their communities and use their time, friendships, and/or expertise with others.

Volunteering is also different from charity, as both describe acts of giving, but the latter remains a more impersonal act. Where volunteers normally help others by devoting their time (as there is physical interaction between volunteers and service recipients), charity is typically an act of offering to help in more tangible forms of money or goods (e.g., clothes, food), and givers and receivers do not necessarily interact with each other. Further, Wolpert (1976) observed that charity normally targets those "in need", which by contrast confirms who the "giver" is. This notion is more unclear in volunteering, as both volunteers and service recipients admittedly and reciprocally give and receive something (material, and/or immaterial). Finally here, Hill (2012) found that volunteering but not charity, is associated directly with community collaborations, public service motives, altruism and the desire for self-improvement. Charity instead, is promoted more through personal resources, and is identified with care oriented helping types of values.

Volunteering significantly differs from service-learning, as well. Service-learning is normally described as a pedagogical framework that aims to integrate both academic and experiential teaching (Howard, 1998). Indeed, in most cases, service-learning is typically understood as "academic service learning". The hallmark of service-learning is sharing knowledge and on-site learning, whereas volunteering may be more concerned with community issues and usually with a targeted group of service recipients. Thus, students involved in a service-learning project are required and expected to have a broader vision of a project than volunteers, and they may also have to relate not only with service-recipients, but with other significant community stakeholders. However in some cases, this ideal is rather de-limiting. For example, some studies have observed that students in service learning projects may end up working with a director of a project more so, than with its recipients (e.g., individuals, families) (Bridges, Abel, Carlson & Tomkowiak, 2010). In such cases, academic (universal) knowledge seeking, represents somewhat of a barrier to achieving more personalized individual knowledge that can be acquired more effectively while learning "in the field", service learning could be the integration of both academic and experiential knowledge. Conversely, volunteers may be more interested in meeting individuals and working directly *with* them, rather than developing more new knowledge *about* or for them. Finally here, service-learning activities are normally "credit bearing", meaning that students involved in such learning will benefit academically if they take part in such activities (i.e., when they are not simply required to attend). This poses some concerns about the actual motivation to engage in such activities. Further, one may wonder how more utilitarian motives may reflect on student participation to the project, relationships with its service recipients, and the overall service experience itself.

Correlates of volunteering

Antecedents are factors or variables that represent the perceived and often empirically documented causes of volunteering, or more simply what influences people to volunteer. Research has identified various antecedents of volunteering. Broadly speaking, these can be either individual, social, and/or economic. However, there is not a clear cut relationship between understanding the antecedents of individual factors or characteristics impacting volunteering, the society s/he is born in, and one's socio-economic status. Thus, various perspectives of volunteering antecedents should not be perceived as mutually exclusive, but be perceived more collectively, as they may contribute to better explaining one's different motives for volunteering.

A well cited early approach to conceptually identifying antecedents of volunteering was offered by Penner (2002) who focused on how dispositional variables, both alone and in combination with organizational variables, were related to volunteerism. Dispositional variables are essentially an individuals' attributes, whereas organizational variables include: a) a volunteer's feeling about how s/he is treated by an organization, and, b) the organization's reputation and its personnel practices. Further, he developed a pioneering model that distinguished different stages of volunteerism, including: 1) the decision to volunteer; 2) the development of the volunteer role identity; and, 3) sustained volunteerism. This model is presented in Figure 1.1.

Each stage of the model in Figure 1.1 represents a qualitatively different step; and it is not simply a function of time. This rather detailed model reveals at each stage how dispositional and organizational variables influence each other, how they affect one's participation to volunteering, what variables promote long-term engagement in volunteering, and subsequently how one's volunteering experiences can be enhanced. Dispositional characteristics include individual traits e.g., personality, values, attitudes, beliefs, and motives that belong to persons who choose to volunteer. Later, Gillath and colleagues (2005) assessed the relationship between avoidant attachment, attachment anxiety, and volunteering across three countries (Israel, the Netherlands, and the United States) and found that in all countries, avoidant attachment was negatively correlated with participation to volunteerism and altruism. Attachment anxiety, instead, was not associated with the level of engagement in volunteering, but with one's motives for volunteering. Specifically, higher scores of attachment anxiety were associated with a desire for more social

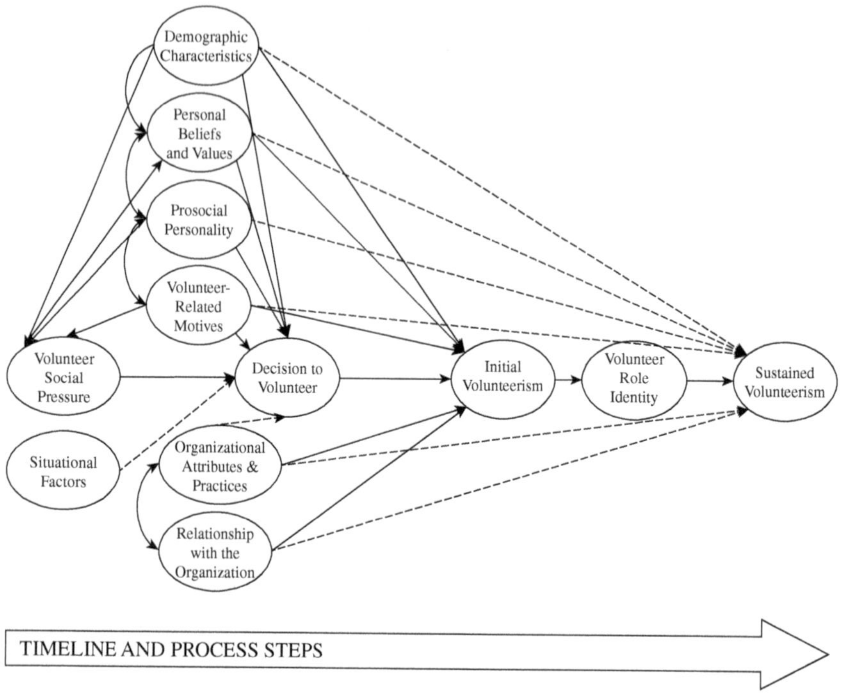

FIGURE 1.1 Penner's model of sustained volunteering

acceptance, self-enhancement, and self-protection in volunteering. Not surprisingly, avoidant attachment and attachment anxiety were also associated with greater loneliness, and more interpersonal problems (p.432). These findings were confirmed in a subsequent study by Erez, Mikulincer, van Ijzendoorn and Kroonenberg (2008). Here, avoidant attachment was inversely correlated with volunteer participation and altruistic motives, whereas attachment anxiety was associated with more self-focused motives for volunteering. These authors suggested that avoidant people may share more individualistic values that are somehow contrary to the communal values that typically ground volunteerism.

In another study, the personalities of hospice palliative care volunteers were assessed according to the so-called "Big Five" personality traits model (i.e., extraversion, agreeableness, openness, conscientiousness, and neuroticism) (Claxton-Oldfield & Banzen, 2010). His results indicated that volunteers scored significantly higher than did the general population on the traits of agreeableness, extraversion, and openness, and significantly lower on the trait of neuroticism. This seemed understandable, as volunteering requires a certain degree of openness to the world, and also to new and unpredictable situations. This same study showed that volunteers scored significantly higher than other respondents on the "empathic concern" and "perspective taking", and significantly lower on the personal "distress", and "fantasy". Penner's framework (2002) (see Figure 1.1) suggested that the initial decision to volunteer is often the result of interrelated socio-demographics and dispositional characteristics, pro-social personality, values, beliefs, and one's motives. It is also influenced by social supports, by other situational factors (e.g., free time availability, emergency response), by organizational attributes and practices, and by volunteering information made available. A volunteer identity is influenced by one's identification with the volunteer's role, and simultaneously to the host organization.

It has been shown that a person can evolve as a volunteer, if s/he receives adequate levels of training and supervision (Deslandes & Rogers, 2008). The identification with the host agency is ensured by effective volunteer management, the perception of a "good match" with one's host agency, and other personal acknowledgements/recognitions offered to potential volunteers (e.g., tangible awards). Penner (2002) suggested that a *decision to volunteer* may be influenced only by an organizational attributes and practices (i.e., the reputation of the local agency), meaning that one organization can be more appealing to a volunteer, than another. However, he also suggested that the decision to *continue volunteering* over time (i.e., sustained volunteering), is greatly influenced by the relationship that develops between the organization and the volunteer. Previous research has indicated that once one's volunteer identity is established, a volunteer is committed to continued volunteering, despite external variables and challenges (e.g., limited free time, financial difficulties, low job satisfaction, etc.).

According to Penner (2002), empathy is the most important factor used to describe one's pro-social personality. In his study, he described empathetic individuals as those who "feel responsibility and concern for the welfare of others" (p.451). Empathy is the capacity to put ourselves "in other people's shoes", meaning to see the world from their perspective. Empathy is a pre-requisite for really "seeing" the other, his/her needs and resources (King Jr. & Holosko, 2012). Being empathic implies that we can see and accept the difference between ourselves and others, and acknowledging these differences are essential for effectively listening to others (Busiol, 2016b). Bekkers (2005) confirmed that empirically, volunteers showed more empathy, and have more human and social capital than did non-volunteers. He also showed how values and beliefs can influence the level of one's overall civic engagement. In fact, volunteers in his sample reported higher levels of education, religiosity, interest in politics (leftist or Christian political parties), and post-materialistic values. Education itself is also one of the most influential variables influencing volunteering, at least in many industrial societies, as more educated people tend to have broader horizons, more curiosity toward the world and other people, and higher job status and mobility (Wilson, 2012).

The relationship between age and participation rates for volunteering are not easy to define, as these may be mediated by other variables such as one's occupation, family status, gender, and employment, etc. However, some research has examined the relationship between age and volunteering, and reported more meaningful associations between one's age and the motives for volunteering (Dávila & Díaz-Morales, 2009). Brody and Wright (2004) and Francis (2011) found that among European or North American youth, important motives for volunteering were values (altruism and concern for others), understanding (learning something new, acquiring skills and experience), and career development (making experiences for professional development). Conversely, protective factors (escape negative feelings and personal problems), and social (creating new relationships) motives were the least identified. It was interesting to note that as one's age increases, career, and/or understanding motives normally decrease, while social and values motives become seemingly more important (Dávila & Díaz-Morales, 2009).

Gender differences in understanding the act of volunteering tend to vary by country, suggesting that they reflect unique cultural and social representations of men and women. However, generally and globally speaking, women are more likely to volunteer than men. This was noted in studies done in the United States, the United Kingdom, Japan, the Netherlands, and Italy, whereas in Sweden, men were reported to volunteer more than women (for a more in-depth review see, Einolf, 2011b). Further, in Hong Kong, women engaged more in volunteering than did men, which may also reflect Chinese cultural values, as often, women take on essential caring roles more than men (Chong, Busiol, & Chung, 2017). As such, gender not only impacts volunteer participation rates; but more importantly, influences the types of preferred volunteering activities chosen. For example, traditionally there is a strong gender-based imbalance in sports-based volunteering activities, where most volunteers are men. Conversely, religious, educational, and human services are more commonly preferred and provided by female volunteers (Cheung, Lo, & Liu, 2016; Musick & Wilson, 2008).

Globally speaking, various religions emphasize altruistic and charitable behaviours, and religiosity is often associated with volunteerism, and is deemed an important predictor of participation in volunteering in some countries or settings. Interestingly, the founding values of volunteering are the same fundamental values of most global sacred scriptures. For example, both Jewish and Christian traditions identify the commandment to "love your neighbour as yourself", as the ultimate expression of their divine laws. Other traditions contain similar teachings that encourage people to love others. Examining informal volunteering in South Asia, Yadama and Messerschmidt (2004) observed that it is easy to recognize the influence of deep religious traditions, together with "…the Ghandian tradition of service to society. In Bangladesh and Pakistan, informal service to one's community has deep Islamic origins; in Sri Lanka, Myanmar and Bhutan, a sense of civic service is informed by Buddhism; and in India and Nepal, a deep tradition of service can be Islamic, Buddhist, Jain, Hindu, or Christian" (p.101S).

Recent research has confirmed that religion holds important influence for individuals volunteering across cultures and societies. Penner (2004) found that religious persons were more likely than non-religious ones to volunteer, even outside of the context of other religious organizations. Analyzing data from a sample of $N = 165{,}625$ people living in 113 countries, Bennett (2015) found that religious individuals were more likely to volunteer than non-religious ones, regardless of one's specific belief commitment. This means that despite various religion-based doctrines, they all foster a sense of altruism, and promote the likelihood of volunteering (with Protestants being the most likely to volunteer, among the world's major religions). Furthermore, researchers describe contributions from two related components, religious beliefs and religious practices (Hustinx, Von Essen, Haers, & Mels, 2015). The former indicate that the values of altruism and caring for others that are normally at the base of any religion, are also the core values of volunteering. The latter, however, suggests that people who engage in religious practices are the most likely to engage in volunteering activities, likely because they have developed larger social networks and have more opportunities to become involved.

Similarly, Einolf (2011a) found a positive association between spirituality and volunteering, in individuals working in charity. Here, the differences between spirituality and religion can be understood, as most spirituality describes a personal relationship with "one's God", or the transcendent outside of a formal belief, and/or an organized group. Religious and spiritual values and beliefs do emerge as important predictors to volunteering. However generally speaking, being a member of an organized religion helps in developing one's social relationships and social capital. Most likely, both factors contribute to participation to volunteering. However, it is not yet clear what factors may be most influential in this interrelationship.

Many religious traditions, missionary work, peace building efforts, and indigenous traditions of mutual aid, are antecedents of modern organized volunteering (Brassard, Sherraden, & Lough, 2010). Nevertheless, as mentioned above, formal volunteering programs in Asia occur less frequently than in European and American countries. Some researchers have observed that whereas Judeo-Christian tradition promotes voluntary associations and philanthropic activities, informal voluntary activities are more common in Buddhist and Islamic traditions (Smith, Shue, Vest, & Villarreal, 1999). Further, the development of volunteer programs may be affected by other important contextual variables like culture, values, beliefs, political systems and political instability, the role of the state in managing and delivering services, and economic growth (Brassard et al., 2010).

Finally here, it has been shown that employment status also affects one's participation in volunteering. Interestingly, part-time workers have been found to be more likely to volunteer, than unemployed or full-time employed ones. However, a more likely determinant for volunteering was one's level of income, showing that people with lower incomes, volunteered less (Wilson, 2012); likely, because they also tended to work longer hours. However, the association between income and volunteering is not linear; as organized volunteering appears to be a prerogative of the middle-class, in many developed countries of the world (Lee & Brudney, 2010).

However, this is a "theoretical model" that was not operationalized by Penner, thus its main value remains heuristic. Furthermore, his model was developed in the U.S., based on a sample that was not representative of the U.S. population itself (respondents were predominately, wealthy, well-educated women of European ancestry, mostly Protestant or Catholic), and it cannot be considered as a culturally universal model. His model accounts for a number of personal, situational and social variables; however, "social" here seems to refer to the volunteers' relatives and peers, i.e., to the community level at best, and not to society, at large. Further, social values and cultural practices are not taken into account by this model, so it is unclear if and how it can apply to contexts different than North America. Additionally, the model was developed in an advanced industrial society; and, it is unclear if and how it can apply in developing countries. Most likely, its utility should be expanded when applied to contexts that present largely different cultures and social norms (e.g., Asian countries), and/or largely different economies (i.e., developing countries).

Sustained volunteering

In the landscape of recent global political and economic downturns, many governments have turned to volunteering as one way to boost to local civic engagement, as an instrument to help revert the further declines of social and economic development. Today, volunteering is no longer an individual's spontaneous act for personal development. Conversely, it is a very meaningful social phenomenon, and as such, it should be considered by all levels of institutions and government offices, as a public and policy concern, using local social capital. Indeed, grassroots initiatives are potentially very influential to local social change and advocacy as noted by Margaret Mead when she said: "Never doubt that a small group of thoughtful, committed, citizens can change the world. Indeed, it is the only things that ever has" (as cited in Lutkehaus, 2008, p.261).

Previous research has also revealed that official promotion, education, and mass media are less likely to influence a person's decision to initiate volunteering, more so than their own friends, family members, mentors, teachers, and other volunteers (Musick & Wilson, 2008). Furthermore, earlier studies revealed that the retention of volunteers is more likely due to organizational characteristics, rather than the psychological characteristics of the volunteer (Penner, 2002). Thus, governments should focus more on economic and social policies that primarily support the process of youth self-determination, as such vision "indirectly" support the development of youth volunteering. Further, based on the experiences of the author, such policies should aim at: 1) creating unique and interesting opportunities for voluntary contributions of individuals, and/or groups (e.g., by providing information on volunteering opportunities, making accessibility to volunteering more available and equitable, targeting and promoting more youth who already volunteer); and, 2) by helping youth to develop an intrinsic and unique personal volunteer identity. This may be achieved by helping youth volunteers feel more confident about their skills and abilities, as well as help with their role clarification within their host organizations. This implies that agencies should in turn, dedicate more resources to train and manage their volunteers to increase their effectiveness.

The outcomes of volunteering

Empirical literature from both Eastern and Western countries has reported data on the positive outcomes of volunteering (and in turn, society). In Western countries (for an in-depth review, see Wilson, 2012), volunteering was found to have positive effects in reducing depression, buffering against stress, improving self-esteem, and improving the mental health of volunteers, likely because it offered them more psychological options and resources. Further, volunteering showed positive effects on volunteer physical health, including the reduction of hypertension and lowering overall mortality rates. Furthermore, volunteering helps one become a "more active citizen". Findings from previous studies showed that youth who volunteer, develop more positive pro-social behaviours, and are less likely to take negative risks (for a review see Shah, Suandi, Hamzah, & Ismail, 2015). Not only does volunteering help many youth become more aware of social problems in their own communities and learn more about diversity; it may also help them to develop more other-oriented values (altruism), and promote stronger personal national identities (Youniss, McLellan, & Yates, 1999). Finally here, in North American societies where organized volunteering is more prevalent, it provides opportunities to obtain an educational degree, and for some, a more rewarding (also economically) job; however, this is not necessarily true in non-Western contexts.

Finally, volunteering may have an impact not only on participants directly involved in the project, but on the community at large. For example, volunteering with people with disabilities may indirectly contribute to increase community awareness about disability issues, because through the project, disabled persons are presented in healthy ways. Thus, by providing opportunities for interactions between people with and without disabilities, a project like this may help break down stereotypes in the community (Miller, Schleien, Rider, Hall, Roche, & Worsley, 2002). A recent review of research by Wu (2011) showed that the social impact of volunteering can be described by four non-mutually exclusive factors: 1) strengthening social connections, as the nature of volunteering is to bridge different parts of society, normally in the form of community partnerships, funding, networking, advocacy, and/or invitation to participate in events.; 2) building strong, safe, cohesive communities; 3) volunteering programs link people and contribute to creating social networks; and, 4) they offer people a chance to identify and understand various social problems in their respective communities. Having a better knowledge of their neighbourhoods, people are also more likely to understand the importance of social participation, and communities become more cohesive. By enhancing civic engagement through volunteering, individuals likely feel more integrated within their communities and develop more common interests and public engagement becomes more significant to them. Finally, by delivering public goods and services, volunteering programs normally offer services that are not otherwise available in the community, or that users cannot afford due to their economic situation, or lack of proximity or access to some communities.

Concluding remarks

This chapter has attempted to understand volunteerism from different angles, from psychology to sociology, from Western to Asian, from scientific research to applied work, from individual to organizational and community, and finally from antecedents factors for behaviour to outcomes. All these perspectives present us with dimensions to understand volunteerism. However, volunteerism still remains as a curious human phenomenon. It is a behaviour that people usually do with no press of circumstances and no bounds of obligation, although it does have opportunity cost and it is effortful. Another interesting point is that the forces that initiate actions of volunteering are not necessarily those that sustain them. So, why is it like this? The myths must lie in some sort of chemical interactions among some important processes involved. The unveiling of these processes will not just inform us how one sustains his/her volunteering behaviour, but will also holistically tell us why human being as a whole from the past to the present can sustain and expand our acts of volunteering, meaning current volunteering still remains the most important and most likely the simplest way for an individual to initiate a connection with his/her community or with a societal issue. The three highly interdependent factors also require the positive responses from one another in order to create an optimal process for "volunteering" to be recognized, identified and sustained as a social phenomenon:

1. Volunteerism has a Personal Process: it reflects the altruistic nature of human self-determining to contribute to the well-being of others. Without such initial drive and the purity of motivation, volunteerism could hardly happen or actualize in human relationships. However, individuals need many antecedent and supportive factors for them to make a decision to join, try, and to sustain. So, the organizational values, structure, management, programming etc. have to be aligning with these personal goals in order to sustaining those individual goals. In the process, as the Volunteering Sustainment reports, a chemical interaction among the individual acts and the organizational support will be generated. From the decision to volunteer to "role identity", it is said that the most important factor is the "organizational support", dispositional and situational factors are no longer the important forces for the individuals to sustain volunteering acts.
2. Volunteerism has an Organizational Process: since most volunteering behaviours happen in an organizational setting, the hurdle for one joining an organization must carry many meanings for the individuals. It reflects the individual perspective of seeing the limitation of one's effort to effect a change in the society, instead, attaching to an organization will facilitate "beginning" volunteers to be more knowledgeable on how to contribute to a bigger social goal. By identifying an organization or a project, individuals experiment on how to incorporate macro social values and goals into their personal values and goals. It also provides group dynamics, training,

knowledge, and culture for volunteers to sustain their individual interest. An organization also provides a specific focus on a social problem, whether a specific target group, elderly, children, women, disabled etc., or for environmental, poverty, peace etc. By engaging in a specific problem or a target group, through supporting an organization, volunteers are connected to the community as a whole. There are instances where individual volunteers after volunteering for some time in an agency will finally be inspired by their volunteer experiences thus gained to innovate their own new project for solving a social problem from a new perspective. However, most volunteers do start their involvement as a volunteer by relating to a project or an organization first. Most volunteer work also occurs within an organizational setting. So, organizations have a very important role in mediating individual motivations to volunteer with the macro society, individuals already learn in the process that collective action is more powerful and effective than individual action. By aligning individual values with organizational values, individuals achieve growth and maturity. However, an organization can support or sustain individual volunteers in the services, and it can also inhibit or discourage their motivations. If the organizational support and management are not sensitive enough to the needs of the individuals, many of them give up volunteering acts because of feeling that they are being rejected, screened out, not recognized, or even not awarded:

> It is found that if a volunteer is satisfied with the organizational support, they will associate with the organization for a longer length as a volunteer, more time as a volunteer. Once sustained, even the organization factor will then subsided, individual volunteers will become a sustained volunteers, they then have the potential to be life-long volunteers or to be able to direct connected with the community level of work, including maybe innovating a project out of their own effort.
>
> *(Studer & von Schnurbein, 2013)*

3. Volunteerism has a Community Process: we all need to feel that we are part of the community and to narrow the gap or "anomie" we feel in the community. As such, "Community as a Process" is understood as a participatory process for citizens in a community to feel a part of and to belong to the community. Volunteerism is said to be the easiest community process for people to get connected and involved in action to solve community problems. Those who volunteer will likely achieve a stronger sense of community and contribute more to social cohesiveness, harmony, and stability. The community also achieves social capital that ties and binds individual and society together. So, volunteering remains a special kind a helping, not replacing professional help, but to be recognized as a caring community if a society promotes and supports volunteering work. It is even suggested that we should incorporate or evaluate a country's volunteer policy to determine its level of development and modernization, or to distinguish developed countries from developing and under-developing ones. A developed country should have a set of

well-defined policies and goals to support organizations and individuals to pursue their volunteering commitment, and to make sure there is no discrimination, and that equality is assured for different groups of people to volunteer. The United Nations Volunteers (2015) even recommends that each country should have a system to record the hours of volunteering achieved in a country, relate the hours to GDP index, incorporate these statistical reports into their policy plan, and recognize citizens' efforts towards community building. All these measures are seen as reflecting governmental support to respond positively to the individual and organizational processes for volunteering.

References

Baqir, F. (2014). "Evolution of Volunteerism in Pakistan." In *Understanding Pakistan*. Volume I. Retrieved from https://www.researchgate.net/publication/266946632_Evolution_of_Volunteerism_in_Pakistan.

Bekkers, R. (2005). "Participation in voluntary associations: Relations with resources, personality, and political values." *Political Psychology*, 26(3), 439–454.

Bennett, M. R. (2015). "Religiosity and formal volunteering in global perspective." In L. Hustinx, J. Von Essen, J. Haers, and S. Mels (Eds). *Religion and volunteering: complex, contested and ambiguous relationships* (pp.77–96). Cham: Springer.

Brassard, C., Sherraden, M. S., & Lough, B. J. (2010). "Emerging perspectives on international volunteerism in Asia." In IVCO Forum Research Paper. Retrieved from https://www.researchgate.net/publication/236961958_Emerging_perspectives_on_international_volunteerism_in_Asia.

Bridges, D. R., Abel, M. S., Carlson J., & Tomkowiak, J. (2010). "Service learning in interprofessional education: a case study. "*Journal of Physical Therapy Education*, 24(1), 44.

Brody, S. M., & Wright, S. C. (2004). "Expanding the self through service-learning." *Michigan Journal of Community Service Learning*, 11(1), 14–24.

Busiol, D. (2012). "The Many Names of Hong Kong: Mapping Language, Silence and Culture in China." *Cultura. International Journal of Philosophy of Culture and Axiology*, 12(2), 207–226.

Busiol, D. (2016a). "Help-seeking Behaviour and Attitudes towards Counselling: a Qualitative Study among Hong Kong Chinese University Students." *British Journal of Guidance & Counselling*, 44(4), 382–401.

Busiol, D. (2016b). "The Development of a Listening Scale." *Research on Social Work Practice* (forthcoming).

Butcher, J. & Einolf, C. J. (Eds) (2017). "Perspectives on Volunteering." In *Voices from the South*. Switzerland: Springer.

Carson, E. D. (1999). "Comment: On defining and measuring volunteering in the United States and abroad. "*Law and Contemporary Problems*, 62(4), 67–71.

Chapman, M. V. (2008). "Volunteer motivation among African American women: A perspective on purpose and meaning." (Unpublished dissertation). George Washington University, Washington, DC.

Charities Aid Foundation (2010). "The World Giving Index 2010." Retrieved from https://www.cafonline.org/docs/default-source/about-us-publications/worldgivingindex28092010print.pdf.

Cheung, C. K. & Tang, K. L. (2010). "Socialization Factors Conducive to Social Work Students' Gain in Competence: Experience in the Hong Kong SAR, China." *Journal of Social Work*, 10(1), 42–58.

Cheung, C. K., Lo, T. W., & Liu, E. S. C. (2016). "Sustaining social trust and volunteer role identity reciprocally over time in pre-adult, adult, and older volunteers." *Journal of Social Service Research*, 42(1), 70–83.

Cheung, F., Tang, C., & Yan, E. (2006). "Factors influencing intention to continue volunteering: A study of older Chinese in Hong Kong." *Journal of Social Service Research*, 32, 193–209. doi:10.1300/J079v32n04_11.

Chong, M. L. A., Busiol, D., & Chung, K. H. E. (2017). "Age, gender and fields of study: do they affect the attitudes of Hong Kong university students toward the elderly?" Unpublished

Clary, E. G., Ridge, R. D., Stukas, A. A., Synder, M., Copeland, J., Haugen, J., & Miene, P. (1998). "Understanding and assessing the motivations of volunteers: A functional approach." *Journal of Personality and Social Psychology*, 74(6), 1516–1530. doi:10.1037/0022-3514.74.6.1516.

Claxton-Oldfield, S. & Banzen, Y. (2010). "Personality characteristics of hospice palliative care volunteers: the 'big five' and empathy. "*American Journal of Hospice and Palliative Medicine®*, 27(6), 407–412.

Cnaan, R. A., Handy, F., & Wadsworth, M. (1996). "Defining who is a volunteer: Conceptual and empirical considerations." *Nonprofit and Voluntary Sector Quarterly*, 25(3), 364–383.

Cornuelle, R.C. (1965). *Reclaiming the American Dream*. New York: Random House.

Dávila, M. C. & Díaz-Morales, J. F. (2009). "Age and motives for volunteering: Further evidence. "*Europe's Journal of Psychology*, 5(2), 82.

Degli Antoni, G. (2009). "Intrinsic vs. extrinsic motivations to volunteer and social capital formation." *Kyklos*, 62(3), 359–370. doi:10.1111/kykl.2009.62.issue-3.

Deslandes, M., & Rogers, L. (2008). "A Volunteer Training Framework." *Australian Journal of Adult Learning*, 48(2), 355–368.

Einolf, C. J. (2011a). "Daily spiritual experiences and prosocial behavior. Social Indicators Research." Retrieved from http://works.bepress.com/christopher_einolf/15.

Einolf, C. J. (2011b). "Gender differences in the correlates of volunteering and charitable giving." *Nonprofit and Voluntary Sector Quarterly*, 40(6), 1092–1112.

Erez, A., Mikulincer, M., van Ijzendoorn, M. H., & Kroonenberg, P. M. (2008). "Attachment, personality, and volunteering: Placing volunteerism in an attachment-theoretical framework." *Personality and Individual Differences*, 44(1), 64–74.

Feit, M. D. & Holosko, M. J. (2013). *Distinguishing clinical from upper level management in social work*. London, UK: Taylor & Francis.

Francis, J. E. (2011). "The functions and norms that drive university student volunteering." *International Journal of Nonprofit and Voluntary Sector Marketing*, 16, 1–12.

Fraser, J., Clayton, S., Sickler, J., & Taylor, A. (2009). "Belonging at the zoo: Retired volunteers. "*Aging & Society*, *29*(3), 351–368.

Gillath, O., Shaver, P. R., Mikulincer, M., Nitzberg, R. E., Erez, A., & Ijzendoorn, M. H. (2005). "Attachment, caregiving, and volunteering: Placing volunteerism in an attachment-theoretical framework." *Personal Relationships*, 12(4), 425–446.

Haers, J. & Von Essen, J. (2015). "Christian calling and volunteering." In L. Hustinx, J. Von Essen, J. Haers, and S. Mels (Eds.). (2015). *Religion and volunteering: Complex, contested and ambiguous relationships* (pp. 23–40). Cham: Springer.

Harris, B., Morris, A., Ascough, R. S., Chikoto, G. L., Elson, P. R., McLoughlin, J., Muukkonen, M., Pospíšilová, T., Roka, K., Smith, D. H., Soteri-Proctor, A., Tumanova, A. S., & Yu, P. (2016). "History of associations and volunteering." In D. H. Smith, R. A. Stebbins, and J. Grotz (Eds.). *The Palgrave Handbook of Volunteering, Civic Participation, and Nonprofit Associations* (pp. 23–58). Palgrave Macmillan, London.

Healy, L. M. (2008). *International social work: Professional action in an interdependent world*. New York: Oxford University Press.

Hill, M. (2012). "The relationship between volunteering and charitable giving: Review of evidence. " CGAP Working Paper London: Centre for Charitable Giving and Philanthropy. Retrieved from http://www.cgap.org.uk/uploads/Working%20Papers/WP%20volunteering%20and%20charitable%20giving%20MH.pdf.

Holmes, K. (2006). "Experiential learning or exploitation? Volunteering for work experience in the UK museums sector." *Museum Management and Curatorship*, 21(3), 240–253.

Hong, S. & Morrow-Howell, N. (2010). "Health outcomes of experience corps: A high commitment volunteer program." *Social Science and Medicine*, 71, 414–420. doi:10.1016/j.socscimed.2010.04.009.

Howard, J. P. F. (1998). "Academic service learning: A counternormative pedagogy." In R. A. Rhoads & J. P. F. Howard (Eds.), *Academic service learning: A pedagogy of action and reflection* (pp. 21–29). New Directions for Teaching and Learning. San Francisco: Jossey-Bass.

Hustinx, L., Von Essen, J., Haers, J., & Mels, S. (Eds.). (2015). *Religion and volunteering: Complex, contested and ambiguous relationships*. Cham: Springer.

International Labour Organization (2011). "Manual on the Measurement of Volunteer Work." International Labour Office, Geneva, Switzerland. Retrieved from http://www.ifrc.org/docs/IDRL/Volunteers/ILO%20Manual%20on%20Measurement%20of%20the%20Volunteer%20Work.pdf.

Kendall, K. A. (2000). *Social work education: Its origins in Europe*. Alexandria, VA: Council on Social Work Education.

King Jr, S. & Holosko, M. J. (2012). "The development and initial validation of the empathy scale for social workers." *Research on Social Work Practice*, 22(2), 174–185.

Lee, Y. J. & Brudney, J. L. (2012). "Participation in formal and informal volunteering: Implications for volunteer recruitment. "*Nonprofit Management and Leadership*, 23(2), 159–180.

Lee, Y. & Brudney, J. (2010). "Rational volunteering: A benefit-cost approach. "*International Journal of Sociology and Social Policy*, 29, 512–530.

Levitt, T. (1973). *The third sector; new tactics for a responsive society*. New York: Amacom.

Liu, E. S. C., Ching, C. W., & Wu, J. (2017). "Who is a volunteer? A cultural and temporal exploration of volunteerism." *Journal of Human Behavior in the Social Environment*, 27(6), 530–545.

Liu, E. S. C., Wu, J., Lo, T. W., & Hui, N. N. A. (2012). "Implementing volunteer program to university students in Hong Kong: Enhancing volunteer participation through service matching and organizational support." In B. C. Eng (Ed.), *A Chinese perspective on teaching and learning* (pp. 165–178). New York, NY: Routledge.

Lo, T. W., Su, S., & Jiang, G. (2009). "Youth empowerment and self-actualization: Experiences in Shanghai, China." In E. S. C. Liu, M. J. Holosko, & T. W. Lo (Eds.), *Youth empowerment and volunteerism: Principles, policies and practice* (pp. 251–267). Hong Kong: City University of Hong Kong Press.

Lupton, R. (2011). *Toxic charity: How Churches and charities hurt those they help (and how to reverse it)*. New York: HarperCollins.

Lutkehaus, N. (2008). *Margaret Mead: The making of an American icon*. Princeton: Princeton University Press.

Miller, K. D., Schleien, S. J., Rider, C., Hall, C., Roche, M., & Worsley, J. (2002). "Inclusive volunteering: Benefits to participants and community. "*Therapeutic Recreation Journal*, 36(3), 247.

Musick, M. A. & Wilson, J. (2008). *Volunteers: A social profile*. Indianapolis: Indiana University Press.

Online Etymology Dictionary. Retrieved from https://www.etymonline.com/.

Pakistan Centre for Philanthropy (2016). "The State of Individual Philanthropy in Pakistan." Retrieved http://www.pcp.org.pk/uploads/nationalstudy.pdf.

Penner, L. A. (2002). "Dispositional and organizational influences on sustained volunteerism: An interactionist perspective. "*Journal of Social Issues*, 58(3), 447–467.

Penner, L. A. (2004). "Volunteerism and social problems: Making things better or worse?" *Journal of Social Issues*, 60(3), 645–666. doi:10.1111/j.0022-4537.2004.00377.x.

Salamon, M.L., Sokolowski, W. S., & List, R. (2003). *Global Civil Society: An Overview*. Baltimore, MD: Johns Hopkins Center for Civil Society Studies.

Shah, J. A., Suandi, T., Hamzah, S. R. A., & Ismail, I. A. (2015). "Why youths choose to become volunteers: From the perspective of belief. "*Athens Journal of Social Science*, 2(1), 51–64.

Smith, B., Shue, S., Vest, J. L., & Villarreal, J. (1999). *Philanthropy in communities of color*. Bloomington: Indiana University Press.

Snyder, M. & Omoto, A. M. (2008). "Volunteerism: Social issues perspectives and social policy implications." *Social Issues and Policy Review*, 2(1), 1–36. doi:10.1111/j.1751-2409.2008.00009.x.

Stebbins, R. A. (2009). "A leisure-based, theoretic typology of volunteers and volunteering." *Leisure Studies Association Newsletter*, 78, 9–12.

Studer, S. & von Schnurbein, G. (2013). "Organizational factors affecting volunteers: A literature review on volunteer coordination. "*VOLUNTAS: International Journal of Voluntary and Nonprofit Organizations*, 24(2), 403–440.

United Nations (2014). "UNV Strategic Framework 2014–2017." Retrieved from https://www.unv.org/sites/default/files/UNV_Strategic_Framework_2014_2017_0.pdf.

United Nations Volunteers (2015). "State of the World's Volunteerism Report: Transforming Governance." Retrieved from https://www.unv.org/sites/default/files/2015%20State%20of%20the%20World%27s%20Volunteerism%20Report%20-%20Transforming%20Governance.pdf.

United Nations Volunteers (2016). "Delivering the grassroots. 2015 Annual Report." Retrieved from https://www.unv.org/publications/unv-annual-report-2015-delivering-grassroots.

Wilson, J. (2012). "Volunteerism research: A review essay. "*Nonprofit and Voluntary Sector Quarterly*, 41(2), 176–212.

Wolpert, J. (1976). "Opening closed spaces." *ANNALS of the Association of American Geographers*, 66(1), 1–13.

Wong, L. P., Chui, W. H., & Kwok, Y. Y. (2011). "The Volunteer Satisfaction Index: A validation study in the Chinese cultural context. "*Social Indicators Researcher*, 104(1), 19–32.

Wu, H. (2011). "Social impact of volunteerism." Points of Light Institute. Retrieved from http://www.pointsoflight.org/sites/default/files/site-content/files/social_impact_of_volunteerism_pdf.pdf.

Yadama, G. N. & Messerschmidt, D. (2004). "Civic Service in South Asia: A Case Study of Nepal." *Nonprofit and Voluntary Sector Quarterly*, Supplement vol. 33, no. 4, December 2004, 98–126. doi:10.1177/0899764004270512.

Youniss, J., McLellan, J.A., & Yates, M. (1999). "Religion, Community Service, and Identify in American Youth." *Journal of Adolescence*, 22(2), 243–253.

Žižek, S. (1997). *The plague of fantasies*. New York: Verso.

2

HISTORY OF VOLUNTEERISM IN ASIA

This chapter presents and contextualizes the origins of Asian volunteerism and examines how it emerged and evolved, including both past and current trends. Historically, organized volunteering emerged more in Western contexts, and previous studies suggest that it was related to core Judeo-Christian values and national individualistic traits, more so than Asian ones (e.g., Chinese), as their traditional values (which are more family/group oriented) are more collectivistic in nature. Nevertheless in recent years, there has been a significant increase in awareness toward formal volunteerism in Asia and its evolution and participation rates are growing rapidly (Liu, Holosko, & Lo, 2009). The chapter briefly and initially describes how volunteerism emerged in Asia. Subsequently, it examines why organized volunteering has been relatively new to Asian countries. Further, it examines what particular precipitating events (e.g., environmental disasters, etc.), and at what particular points in time, have brought volunteerism more to the forefront and attention of public opinion in Asia, and how such perceptions about volunteerism have been subsequently affected by these events. Finally, it describes what types of volunteering is most common in various Asian countries today, in particular as related to Hong Kong.

Volunteerism in Asia

Currently, there have been no comprehensive studies on the history of volunteerism in Asia. Geographically, Asia is a very large and complex geographic area that includes a wide variety and large number of cultures, religions, political systems, languages, and economies, which makes it rather difficult to describe the evolution of Asian volunteerism. For instance, countries like Korea, Indonesia, Cambodia, Myanmar, Vietnam, and the Philippines have longer histories of invasion, conflict, colonization, and/or dictatorships. Ironically, it is under such circumstances that organized volunteerism initially developed in these countries, as a form of civic resistance against their various oppressors (Co, 2004).

One could posit that in Asia, volunteering steamed from a military tradition, before extending to a more holistic national civic dimension. Indeed, volunteers played essential roles in the Vietnamese wars for independence, and the war against the U.S., by transporting food to the battlefields, by opening roads to facilitate passenger transportation, and by hiding soldiers. More recently, starting in the 1990s, volunteering was eventually identified by the Vietnamese Communist party as an essential component for re-building the country. Similarly in the Philippines, volunteerism initially emerged as a "call of duty" for defending the country from aggressors, who through history were either Spanish, American or Japanese. Although the Philippines obtained its independence in 1946, during the 1970s and until 1986, it also experienced many dictatorships. During these years, the church was the strongest (if not the only) institution encouraging and organizing voluntary work and offering support to orphans, the homeless, the injured, and the poor. Paralleling other Asian countries, in the Philippines, the voluntary sector flourished with the end of these earlier regimes, and the restoration of democracy (Co, 2004). Conversely, one could say that volunteering originated in direct response to colonialism, occupation, and suppression, and later evolved in post-colonial states, particularly when the state gradually receded and allowed for the provision of civic and health services to non-state, and/or non-governmental organizations.

Indonesia

In Indonesia, the spirit of volunteerism has been described as stemming from the practice of *gotong royong*, meaning mutual aid. This communal practice has been best described among the people of Java. Today, this culture of giving, finds idealized manifestations in the construction of mosques and cultural centres, as well as in donations of food and goods, to celebrate social events such as births, and/or weddings (a practice which goes by the name of *kenduri*), and/or donations of land to future generations, and/or religious purposes. A similar practice goes by the name of *arisan tenaga,* or simply *arisan* (rotating-credit associations) in South Sulawesi, indicating a form of mutual assistance in cultivating land among various villagers (Agerhem & Cross, 2004; Sujarwoto & Tampubolon, 2013).

Singapore

An interesting phenomenon occurred in Singapore, where local youth engaged more in short-term volunteering internationally, than locally (Krishna & Khondker, 2004). Much international cooperation and volunteerism is promoted by the Singapore International Foundation (SIF), an NGO or more precisely a GONGO (governmental non-government organization), established in 1991. The SIF sends volunteers abroad mainly through three programmes: a) Singapore Volunteers Overseas (SVO), where trained and skilled youth normally spend one to two years volunteering in host communities serving as teachers, healthcare workers, social workers, and training the trainers. SVO specifically focuses on transferring skills and capacity-building; b) the Youth Expedition Project (YEP), which offers youth between 17 and 25 years old opportunities to discover different cultures and societies, raise awareness about socio-economic development issues, and awaken a sense of social responsibility; and, c) the local Humanitarian Relief Programme (HRP), which involves skilled youth (often engineers, medical doctors, counsellors, nurses) in disaster relief activities.

The emphasis on international volunteering has come under some criticism in Singapore, particularly because the above noted programmes are partially financed by the state. For example, the media described the participants of these programmes as "pampered children" who should volunteer at home, rather than engage in costly and short-term programmes in underdeveloped international countries. However, although the strategy of promoting overseas volunteering may be due to the specific socio-political context of Singapore, it is also a way for indirectly encouraging more volunteerism at home. As Krishna and Khondker (2004) reported, many youth in Singapore may hold the perception that the state is dominating every aspect of their life, so there is no room for them to personally offer their voluntary contributions. However, when volunteering abroad, they may also have the chance to re-examine the roles that they can play locally, in their home country. Furthermore, their international volunteering may serve as a strategy to cultivate a sense of increased national pride and identity as Singaporeans, which is a key component of the visionary ongoing nation-building projects of Singapore. In last fifteen years, the Singapore Ministry of Education has financially supported numerous schools to send their students to do international volunteering; as this is part of a long-term strategy of "planting future seeds" in youth's minds, which is expected to have increased positive and sustainable effects in the long run, when their youth return home. Thus, volunteering abroad in the specific context of Singapore, may actually represent an important first step toward a long-lasting engagement in future volunteering (Brassard, Sherraden, & Lough, 2010).

Japan

In Japan, organized volunteerism is presently still at an early stage of its development, as local volunteering experiences receive little or no recognition. In 2002, volunteers comprised only 9% of the population (Taniguchi, 2010). It appears that a number of reasons contribute to this phenomena. Tatsuki (2000) maintained that the modern Japanese volunteerism movement primarily originated in response to the 1923 Tokyo earthquake, when many university students mobilized to help people in need, and consequently founded the University Settlement House. However, with their war against China and later World War II, all of the country's resources, including charity, philanthropy, and various forms of social assistance came under stricter control of the state. For various economic, social, and political reasons, this system remained in place until after the end of the war, as most societal resources were controlled by a centralized and bureaucratic welfare service system. This endured until another earthquake hit the country, and radically changed the mind-set of many Japanese citizens. The 1995 Kobe earthquake, which killed more than 6,400 people and left another 350,000 homeless, represented a crucial turning point for volunteerism in Japan (Brassard et al., 2010). Tatsuki (2000) noted that this earthquake awoke a national sense of increased active citizenship and community involvement. Likely because of the disastrous impact of this earthquake, many people felt entitled to act on their own and start local voluntary actions, whereas under normal circumstances, a sense of traditional national obedience and conformity would have otherwise prevailed. Additionally, the ensuing large number of volunteers who emerged following this event was interpreted as a shift from a narrower, national self-interest, to more community-based issues and collective actions.

The 1995 earthquake popularized the term *borantia*, and almost overnight changed the national public perception of volunteering. Traditionally in the Japanese language, the term to describe charity and mutual self-help is *hoshi*, a notion that carries with it a strong sense of moral obligation, service, and sacrifice, and reflects the traditional hierarchical Japanese society. However, from the 1970s, the term *borantia* appeared (similar to the English *volunteer*), to describe a new type of associational behaviour. Specifically, *borantia* is associated with freewill and giving, rather than with obligation. As such, this term describes an attitude that is opposite to *hoshi*. The term emerged in a period of time when male Japanese youth were questioning their historic traditional social norms and values, and were in search of new purposes in their lives. The term finally became a symbol of civil society and individual participation after the devastating 1995 earthquake, when public frustration with the government's inability to consider and protect its citizens motivated many to take to their own initiatives and actions (Georgeou, 2010).

In recent years, there has been a growing interest among the Japanese to participate in various forms of local community voluntary work. Nevertheless overall, volunteerism in Japan remains rather low "internationally speaking", and previous studies have suggested that besides demographics, socioeconomic, and social capital variables, and religion (as in many other societies), in this context an important intervening variable is one's interactions with foreigners (Taniguchi, 2010). Historically, Japanese persons have tended to culturally distinguish between both in and out-group members. Currently in Japan, the idea of volunteering with/for strangers is still relatively new and uncommon. Thus, an important contribution to the Japanese voluntary sector is to promote greater levels of interaction with either immigrants and/or with people living in other countries (as today, many Japanese have many opportunities to travel abroad and volunteer) (Taniguchi, 2013). Because Japanese youth are not fluent in English, unlike countries like Singapore where English language is used, their international volunteering efforts are similarly rather underdeveloped (Brassard et al., 2010).

India

In India, the voluntary sector has been shaped by several longstanding societal and historical variables. Some organizations operating in community social development have been inspired by religious doctrines, and values; yet others are instead inspired by Gandhian values. In both cases however, spirituality plays a central role in India's culture. In 2005, the number of community organizations working at various levels in the non-profit sector was estimated to be about 1.2 million, involving almost 20 million paid or unpaid workers (Srivastava & Tandon, 2005). Riley (2002) suggested that the majority of Indian NGOs operate in the southern region because there the presence of Christian welfare organizations is much more prevalent. Recent research showed that Indian students may choose from many volunteering opportunities, either in non-profit agencies, as well as informal volunteering in NGOs and religious institutions. The motives and reasons for volunteering among Indian youth were also studied, with poor and upper-class students pursuing more educational volunteering opportunities, and middle-class students desiring more employment-based opportunities (Ghose & Kassam, 2014).

Nepal

Nepal is yet another illustrative example of how a political system may dramatically delimit (or even prohibit) the establishment of any formal or organized organization (particularly, if it is not administered by the state) for volunteering experiences. In the 1970s, Nepal launched its first nationwide youth civil service movement known as the National Development Service (NDS). It was developed as an integral component of a larger plan, aimed to modernize the Nepalese education system. University students were required to attend training, followed by ten months of volunteering service in rural communities. The programme was surprisingly very successful, and paradoxically, their underestimated success also explained why the NDS was soon dismantled. Ironically, the encounters between young university students and poor villagers awakened their mutual understanding, and opened the eyes of both subgroups. This ongoing exchange somehow enhanced a new sense of social justice and political participation among the population that troubled the existing monarchy, and the few politicos who had power and authority (Yadama & Messerschmidt, 2004). In short here, Nepalese volunteering promotes values of mutual-help, civil rights, participation, accountability, empowerment, and self-efficacy, and all of these are closely related to democratic ideals (that is, where the power is dispersed among the population), and not to any form of an authoritative regime (where the power is concentrated to just a few individuals).

China

In China, *guanxi* (one's own social network) is a complex system based on mutual obligations and nuanced cultural understandings that regulate long-term social and business relations. *Guanxi* describes the close relationships among people from the same social circles; as such, it differentiates insiders from outsiders. *Guanxi* is based on reciprocity and as such, it is capable of mobilizing people to offer help, showing that care and giving support is considered as a form of citizen voluntary activity. Similarly, Japanese voluntary activities were initially obligations determined by the principles of membership and national duty; and in Korea, volunteering was described as being grounded more so on patriotism (Brassard et al., 2010).

Collectively, traditional Chinese, Korean and Japanese cultures greatly emphasize the identification of one's own group identity, as one of the main motives for voluntary activities. Thus, volunteer activities may then be practiced mainly among members of the same cohorts (although significant differences about what defines "one's own group" among these cultures exist), which are also likely to have caused volunteering to remain rather unorganized and undeveloped in these societies. Conversely, voluntary activities in European and North American societies were greatly inspired by more core altruistic and imbedded spiritual, and/or religious values (e.g., religion), rather than about societal norms of membership to a group. Furthermore, in collectivist societies, the group is deemed more important than the individual (Busiol, 2012), so voluntary activities should be beneficial to the former, but not necessarily to the latter.

Particularly in the communist China of Chairman Mao, volunteering was promoted as a means to strengthen national morality, and in turn, it reinforced the leaders' authority, thus empowering the Chinese Communist Party (CCP), and not necessarily Chinese youth. Today, self-actualization is a common term for describing youth empowerment through volunteering (Liu et al., 2009). However, this was not the case in pre-reform China, where self-actualization was instead equated with selfishness. In that context, individual choices and will (which is at the base of all volunteering) were not encouraged, and instead mass movements and campaigns against individual choices were adopted (Lo, Su, & Jiang, 2009). However, things changed dramatically in post-reform China, as the new and emerging economic system had a profound impact on society, and created a newer and higher demand for national social welfare. Major factors influential here included: the increased number of laid-off workers not covered by labour insurance; the increase in industrial injuries; the increased growth of the elderly population requiring social security healthcare and retirement pensions; changes in household structures; the increased number of one-child families; and, the increase in the number of migrant workers. Furthermore at the same time, traditional forms of volunteering were declining, particularly among youth, as their days were now busy with longer working hours. In this context, Chinese volunteering was eventually re-discovered, as a means of "giving back" to the community and society. This was coupled with the newer freedoms experienced by youth (i.e., freedom to choose a job, instead of doing a job assigned by the state; freedom to travel, and freedom to participate in their own communities), and their consequential needs to give more meaning and purpose to their own lives. This new-found freedom of choice was in fact unknown to many as historically, the concept of individual importance is still very unfamiliar to Chinese culture.

In this new Chinese cultural scenario, volunteering represented a way for discovering more about oneself (e.g., values, aspirations) and others, and for reflecting about life itself (e.g., what are we living for?) (Lo et al., 2009). From the 1980s, volunteering was recognized as rather noble in Chinese communist society (Zhuang, 2010). However, it was in the 1990s that organized volunteering started to grow significantly in mainland China, particularly in the faster growing and developing cities: Shenzhen initiated the first volunteer association in this regard, called the Shenzhen Volunteer Association which was established in 1989, and the Youth Volunteer Work Federation was launched in 1990; Beijing founded the Loving Heart Association, in 1993, and the Youth Volunteer Action, in 1994; and, in Shanghai the Shanghai Volunteer Association was founded in 1995. More recently, the Beijing 2008 Olympic Games represented an important milestone in the history of volunteerism in China. The enormous number of participants supporting the Olympics with some 70,000 volunteers, mostly university students, were selected from more than one million applicants, which popularized and widened the understanding of volunteerism in Chinese society, contributing to increased participation to the importance of volunteering overall (Zhuang, 2010).

Hong Kong

In Hong Kong research confirmed that volunteering helped youth prepare better for employment, and also to becoming more responsible adults (Liu, 2014). A study among Hong Kong university students revealed a significant correlation between volunteering and social responsibility, defined as the sensitivity and respect for the society in which one resides (Cheung, Lo, & Liu, 2015). Fostering a higher sense of social responsibility among youth is important for offsetting much existing inequality and conflicts in society, as well as for preventing some negative effects of globalization such as the reduced identification with one's own society. In another study, youth volunteers showed a higher sense of purpose in their lives and more pro-social values, than did non-volunteers of similar ages (Law & Shek, 2009). Furthermore, volunteering has been associated with building trust, cooperation, providing more work experiences, having opportunities for career development, and revealed positive effects on one's mood overall (Cheung, Lo, & Liu, 2012;, ; Cheung, Lo, & Liu, 2016; Liu, Ye, & Yeung, 2015). In another Hong Kong study by the Agency for Volunteer Service (AVS) in partnership with the Hong Kong University Centre for Civil Society and Governance, it was found that the younger the volunteer, the longer they served as volunteers; and the longer volunteers served, the higher their overall volunteer hours (Centre for Civil Society and Governance, The University of Hong Kong and Policy 21 Limited, 2010). Finally here, for some Chinese youth, volunteering may represent a strategy for coping with one's own personal life challenges. The impact on other people's lives may be limited, but nevertheless the economic and social consequences of these various voluntary activities seemed significant, as they helped some youth volunteers address local problems such as social isolation, marginalization, substance abuse, and depression (i.e., self-oriented and protective motives).

International volunteering in Asia

International volunteering is defined as an organized voluntary activity by volunteers who go abroad. The organizations supporting and coordinating such projects may be either public or private, and often volunteers receive little or no compensation for their service (Brassard et al., 2010). Within international volunteering, overall there are a few volunteer activities such as: 1) a "gap year" – in most cases this involves high school or college students who volunteer for "any period of time between three and 24 months in which an individual takes "'out' [time] from formal education, training or the workplace, and where the time out sits in the context of a longer career trajectory" (Jones, 2004, p.8); 2) international service-learning – where "a structured learning experience combines community service with explicit learning objectives, preparation, and reflection" (Seifer, 1998, p.274); and, 3) "voluntourism" – or volunteer tourism.

Brassard and colleagues (2010) suggested that the emergence of international volunteering is due to several factors, including: 1) globalization – particularly due to migration, the exponential growth of social media, and international study programs; 2) colonization; 3) the global response to natural disasters – like tsunamis, earthquakes, and/or floods; 4) the development of national volunteering – where most participants volunteer at home first, and then go abroad; and, 5) political and economic factors – such as a growing middle class, and travel costs reducing. For example, international volunteering in Asia greatly increased after a tsunami hit Indonesia, Thailand, and Sri Lanka, the Maldives, and part of India, on the morning of 26 December 2004. Not only did this disaster wash away entire communities and villages in a few short minutes, but it also destroyed some of the most exotic holiday destinations of many (mainly foreigner) travellers, and also killed many tourists who were visiting there on vacation. Additionally, when this tsunami hit, many people were able to record videos of these events with their own phones (unlike before), and post them immediately on the Internet. This resulted in an unprecedented number of amateur reports and stories directly from the field, being watched globally. As a consequence, many people were shocked, and some individuals started thinking about combining their holidays with volunteering in one of these countries.

Finally, this massive international response was also possible because in recent years tourism has become more of a mass phenomenon. Notwithstanding these issues, international volunteering also presents some challenges and limitations. For example, there may be a lack of coordination between sender and hosting organizations, which may cause mismatches between the expectations of volunteers and the needs of service recipients. Further, most host organizations lack the capacity in terms of human/financial resources to assess the impact of international volunteering activities on their host communities. Finally here, some governments prefer not to prioritize international volunteering, as they worry that foreign volunteers may take away possible jobs that locals could do (Brassard et al., 2010).

Voluntourism

Voluntourism is a relatively new trend, and it has emerged in the last 20 years as a combination of *volunteering* and *tourism*. Voluntourism or "volunteer tourism" is shorter-term voluntary work for those who conceive of volunteering, not as the only purpose of their vacation traveling. Voluntourism originated in Europe and later was popularized among North America and Australia. Recently, it has grown in some wealthier non-Western nations, and frequently includes Asian participants from places like Hong Kong and Singapore (Lo & Lee, 2011; Sin, 2009).

According to Wearing and McGehee (2013), volunteer tourists normally engage in short-term projects that last less than four weeks and focus on, but are not limited to, economic and social development, medical assistance, conservation projects, or education. Although volunteer tourists often have positive motives for volunteering, including altruism, cultural understanding, self-growth, some have suggested that voluntourism is a new form of colonialism, in that it serves the needs of the (Western) clients, more so than the actual host communities. For instance, in most cases, many of these volunteers lack necessary skills, although they may feel that they will be valued experts, coming to help vulnerable persons. Second, they may not be very culturally sensitive; and thus, they may import their own values and habits that the indigenous locals may not find adequate or useful (Tuovinen, 2014). It is deemed that this particular type of volunteering in some instances can do more harm than good. For example, some host communities may become dependent on the "business of voluntourism". In fact, organizations operating in volunteer tourism are likely to be more oriented toward business and profits, than humanitarian or social capital purposes. Furthermore, voluntourism may undermine the dignity of the local communities, and promote an "assistance dependency mentality", among local stakeholders (Guttentag, 2009). Taken together, these consequences are actually contrary to the mission or aims of volunteering (as indicated in chapter 1).

This was particularly evident and noticed in countries such as Cambodia, where volunteer tourism has become a very profitable business, in recent years. According to Tuovinen (2014), the number of orphans in Cambodia decreased, but the number of orphanages simultaneously increased. Interestingly enough, in these same years, the number of visitors to Cambodia tripled. Not surprisingly, more than two thirds of Cambodian orphans hosted in these institutions actually had at least one living parent, but came from poorer families in rural areas and, therefore, were sent/sold by their relatives to these orphanages, with the hope of a better life, and more opportunities of receiving an education. However, some of these children became more of a tourist attraction, and orphanage visits in most cases were actually businesses that were rather exploitative of these children (Tuovinen, 2014).

Thus, voluntourism has the potential for some negative consequences that are intrinsic to its various forms of volunteering. In summary, voluntourism is: 1) mainly a Eurocentric import; 2) volunteers and agencies may actually benefit more than the service-recipients themselves; 3) it is done with little or no training, suggesting that many people feel entitled to volunteer just because they want to, and have no perception of potential negative consequences of their actions; and, 4) it creates a circle in which service-recipients (e.g., children) are a consequence of volunteering (e.g., they increase in number as the number of volunteer increases), and as such, they are induced to remain in this condition of need rather than evolve.

Conclusion

Volunteerism is commonly recognized as an early form of social service in supplementing resources to the community. It is also recognized as an early seed facilitating the development of social work as a profession basing on the American experience (Hepworth & Larsen, 1986). It is therefore quite relevant for us to borrow the knowledge on how social work became internationalized and exported to Asian to conclude on the Asian experiences in adopting and applying systematically volunteerism to their communities. In discussing the Internationalization of Social Work, it is said that it has gone through four stages of development, starting with the Pioneering stage, where social work was imported from the U.K. and be applied in the U.S.; then the Imperialistic stage, where social work was exported from the U.S. to European countries (mainly English-speaking countries); then the Indigenization stage, where social work was exported to non-English speaking countries including Asian countries; and finally the International Social Development stage, where the Eurocentric and non-Eurocentric cultures will exchange and network to discuss on the consequences of indigenization, and put lights on its future development (Mayadas and Elliott, 1997; Ip, 2006). If we put this to examine the experiences of Asia in implementing and developing volunteerism, we can easily find that volunteerism (specifically formal volunteerism), like International Social Work, was firstly pioneered and imperialized in the Western cultures, across both cultures of the U.S. and other European countries. It then got indigenized or adopted for implementation in Asia countries by many different paths and journeys. Our reviews earlier on how different Asian countries have been developing volunteer service will serve as a proof that it has successfully transplanted to many Asia countries. The argument left for discussion is "whether have we entered the International Social Development" stage, that we are having equal, intensive and parallel networking and exchanges between the Eurocentric countries and Asian countries to share and communicate on our experiences and consequences of indigenizing volunteerism (Midgley & Toors, 1992; Ip, 2006). Among Asian countries, are we having enough reflections and doing critical empirical studies to examine the impact of this borrowed idea to our cultures? If not, do we know how our service recipients perceive this type of helping, is volunteer service dominating, overpowering, and judging service recipients? How about our volunteers? Do they feel pressurized to be a volunteer and criticized for not being one? All these are obvious gaps of knowledge here in Asia, which are limiting us to confidently draw a conclusion on how well we have been indigenizing our work in local communities, meaning that the existing services might risk being "not appropriate" for our service users, but remain an unfamiliar and imposing culture (Midgley & Toors, 1992). If we conclude that volunteerism is still undergoing its indigenizing stage of development here in Asia, we have to admit that knowledge building and empirical studies are of utmost importance for us to move on indigenizing our work. This gives a supporting ground for this book, in its following chapters, to narrow its focus from Asia to Hong Kong, and then from the macro volunteer development in Hong Kong to the creation and implementation of only one frontline experience in Hong Kong. It is hoped that this attempt will contribute in building some grounded knowledge and drawing conclusions on local practice wisdom, for shedding light on how to advance future volunteer work.

References

Agerhem, S. & Cross, S. R. (2004). "Volunteering in South Asia and South East Asia." International Federation of Red Cross and Red Crescent Societies. Asia Pacific Service Center, Kuala Lumpur, Malaysia. Retrieved from http://www.cruzroja.es/pls/portal30/docs/PAGE/6_VL_2006/BIBLIOTECA/PAISES_REGIONES/ASIA/IFRC_VOLASIA_2004195809.PDF.

Brassard, C., Sherraden, M. S., & Lough, B. J. (2010). "Emerging perspectives on international volunteerism in Asia." IVCO Forum Research Paper. Retreived July (Vol. 1, p.2014). Retrieved from https://www.researchgate.net/profile/Benjamin_Lough/publication/236961958_Emerging_perspectives_on_international_volunteerism_in_Asia/links/0c96051ae39a417154000000.pdf.

Busiol, D. (2012). "The Many Names of Hong Kong: Mapping Language, Silence and Culture in China." *Cultura. International Journal of Philosophy of Culture and Axiology*, 12(2), 207–226.

Center for Civil Society and Governance, The University of Hong Kong (2010). "Volunteering in Hong Kong Survey Research." Retrieved from http://www.avs.org.hk/symposium/pdf/HKU%2520PPT_Press%2520Conf_eng_final.pdf.

Cheung, C. K., Lo, T.W. & Liu E. S. C. (2015). "Relationships Between Volunteerism and Social Responsibility in Young Volunteers." *Voluntas: International Journal of Voluntary and Nonprofit Organizations*, 26(3), 872–889.

Cheung J. K., Lo, T.W., & Liu, E. S. C. (2012). "Measuring Volunteering Empowerment and Competence in Shanghai." *Administration in Social Work*, 36(2), 149–174.

Cheung, C. K., Lo, T.W. & Liu, E. S. C. (2016). "Sustaining Social Trust and Volunteer Role Identity Reciprocally over Time in Pre-adult, Adult, and Older Volunteers". *Journal of Social Service Research*, 42(1), 70–83

Co, E. E. A. (2004). "Civic service in East Asia and the Pacific." *Nonprofit and voluntary sector quarterly*, 33(4_suppl), 127–147.

Georgeou, N. (2010). "From Hōshi to Borantia: Transformations of Volunteering in Japan and Implications for Foreign Policy. "*VOLUNTAS: International Journal of Voluntary and Nonprofit Organizations*, 21(4), 467–480.

Ghose, T. & Kassam, M. (2014). "Motivations to volunteer among college students in India." *VOLUNTAS: International Journal of Voluntary and Nonprofit Organizations*, 25(1), 28–45.

Guttentag, D. A. (2009). "The possible negative impacts of volunteer tourism." *International Journal of Tourism Research*, 11(6), 537–551.

Hepworth, D. H. & Larsen, J. A. (1986). *Direct Social Work Practice*. Belmont, California: Wadsworth Publishing Company.

Ip, K. S. (2006). "Indigenization of social work: An international perspective and conceptualization. "*Asia Pacific Journal of Social Work and Development*, 16(1), 43–55.

Jones, A. (2004). "Review of gap year provision." London: DfES. Retrieved from http://217.35.77.12/archive/england/papers/education/pdfs/RR555.pdf.

Krishna, C. K. & Khondker, H. H. (2004). "Nation Building Through International Volunteerism: A Case Study of Singapore." *The International Journal of Sociology and Social Policy*, 24(1/2), 21–55.
Law, B. M. & Shek, D. T. (2009). "Beliefs about volunteerism, volunteering intention, volunteering behavior, and purpose in life among Chinese adolescents in Hong Kong." *The Scientific World Journal*, 9, 855–865.
Liu, E. S. C., Holosko, M. J., & Lo, T. W. (Eds.). (2009). *Youth empowerment and volunteerism: Principles, policies and practices.* Hong Kong: City University of Hong Kong Press.
Liu, E. S. C. (2014). "Youth's Perception on the Impact and Meaning of Working with Children." *Journal of Psychology & Psychotherapy*, 5(2). doi:10.4172/2161-0487.1000177.
Liu, E. S. C., Ye, C. J. & Yeung, D. Y. (2015). "Effects of Approach to Learning and Self-perceived Overall Competence of University Students." *Learning and Individual Differences*, 39(April), 199–204.
Lo, A. S. & Lee, C. Y. (2011). "Motivations and perceived value of volunteer tourists from Hong Kong." *Tourism Management*, 32(2), 326–334.
Lo, T. W., Su, S., & Jiang, G. (2009). "Youth empowerment and self-actualization: experiences in Shanghai, China." In E. S. C. Liu, M. J. Holosko and T. W. Lo (Eds.), *Youth empowerment and volunteerism: Principles, policies and practices* (pp. 251–273). Hong Kong: City University of HK Press.
Mayadas, N. S. & Elliott, D. (1997). "Lesson from international social work." In M. Reisch & E. Gambrill (Eds.), *Social Work in the 21st Century* (pp. 15–28). California: Pine Forgepress.
Midgley, J. & Toors, M. (1992). "Is international social work a one-day transfer of ideas and practice methods from the United States to other countries?" In E. Gambrill & R. Pruger (Eds.), *Controversies in social work* (pp. 35–46). Boston: Allyn & Bacon.
Riley, J.M. (2002). *Stakeholders in rural development: critical collaboration in state-NGO partnerships.* New Delhi, Thousand Oaks, London: Sage Publications.
Seifer, S. D. (1998). "Service-learning: community-campus partnerships for health professions education. "*Academic Medicine*, 73(3), 273–277.
Sin, H. L. (2009). "Volunteer Tourism – 'involve me and I will learn'." *Annals of Tourism Research*, 36(3), 480–501.
Srivastava, S. S. & Tandon, R. (2005). "How Large Is India's Non-Profit Sector?" *Economic and Political Weekly*, 40, 1948–1952.
Sujarwoto, S. & Tampubolon, G. (2013). "Mother's social capital and child health in Indonesia." *Social Science & Medicine*, 91, 1–9.
Taniguchi, H. (2010). "Who are volunteers in Japan?" *Nonprofit and Voluntary Sector Quarterly*, 39(1), 161–179.
Taniguchi, H. (2013). "The influence of generalized trust on volunteering in Japan." *Nonprofit and Voluntary Sector Quarterly*, 42(1), 127–147.
Tatsuki, S. (2000). "The Kobe earthquake and the renaissance of volunteerism in Japan." *Journal of Kwansei Gakuin University Department of Sociology Studies*, 87, 185–196.
Tuovinen, H. (2014). "Shadows of voluntourism and the connection to orphanage business in Asia and Cambodia." (BA thesis). Haaga-Helia University of Applied Sciences, Helsinki, Finland.
Wearing, S. & McGehee, N. G. (2013). "Volunteer tourism: A review. "*Tourism Management*, 38, 120–130.
Yadama, G. N. & Messerschmidt, D. (2004). "Civic service in South Asia: A case study of Nepal. "*Nonprofit and Voluntary Sector Quarterly*, 33(4_suppl), 98–126.
Zhuang, J. (2010). "Beijing 2008: Volunteerism in Chinese culture and its Olympic interpretation and influence." *The International Journal of the History of Sport*, 27(16–18), 2842–2862.

3

HISTORY OF VOLUNTEERISM IN HONG KONG

This brief historical account presents a discussion of the relationship between international, national, and local trends that have impacted Hong Kong's volunteerism. How local communities received and implemented these policies, and how Hong Kong citizens become involved in volunteering will be described. This helps contextualize the evolution of volunteerism in Hong Kong and promotes how to think more about the "big picture", meaning not simply from the perspective of the volunteer, and/or the service receiver, but also collectively from community, societal and political perspectives. Finally, the chapter provides some insights on how local policies "trickle down" to community and individual levels, and how they impact local volunteering activities in Hong Kong.

Global trends in volunteerism

Why local governments should promote volunteering

Volunteering reflects a form of pro-active citizenship, which is directly related to the concepts of altruism, social inclusion, and justice. These in turn, can significantly contribute to a more cohesive, tolerant, and equitable society (Cuthill & Warburton, 2005). For instance, when examining findings from previous research, Haski-Leventhal, Mejis and Hustinx (2010) identified four main reasons why all governments should promote youth volunteering: 1) it increases the quality of life and career opportunities of volunteers (individual positive effects); 2) it improves the quality of local services, and makes them more affordable; 3) it reinforces social capital and social cohesion, and helps to reach out to disadvantaged groups; and, 4) it enhances civil engagement among youth, which strengthens the overall community. Today, many contend that local governments should do more research on volunteering to realize their various cultural, social, and economic outcomes. Such research could then be used to make more informed national and local policies about volunteerism, in general.

Government policies in other countries

Volunteering can be conceptualized along three interrelated, and braided dimensions: willingness, capability, and one's availability to volunteer (Haski-Leventhal, Meijs, & Hustinx, 2010). Willingness to volunteer is influenced by individual motives, values, attitudes, as well as social norms, benefits, and incentives. Capability refers to the actual skills and knowledge required for volunteering. Finally, availability indicates whether one can offer the time, and is emotionally available, to commit to the volunteering experience in a meaningful way (p.147).

First, governments can promote volunteering by enacting more proactive policies that enhance local youth *willingness* to volunteer. For example in 1993, the U.S. passed the National and Community Service Trust Act with its goal to establish the Corporation for National and Community Service (CNCS), to enhance more local volunteering opportunities (Frumkin & Jastrzab, 2010). Today, this agency engages more than 5 million citizens, and offers many diverse programmes to address various local issues like poverty, education, and the environment. Similarly, the U.K., agreement (Compact) between the government and the voluntary sector was signed in 1998, and renewed again in 2010 (National Council for Volunteer Organizations). It was developed by representatives from leading voluntary, community, and minority organizations. It also established guidelines about several Hong Kong national priority areas such as funding arrangements, policy design, promoting equality, strengthening independence, and increasing more direct involvement in delivering local services. In South Australia, the government appointed a "Minister of Volunteering", and decided to promote more local volunteering by awarding volunteers for their service contribution.

Furthermore, empirical research has indicated that friends, family members, mentors, teachers, and other volunteers directly influence a person's decision to volunteer, more so than official campaigning, and/or the mass media (Musick & Wilson 2008). In a large study conducted in Hong Kong (Law & Shek, 2009), it was shown that a youth's intention to volunteer and their volunteering behaviours were significantly influenced by strong beliefs about family. Thus, in Hong Kong volunteering policies should ideally target youth's familial connections and related networks, in order to influence their volunteering willingness and to participate. For example, local policies could reward volunteers who involve others from their social networks (e.g., friends, neighbours, and/or family members) in volunteering.

Additionally, more or all local governments should increase one's *capability* to volunteer, by supporting more research, and dissemination of knowledge about volunteering, coupled with developing local training centres for volunteers and volunteer managers. For example, the European Union (EU) has had several public calls for proposals for tender, under the "EU Aid Volunteers" initiative. In addition, most governments do have the power to ensure that people with disabilities, disadvantaged, or excluded groups may also volunteer. Alternatively, many local governments could also support various travel costs, medical insurance, and some accommodation for local citizens who wish to volunteer (ECHO, 2014).

Finally here, local governments in many countries could enhance a youth's *availability* to volunteer by offering tax deductions, and/or other financial incentives, so that such youth could work less, and have more free time for volunteering (Haski-Leventhal et al., 2010). In the U.S., the Serve America Act awards disadvantaged youth with money for completing volunteering programmes. Specifically, the Act aims at involving low-income students and out-of-school youth, with the hope to improve their lives and communities. Finally, schools and institutions that have the best records of students volunteering are eligible for additional grant funding.

Major obstacles impeding youth volunteering

According to the United Nations (United Nations Volunteers, 2013), there are many identified barriers to youth volunteering. First, there is a concern that volunteering may remain accessible only to the so-called elite or privileged members of a community, for two main reasons: 1) social and economic exclusion, as only a few individuals may be able to volunteer, instead of having paid jobs; and, 2) in some communities, voluntary activities may be not accessible to various minority groups, young women, and/or youth with special needs. As a consequence, these already marginalized youth (those who may potentially benefit the most from volunteering) may find it more difficult to access volunteering in their respective communities. Conversely, although many non-profit organizations rely heavily on local volunteers, they tend to do a poorer job in managing their volunteers' time and talents. For example: a) the needs of host agencies may not always match the expectations and skills of volunteers; and, b) some agencies may provide limited coaching and mentoring opportunities for their volunteers. Overall, such poor management might negatively affect the overall volunteering experience, and the extant literature reveals that volunteers who are not satisfied by their experiences, are less likely to volunteer in the future. In the U.S., in order to address this problem, some current policies (e.g., the Serve America Act, 2009), provide grants to support for the active recruitment, matching, training, and supervision of volunteers. The act's aim is not only to recruit new volunteers, but more importantly, retain them. Finally here, other barriers to the development of volunteering noted in the literature include: a) a lack of information about volunteering opportunities; b) youth are minimally involved in programme design and implementation; and, c) there is limited extant evidence-based research about the precise impact of volunteering on peace, community and human development.

The situation in Hong Kong

Obstacles to youth volunteering in Hong Kong

As indicated above, there are numerous obstacles or challenges to volunteering globally, and some are very apparent in Hong Kong. Kam (2009) maintained that historically, youth services in Hong Kong were developed to reduce "anti-social", and/or "deviant" behaviours. Similarly, To (2007) observed that social work in Hong Kong is based primarily on a *deficit* model, and that local social workers have long been criticised for placing more emphasis on helping youth adapt to their environments, rather than supporting them to develop critical thinking skills to help change the system. It is also known that local social services often reflect a "blaming the victim mentality"; however, these are normative and are aimed at "correcting", and/or treating victims, rather than changing the prevailing social conditions that cause their social problems. As such, local health and human service agencies are more inclined to solve more immediate problems, rather than planning longer-term prevention-based strategies, and/or empowering local programmes to promote more positive youth development. Putting this general background of social welfare in Hong Kong to youth volunteerism, it is speculated that Hong Kong is found to be increasing its number of volunteers quickly but is not able to sustain volunteers, or optimize volunteers' development through volunteering. As reported by the World Giving Index (Charities Aid Foundation, 2010), Hong Kong ranked number 18 among the top 21 countries in the world. At the same time, Hong Kong young volunteers are found by a local study to be unable to become "long-term engagement" volunteers, because of a "lack of time", "not feeling respect and a lack of understanding from the society", "insufficient support from the host organization", etc. (Chinese YMCA, 2016). As a result, many Hong Kong youth are often seen as passive receivers, rather than cherished local resources. Similarly, their participation is often perceived as "technical supporters" and may be taken as a burden on professional human service employee workloads. Thus, more thinking and research should be carried out to understand how local policies should be made to promote a fundamental shift in mentality; as youth volunteering should be taken as inclusive and empowering, rather than exclusive and marginalizing.

Promoting local volunteerism

In September 1997, the Social Welfare Department (SWD) set up the Central Office for Volunteer Service (COVS), in order to facilitate volunteer development in a more co-ordinated manner. In 1998, the Volunteer Movement (VM) with its aim to develop local volunteer service opportunities was formally launched by the SWD, in coordination with a number of non-governmental organizations/institutions. In 1999, the "Steering Committee on Volunteer

Movement" was created, and was subsequently re-named the "Steering Committee on Promotion of Volunteer Service" (SCPVS) in 2002. Since then, the SCPVS has worked extensively to promote a culture for local community volunteering experiences in Hong Kong. However, their objectives have expanded over time, and various other strategies were developed. The implementation of strategies targeted at district levels are currently supported by a few "District Coordinating Committees on Promotion of Volunteer Service" (currently eleven), that operate through their " Designated Offices on Volunteer Service", in each district. Specifically, they provide assistance to agencies/organizations to develop volunteer teams in the designated Hong Kong district. The local organizational structure of these various government agencies promoting volunteer activities is illustrated in Figure 3.1.

From 1999 to 2005, the SCPVS presented the concept of volunteering (as being relatively new to the local culture), as a way of fulfilling one's personal self-empowerment. Basically, the committee made efforts to popularize volunteering through a vigorous and strategic public promotional campaign (e.g., leaflets, websites, user guides, database, hotline, banners, etc.). Here, the committee decided to initially target three local sub-groups, each represented by a specific sub-committee: 1) youth; 2) commercial corporations; and, 3) community organizations (Steering Committee on Promotion of Volunteer Service, 2016). Figure 3.1 describes the current organizational strategy of the SCPVS.

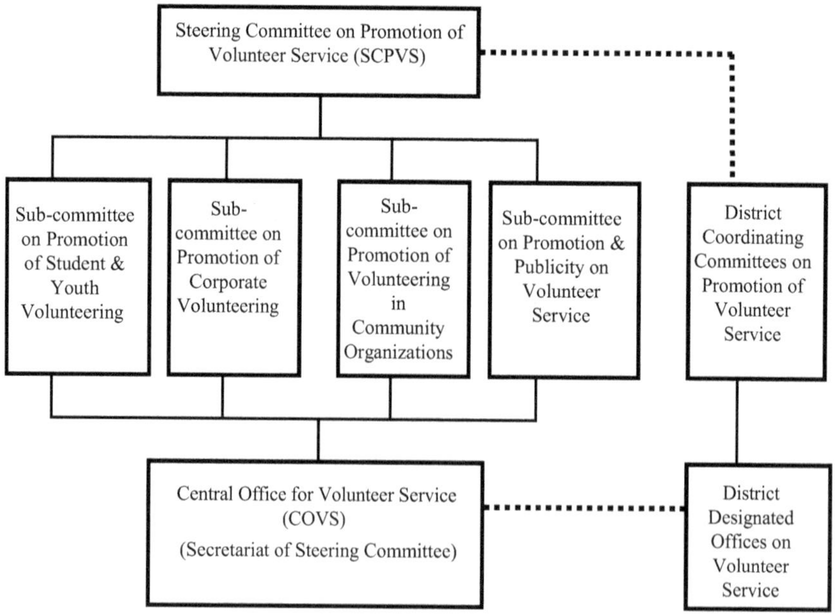

FIGURE 3.1 The organizational structure of the Steering Committee on the Promotion of Volunteer Services (SCPVS) in Hong Kong

Since 2010, given the growing annual number of Hong Kong volunteers, the SCPVS initiated a rather creative idea. The concept of "Level 3 Volunteering" was launched, with its aim to bring together the spirit and values of volunteering into one's everyday life (whereas for instance, "Level 1" of volunteering was considered more episodic/"one-off" volunteering, "Level 2 Volunteering" was those sustainable volunteer projects rooted in Hong Kong already). Building on their success, the same goal was sequentially re-created with the slogans used in 2011 "Volunteering – New Attitude to Life", 2014 "You and Me Together", and 2015 "Volunteering – New Experience in Life". These all highlighted the benefits and the potential enrichment derived from community volunteering. During this time, the committee made concerted efforts to diversify local volunteering opportunities, by launching different local programmes, projects and schemes. Furthermore, various awards were offered to individuals, families, and organizations, based on the times that they devoted to their voluntary activities. Other initiatives, such as training and local competitions were offered by each sub-committee listed in Figure 3.1. In order to reach the targeted core youth, the SCPVS also liaised with schools, parent-teacher associations, youth organizations, and subsequently organized public speeches, for sharing first-hand experiences of local volunteering. From 2016 onward, the committee's objectives evolved to promote the mutual benefits to both services recipients and volunteers, so that everyone could consider becoming a volunteer in their daily life; encourage diverse and new volunteering opportunities that might respond to emerging social needs; recognize good practices and timely knowledge; and, strengthen networks with community stakeholders for better coordination and collaboration (Steering Committee on Promotion of Volunteer Service, 2016).

After laying out the general background about volunteering in Hong Kong, its obstacles and the government promotional work, the rest of this chapter will focus on discussing how the roles of Hong Kong Government (details on the work of SCPVS), and a local non-government organization which was specifically set up for promotion of volunteer work (the introduction of the work of Agency for Volunteer Service) have helped develop volunteerism in Hong Kong.

SCPVS in Hong Kong

In order to have the insider perspective to the committee work of SCPVS, in 2018 the author (of this text) conducted a two-hour focus group with two key stakeholders of the SCPVS, the Chair of the Sub-committee on Promotion of Student and Youth Volunteering who was also a member of SCPVS, and one SWD member of staff supporting the work of this sub-committee as well as SCPVS. They were asked about their experiences with the history of the committee, appointments to the committee, their roles and responsibilities, and perceptions about the committee and its work in Hong Kong's volunteering history. Their candid responses are presented herein as a composite account of all information thus collected.

About the background of the Volunteer Movement (VM) and the setting up of the SCPVS

After the 1967 riots, the Hong Kong government started to pay much more attention to youth policy, overall. The government decided to establish more government branches for youth development, to give youth more channels to participate in local social development in positive ways to exert their energy, and to express their voices and opinions. Over time, it was also realized that it was important for the government to emphasize youth work. Volunteerism started a century ago in Hong Kong. Before the establishment of the Hong Kong Government, there were already many volunteer and religious groups who came to provide social services in Hong Kong. But 1967 was a very important historical time, driving the government at that time to set youth policy as a priority. One of their main goals was to encourage youth to participate in building their communities, showing them how to use their energy and strengths positively, such that volunteerism became a very important community concept. According to various documents, 1998 was recorded as the year of the official Volunteer Movement (VM). In fact, volunteer service was already happening in many departments earlier, e.g., in the Social Welfare Department, in many youth services, and youth volunteering already existed. But in a more systematic way, it used the VM to co-ordinate the territory to widen volunteer services, to promote and collect data on volunteer hours, and to award outstanding services. A steering committee was then formed in 1999. Many community leaders and experts were invited to sit on the committee and offered their opinions. The existing Steering Committee continues to advise on the vision, direction, strategies and ideas for the government on how to continue developing local volunteering in a very strategic way in Hong Kong.

The first chairperson of the first Steering Committee was Mrs. Tung (wife of the then first Chief Executive of Hong Kong), in 1998. She became the leader of all volunteer services in Hong Kong. Since then, all wives of Chief Executives are routinely appointed as Chair for a term. All who are appointed as the members are in fact the well-known community leaders, many are from the media, all of whom are very enthusiastic about community building. They lead us, and also different sub-committees. Conclusively in Hong Kong, there are some pressing social issues in the community, and so volunteering is always being expanded. However, volunteerism and social welfare in fact has a very long history in Hong Kong, and Hong Kong social work has a long history of developing local volunteerism. Social welfare is mainly run by NGOs, but NGOs do not have all the resources they need for their services, and so they have to rely heavily on volunteers for fund-raising and for offering their services. Volunteerism is therefore widely recognized and driven by the government. When the government supports the development of NGOs, it fully recognizes that not all resources are limited, but volunteerism is highly regarded as a valuable resource to fill in all possible gaps. When NGO proposals are handed to the government, and if volunteers are included, the government will buy into the idea.

The rationale for the formal establishment of the volunteer policy in 1998

Why was it implemented in 1998? This is related to when Hong Kong was handed over to Chinese sovereignty in 1997. The return of Hong Kong to China was a very challenging transitional period and the government was concerned about how to stabilize our uncertain society, and so, the year 1998 carries special meaning. Volunteerism was already established before 1998, but how to build a caring community was very challenging in Hong Kong during this transitional period. The senior officers of the government thought it was important to further implement volunteerism, but by which department and how? Since the contributions of volunteering to welfare services was happening in the welfare sector, naturally, people thought that the promotion of volunteers should be actualized by the SWD, and the director of the SWD was invited to take over this task.

But in fact, the promotion of volunteers as a macro concept was nested with the local Home Affairs Bureau (HAB). So policies were established by HAB, but the administrative executor for it was SWD. The Bureau and Department has two layers of structure; when the department wants to expand and secure new resources, it has to be approved by HAB. HAB gives advice, and will not implement the strategy. When SWD receives the task, it is the director of the SWD who will create the recommended method and procedures. Then, the Bureau will advise and endorse. The idea of setting up a Steering Committee and the sub-committees were all from the SWD. A member of the Steering Committee is a staff member from the HAB, there is also a member from the Labour and Welfare Bureau, Education Bureau, etc. Another member from HAB is also a member of the sub-committee. In this way the Bureau and Department maintain their close communication. Education is involved because much youth volunteering happens in the education sector. So, HAB is the policy-making body, and SWD is the implementer/executor of the policy. There is in fact a Youth and Community sector in HAB, and they will send representatives to the VM Steering committee and sub-committees. HAB also has a team that takes care of volunteer services. Why is HAB the policy-making body? It is because volunteer service is very often seen as being in the welfare sector, but volunteerism is not only owned by the welfare department.

In Hong Kong, many volunteers work in the areas of leisure, sports, environmental protection, tourism, cultural conservation, and international events like the East Asian Games, and the Olympics, which all are in the areas of Home Affairs. SWD is only responsible for building a caring community, so it gives people the impression that volunteerism is visible in our local welfare sector. In addition, most regular and systematic users of volunteers are our local NGOs, and SWD has a close linkage with NGOs, and so using SWD as an executive arm is highly appropriate. However, the coverage of volunteering is in fact much wider than just welfare. So, if VM policy resides within the Labour and Welfare Bureau, it in fact could not take care of all the international events, etc. But that way in which volunteers are promoted and awarded from those international events or others by the HAB, has to come back to the participating platforms initially created by SWD. However, the industrial sector also promotes volunteers, international games, and volunteer recruitment. Those promotional and recruitment efforts are done by themselves, not by the SWD. So from the perspective of SWD, it will not just promote volunteerism via the welfare sector, but it will include all sectors that are using volunteers, so its promotional work is indeed macro-based.

It is interesting to note that currently, there is no formal structure for SWD working with under HAB, except for the VM. Volunteerism is only one way to access more community development. The VM as an HAB policy is put under community development in HAB. Since VM promotes volunteerism in the community, and to the government, it does not really matter how it is structured, as the main goal is to make it work and be promoted. So, in reality it is executed by SWD, but owned by HAB. In SWD, VM is under the Assistant Director of Youth and Corrections Branch (ADYC), and so it has a very strong relationship with youth work. But to the external community, volunteer promotion is for all sectors and affects all levels, not just youth and welfare. After the 1967 riots, SWD set up the Youth and Community Branch and focused it on youth development, and so when we want to further develop volunteerism, it is likely VM will be put under the Youth branch in SWD. Of course, volunteerism in fact can happen in uniformed groups (e.g., the Scout Association of Hong Kong, The Hong Kong Girl Guides Association, etc.), women's groups, elderly groups, etc. But currently, volunteerism is a natural fit to be placed under the youth branch. Beneath the steering committee, we have four sub-committees, namely youth, corporation, community (for uniformed group, neighbourhood groups, Red Cross etc.), and promotional groups (these four groups are the original system, which has been kept over many years). So, for the steering committee, it is clearly a macro concept also.

The rationale on why the volunteer movement places such a strong emphasis on youth

From the government's point of view, a good policy sometimes is just a concept to build from within the local community. It is generally believed that the government should adopt a non-intervention type of approach, as far as possible. Currently most of the sectors in Hong Kong especially among NGOs are doing a very good job in promoting volunteerism, because they know it is a very important part of their community implementation work. What they expect from the government is to support, distribute resource, and have a fair recognition system. In Hong Kong, there are three kinds of annual awards ceremonies: one for youth, one for the whole community (elderly, housing estate neighbourhood caring projects, etc.) and one for corporates (using an approach of competition among corporates).

The steering committee and its members have many chances to represent Hong Kong to visit other countries and have volunteerism exchanges. Very positive feedback is received that Hong Kong is quite unique, organized (this is well documented in international exchanges and conferences and by reports and books) and has clear goals and divisions of labour. The current government policy (as observed by the interviewees) of Hong Kong is that if the government gives more pro-active directions to the community, all will likely follow, though no typical effort is out there for exploring the real needs of the community at the same time. Not NGOs, but more accessible funds and charitable sources, such as the corporations also support many new projects in the Hong Kong community. A culture of taking initiatives to serve the community has built in our community; and after taking initiatives, they then will do things according to their own agenda and vision. That is the great thing about a good macro policy!

The changes between volunteers and government, and between the community and the government after the policy implementation

It has become more systematic overall, especially in the educational sector. The educational sector is very responsive to new policy; the VM policy has in fact directly impacted the community educational goals. Schools always act according to external and mandated requirements. Once it is said that it is a requirement to enter university, all schools will implement it, and make it compulsory. After knowing that our universities in fact do not count this as requirement, for many schools, it has already become part of their curriculum, and part of their co-curricular activities. So, it does have an impact on all of our schools and the education system. To the larger community, all NGOs themselves already have their own award systems, where they compete, and report their hours. This has served to become a motivational factor for bigger awards.

For those who are willing to compete, it has become a rather formalized and structured culture. Before, it was mainly an informal system. Hong Kong is very advanced in some areas, as we have formal and informal recognition, training, and benchmarks for personal development. Even for the volunteers themselves, they may look for personal challenges, growth, enhancement, sustainment, and management etc., all of which are popular topics in Hong Kong today. Most organizations already understand that it is simply an award system, but it needs to present a "whole package" in order to attract and manage our volunteers. The Agency for Volunteer Service (AVS) has an institute that promotes volunteers. In the 1970s, it set up the Association of Volunteer Service, then changed that to the Agency for Volunteer Service (AVS). It is an NGO which focuses on volunteer promotion. It is also a member of the IAVE (International Association on Volunteer Effort). The Hong Kong government is not a member of IAVE, but AVS represents the Hong Kong community participating in international exchanges. It has an important community role, and has HAB as its own "direct funding source". Whenever HAB wants to recruit volunteers for any international events or games, e.g., promotion of tourism in Hong Kong, HAB will approach AVS, instead of approaching NGOs. Some in Hong Kong are even confused about whether SWD is under AVS (partially, also because the Chinese name of AVS may misleadingly suggest that AVS is more important than the SWD). But actually, it is the opposite; AVS is an NGO that receives subventions (on some projects) from the SWD. But to some larger NGOs, AVS is just a small NGO, and it does not work for SWD or the government. But among other smaller NGOs, and when co-ordinating some city-wide events, it does carry the co-ordinating role more comfortably. It is an NGO which has a specialty, as AVS sits in the steering seat as the "local expert", in many committees in Hong Kong for promotion of volunteerism locally and internationally. There are representatives from HAB and from the local community, because of their knowledge of how to promote and run events in the community. There also have representatives from business, from women's groups, and from non-subvented NGOs too. So, the steering committee is a very inclusive structure with aggregated representation in its membership.

After the policy development, the Hong Kong Government often creates many platforms for different sectors to meet and to collaboratively exchange ideas, resources, and strategies to raise all of our horizons. It is to avoid each sector will be doing things without collaboration with other sectors. Many awards, e.g., awards granted by the Hong Kong Federation of Youth Groups, AVS, etc., are awarded (to awardees) from other organizations too, not just from their own organization. That is the way to make the concept of volunteerism territory-wide, not just organizational.

The local business sector is also becoming very active. Environmental work is on the rise, and political parties are strategically also using more volunteers. The patients' advocacy group is also a new trend. Local volunteer work is now not just localized in social welfare, but all over our community. Social capital and enterprise bring new challenges to growth in Hong Kong. Secondary schools and universities etc., are doing many and various types of volunteer projects. There are also new ideas and discussions happening about local volunteering and the spirit of volunteering. It is time for Hong Kong to think about how to define and better categorize volunteers locally. Indeed, Hong Kong is actively promoting volunteering for today, and for our future. Forward looking, youth and corporate areas are the two foci areas we need to continue to develop. Corporate Social Responsibility (CSR) is also on the rise, as elderly and early retired groups are also getting attention. Since the coverage of volunteering is expanding, forward looking, Hong Kong is also in high demand for more quality training, organizational management skills, service learning for education and students, all are in need of new knowledge inputs. In short, these are our future directions for volunteering in Hong Kong. We are all proud to be a part of this legacy of volunteering in a city that has shown it truly cares for the social welfare of its citizens!

Agency for Volunteers Service (AVS)

Agency for Volunteer Service (AVS) has been the most prominent Hong Kong NGO with the core mission in promoting volunteerism from 1970 until today.

Volunteerism in Hong Kong would likely not have progressed and developed without local and community efforts in setting up agencies that interpreted community needs, organized volunteer services, and mobilized volunteers. Such volunteer associations also normally offer referral services for individuals who wish to volunteer, and match volunteers to the hosting organizations which require volunteer services. Furthermore, in order to strengthen volunteers' competencies, and to enhance the quality and professionalism of Hong Kong's volunteer services, organizations like AVS also provide training and other developmental programmes for volunteers. Although often overlooked, the establishment of volunteer associations focusing on promoting and training are an essential component of a nation's volunteerism.

This sub-section first tables a historical account of why in 1970 (and not earlier) there was an attempt to establish a volunteer association in Hong Kong, and how this contributed to changing the perceptions about volunteerism among local people. Second, the milestones and major achievements of AVS are presented and contextualized in light of the overall history of volunteerism in Hong Kong. Finally, it discusses how the mission and the vision of AVS has changed over time, and what its future holds. This sub-section presents the "other side" of government-mandated volunteerism, where local agencies promote volunteerism.

To complete the "bigger picture" of Hong Kong's volunteering history, the author interviewed senior members of AVS that promotes volunteerism both locally and internationally. The author conducted a focus group in 2018 with three long serving and key members of AVS that included its chairman, its treasurer and its CEO. Here are their composite responses, from their day-to-day work, through the organizational lens of AVS.

The history of AVS

The HK Council of Social Service (HKCSS) received an invitation from the Social Welfare Department in 1967 to promote volunteering in HK. There was already a sub-unit for volunteerism in HKCSS by that time. One of those new ideas to further promote volunteerism was to create an NGO specifically for it. One of the staff in the sub-unit for volunteerism in HKCSS was then appointed to be the first CEO of this new agency to help actualize and create the Association of Volunteer Service in 1970. It was re-named the Agency for Volunteer Service in 1981.

Before 2000, its scope was limited to smaller scale work. From 2000 to 2011, it finally succeeded in re-organizing itself to cover a more macro level of work. Since 2000, in four landmark years (2000, 2002, 2006 and 2011), board members and staff worked together in several brainstorming sessions to come up to some new directions for development. Its original role of promoting volunteering was kept as its most important goal. Besides that, it decided to become more proactive and sustainable in its future development and thus established VMV (Values, Mission, and Visions) to its work. The new directions also emphasize partnerships, quality, and resources building.

The relationship of AVS with the government

Before 2000, AVS was funded under the SWD for the "Promotion of Volunteering". After 2000, it was under Home Affairs Bureau (HAB) together with uniform groups and the Hong Kong Award for Young People. Besides annual funding, AVS also receives project-based funding, e.g., for the World Trade Conference Hong Kong Ministerial Conference in 2005, ITU Telecom World in 2006, Life Buddies Mentoring Scheme in 2015–8, etc. Thus, AVS often partners with the government for the provision of volunteers for these city-wide projects. However, as an NGO, it still enjoys the freedom of independence in autonomous management and in setting its organizational goals. For example, when AVS decided to globalize its network, it did not have to consult with the government but just pursued it in the way its members thought that was the right direction for Hong Kong. AVS has then set up the Volunteer Talent Bank for local people with specialized and professional skills, and now has registered 1,200 volunteers. These groups of volunteers are self-managing and AVS staff only give them basic support for implementation. Its training programme is also unique. It is a project supported by The Community Chest of Hong Kong and each year it provides over 400 sessions to individuals and organizations from difference sectors.

The major contributions of AVS to Hong Kong

Foremost, its services cover the Hong Kong Government, local NGOs, and Hong Kong citizens. Its Volunteer Referral Service is one of the oldest services delivered so far, and is its "signature program". All individual volunteers have to register on-line or through its App (which is especially helpful for first-time volunteers), followed by training and then service matching. When registered, volunteers can select service opportunities according to their choices, and AVS will do the referral based on the criteria of the requesting or partner agencies. NGOs like this Volunteer Referral Service very much because if they recruit volunteers by themselves, they are unlikely to be able to recruit such a large number of trained volunteers, but AVS is able to do it because it already has a large number of volunteers registered in its volunteer pool. It also caters for large numbers or smaller numbers of volunteers needed by different NGOs, government bodies or community projects. During the East Asian Games in 2009, the government intended to recruit 6,000 volunteers, and finally there were over 14,000 volunteers registered. AVS did rounds and rounds of interviews in order to select the 6,000. During the SARS in 2003, within days, there were over 6,000 registered in support of the elderly, deprived groups, various medical and education sectors. Currently, AVS has around 7,000 registered per year. Besides individual registration, AVS also runs corporate registrations, which have around 100,000 volunteers per year.

Here, after registration, volunteers will receive training from its Hong Kong Institute of Volunteers (IoV) and service opportunities they are interested in. Volunteers are managed with the support of committed volunteer leaders and each year will be recognized and presented awards if they meet the standard number of service hours, for their long service and outstanding performance as well. IoV was set up in 2003 with funding from The Community Chest of Hong Kong. It is managed by six staff-trainers with about 40 volunteer trainers. Aimed at strengthening volunteers' competence and the quality and effectiveness of volunteer service, besides offering regular training to volunteers, IoV also tailors training programmes to NGOs, government bodies, education institutes, and private sector companies on volunteer concepts, service skills, leadership, and volunteer service management (VSM). VSM training is specially designed for volunteer managers and administrators who have the responsibility to coordinate, organize, and work closely with volunteers in service delivery. Training is considered a very important and essential part of local work energizing the volunteer process.

In promoting the good practice of volunteering, AVS has developed the Hong Kong Volunteer Charter and a set of practice reference guide for volunteers and volunteer-involving organizations. In addition, AVS fosters volunteerism through various means in its promotion, public education, and volunteer recognition programmes. It launches the Hong Kong Volunteer Award, Heroic Volunteer Award, Professional Volunteer Service Accreditation Programme, Leadership Bauhinia Volunteer Award to promote volunteer values and to raise public awareness and societal recognition on volunteer contributions. To promote cross-sectoral collaboration for the development of volunteerism, AVS set up the Hong Kong Council of Volunteering in 2004, provide a platform for exchange and cooperation to broader participation in and across sectors. The Council is composed of representative organizations from different profession, business, education, and religious sectors.

International connections

AVS is the first organization in Hong Kong to echo the United Nations International Volunteer Day by organizing celebrations and promoting volunteering locally since 1992. AVS is the International Association for Volunteer Effort (IAVE) Representative for HKSAR since 1998 and also a founding member of its Global Network of National Volunteer Centres. IAVE is an international organization in promoting, strengthening, and celebrating volunteering around the world. AVS organizes Hong Kong delegations to participate in its international and regional conferences each year for exchange and networking with volunteer leaders worldwide. It hosted the IAVE Asia Pacific Regional Volunteer Conference in Hong Kong in 2005 with very positive feedback.

AVS maintains close connections and partnership with major volunteer organizations in the Greater China Region and receives many delegations and visiting groups from mainland China. In 2017, AVS organized the Cross-Strait, Hong Kong, and Macau Youth Volunteering Forum participated by volunteers and youth leaders from the four places. AVS became a cooperation organization of United Nations Volunteers in 1998 to promote the UNV programmes and to encourage the participation of professionals and youth in volunteering overseas. To further youth volunteerism, AVS from 2015 started the UNV-Hong Kong Universities Volunteer Internship Program funded by the Hong Kong Government sending local undergraduates to serve a six-month assignment in development countries contributing to peace and development.

The major changes in volunteer work in Hong Kong in recent years

To understand the landscape of local volunteering, AVS conducted surveys. It found that Hong Kong has a healthy and steady growth of volunteering. In its 2009 survey, the volunteering percentage of local citizens was 36%, representing 14 percentage point increase from 2001. The total number of volunteering hours was 87 million, the economic value of which was HK5.5 billion at the time. Volunteers in Hong Kong were found be to better educated, younger, with higher income, and better social status.

It was found that there has been increasing diversity of volunteering as more volunteers begin to be involved in areas like environmental service, sports, mentoring, counselling, and skill transfer or coaching. Volunteers now see their altruistic behaviour as a means for self-actualization and find the experience fulfilling and meaningful.

The major obstacles and challenges ahead for volunteerism in Hong Kong

Hong Kong people are much busier than before. However, with the rapid advancement in information technology, AVS suggests that more active use of the internet, social media, and mobile applications will be helpful to promote, recruit, and organize volunteers. On the other hand, it also finds the higher demand for quality service from NGOs and demands from volunteers for more dynamic and meaningful service opportunities.

Regarding the trends of volunteering, AVS observes that there is high potential for employee volunteering in the business sector. More retirees or young-olds can be engaged in volunteering. The use of electronic means will make volunteering more accessible and convenient, and will encourage cross-border and international volunteering.

As an organization advocating volunteering, AVS recognizes the need to review and renew current efforts to adhere closely to societal pulses, to meet the changing community needs over time and to be reflective and creative in strategic planning in fostering the development of volunteering for a sustainable future. It is in its vision and mission that AVS will continue the effort to deepen public acceptance, make volunteering embedded as a way of life, to diversify volunteer service opportunities, and most importantly to create an enabling environment for volunteers to participate and contribute with recognition and satisfaction. Through community partnership, AVS is dedicated to taking volunteerism to new heights in the years ahead.

References

Charities Aid Foundation (2010). "The World Giving Index 2010." Retrieved from https://www.cafonline.org/docs/default-source/about-us-publications/worldgivingindex28092010print.pdf.

Chinese YMCA (2016). "Over half of Hong Kong's youth want to volunteer but lack of time." Retrieved from http://www.ymca.org.hk/en/ywvblt.

Cuthill, M. & Warburton, J. (2005). "A conceptual framework for volunteer management in local government." *Urban Policy and Research*, 23(1), 109–122.

ECHO (2014). "Fact Sheet – EU Aid Volunteers." Retrieved from http://ec.europa.eu/echo/files/aid/countries/factsheets/thematic/euaidvolunteers_en.pdf.

Frumkin, P. & Jastrzab, J. (2010). *Serving country and community: Who benefits from national service?*Harvard: Harvard University Press.

Haski-Leventhal, D., Mejis, L. C., & Hustinx, L. (2010). "The third-party model: Enhancing volunteering through governments, corporations and educational institutes." *Journal of Social Policy*, 39(1), 139–158.

Kam, P. K. (2009). "From social control to empowerment: Toward a youth empowerment approach in services for young people." In E. S. C. Liu, M. J. Holosko and T. W. Lo (Eds.), *Youth empowerment and volunteerism: Principles, policies and practices* (pp. 109–134). Hong Kong: City University of HK Press.

Law, B. M. & Shek, D. T. (2009). "Family influence on volunteering intention and behavior among Chinese adolescents in Hong Kong." *Adolescence*, 44(175), 665–683.

Musick, M. A., & Wilson, J. W. (2008). *Volunteers: A social profile*. Bloomington: Indiana University Press.

National Council for voluntary Organizations (NCVO). Retrieved from https://www.ncvo.org.uk/search?q=compact&x=14&y=14.

Steering Committee on Promotion of Volunteer Service (2016). "Development of Volunteer Movement and Promotion Direction from 2016 Onwards." Retrieved from http://www.volunteering-hk.org.

To, S. M. (2007). "Empowering school social work practices for positive youth development: Hong Kong experience. "*Adolescence*, 42(167), 555–567.

United Nations Volunteers (2013). "UNV Youth Volunteering Strategy 2014–2017 Empowering Youth through Volunteerism." Retrieved from https://www.unv.org/sites/default/files/UNV%20Youth%20Volunteering%20Strategy.pdf.

PART II

Examples of theory into practice: Implementing the City-Youth Empowerment Project and its five selected programmes

4

CREATING AND SUSTAINING A VOLUNTEER PROJECT: THE CITY-YOUTH EMPOWERMENT PROJECT (CYEP)

The City-Youth Empowerment Project (CYEP) was established in 2005 at the City University of Hong Kong (CityU) in the Department of Social and Behavioural Sciences (SS Department). From its inception, CYEP has grown from roughly 150 enrolled volunteers to an annual highest enrolment of over 2,000 in 2015/16; and the annual total number of service hours reached over 30,000 in 2015–16 (see Table 5.3).

Within thirteen years of its implementation (2005–2018), it has evolved and grown to be a non-credit bearing service-learning project open to all CityU students. One of the most valuable intended outcomes of CYEP is to transfer values and experiences heavily anchored in fundamental social sciences knowledge to students who are of other disciplines – in order to promote civic engagement, effective direct helping skills, community integration, and the caring mission of CityU. Its aim is to mobilize students to serve the vulnerable individuals, to enhance civic and social commitment, and to integrate community practice-oriented knowledge for service learning. With an overarching mission of promoting social change in local communities, understanding socially-unique values and structural obstacles, social inclusion is gained through community volunteer services. Over the years with the input of both theoretical concepts and skills on positive youth development, youth empowerment, sustained volunteerism, and community capacity building, CYEP has built a simple and person-centred human connection infrastructure that has successfully organized students' energy on campus to meaningful group synergy and institutional mission. "Youth empowerment" is already a popular discourse describing student activities on our campus. CYEP has a long history of serving over 30 community projects with most of the target groups and locations around CityU, and mostly in Shek Kip Mei and Shum Shui Po areas (some older and congested districts in Hong Kong). The slogan for the project in early period was "We are City-Youths. We Volunteer". It was later modified in 2011 to "Connecting Communities through Service and Learning", and from 2013 to "Serve, Learn and Change".

Psychologically and developmentally we have learned that, youth volunteering is a meaningful process which recognizes youth's self-determination to not only relate to their society, but reciprocally when they serve the society, the society also serves as a good platform to actualize youth's needs to be better connected with the society (Risler & Holosko, 2009). CYEP leans heavily on such youth empowering through its Volunteering Process Model (VPM) for contextualizing its creation, rationale, and development process. Borrowing the VPM from Risler and Holosko (2009) but with an emphasis on the reciprocal relationship among volunteers and the social environment, and among volunteers and different target groups they served, we modified their model to be a Reciprocal Volunteer Process Model (RVPM). The uniqueness of the RVPM is that we see the volunteering process as a two-ways process, a mutual process for volunteers and the service recipients. We also embrace two groups of people as targets for empowering: the university students who will benefit from serving, and the NGOs and their service recipients, who will benefit from connecting with the university volunteers and the university environment. The role of the CYEP is to create a process and to heighten some interactions for both the volunteers and the serving target groups to benefit.

The earlier years: implementing cross cultural learning programmes

Since I was the key person who created this initiative, I will tell the story of CYEP by telling my own personal story. I joined the tertiary education sector to be a teacher for social work programmes after working as a youth social worker in an NGO for almost ten years. My first goal after joining CityU and its Department of Applied Social Studies (renamed to Department of Social and Behavioural Sciences in 2018) was to transform myself from a social worker to an educator. It took about ten years for me to achieve competence in my new role. This adjustment period in my new role had given me a small space to enjoy classroom teaching. However, it had also given me some time to notice many "social problems" around me in this new environment. Very soon, I began to actively engage in many student activities. My first endeavour was in 2000, when I became the convener of the "Maximizing Students' Learning Group" in our department. Here, I initiated a new co-curricular programme called the "Cross-cultural Learning Program" (CCLP). For the following three years (2001, 2002 and 2004, 2003 CCLP was cancelled due to the outbreak of SARS in Hong Kong), CCLP had in total organized 27 student groups with 328 participating students attached to universities or NGOs in different Asian countries or different cities in mainland China for cultural learning, community service, and to study or research on different social problems in those cities for three weeks. Each of the 27 groups was also coached and led by a teacher from our department as adviser and those leading teachers would also accompany students in cross-the-border exchanges for at least seven to ten days helping to negotiate and arrange with our overseas partnering organizations and universities to offer different learning activities for our student groups. In these three years, CCLP programmes were implemented in mainland China, Cambodia, Taiwan, Singapore, and Japan.

Becoming a residence master at CityU

In 2002, I served as the residence master in one of the first three residence halls for undergraduate students in City University of Hong Kong. It was the first experience for CityU to offer residential halls for undergraduate students and it planned to build 11 halls in four phases in the next ten years. When we started to implement hall management in its first phase, we were faced with many student problems. For most students, it was the first time for them to live far away from home and it demanded new adaptations. On dyadic and group levels, co-existence among students and the issues of collective life style were not easy for anyone. The communication between the students and the university were also challenging. As a whole, we were confronted with positioning what hall culture we wanted to cultivate for our students. At that time, the Vice-President (Undergraduate Education) of CityU was Professor Edmond Ko, who also started the student residences. One day, a group of colleagues including Professor Ko, talked about student problems in the residence halls, and suggested ways to help students to further benefit from hall life. One of the suggested ideas then was to offer some volunteering work. Since I was a social worker, it was automatic for them to expect me to follow up on the idea of implementing a volunteer project in the student residence. Someone suggested that maybe I would contact some local NGOs and secure some volunteer works for our residents to serve others. However, I told them that setting up a project is never an easy thing, and I offered to commit to do this, only if they granted me staff, and some funding. It was then agreed that I would draft a proposal to suggest how to create a volunteer project for the student residence. One week later, I prepared a two-page proposal, asking for two staff, and it was in that moment that the City-Youth Empowerment Project (CYEP) was born.

Anchoring CYEP in academic exchanges

In 2004, I decided to launch an international conference so that students and teachers who had participated in the CCLP programs will continue to discuss on the meaning and impact of our on-going cross cultural learning. The first one (in 2004) therefore was called *International Conference on Youth Empowerment: Cross-Cultural Exchanges*, which reflected the work done in the CCLP. The students who had joined the CCLP were recruited to be student helpers to run the entire programme, and more than 250 delegates from all over the world participated in this conference.

The year of 2005 was a very special converging point in my career. I had been a teacher in social work programmes for some 15 years. I launched a series of cross-cultural learning programmes, and was convinced that community service and international exposure are useful transformational processes for university students. I stressed youth empowerment conferences as a guiding principal for transforming university students and received very positive academic and community support for this theme. Wearing several hats, I gained a more holistic view on the generic "educational" challenges of university students.

Sometime in early 2005, the CYEP proposal was approved and a first sum of seed money was received to formally launch the project. Originating from a teaching and learning project with a mission to mobilize students to volunteer in the community, it was initially open only to those students who lived in student residences. However, it quickly became evident that this form of student engagement with the community was beneficial to the personal and academic development of participating students, as well as to the community at large, especially to those whose accessibility to adequate resources was low and limited. In 2018, CYEP is a university-wide service-learning project, under the Department of Social and Behavioural Sciences, with the mission to mobilize and organize CityU students to serve underprivileged communities through various volunteering services. The project also aims to enhance students' civic commitment and understanding of social issues, and to integrate practice-oriented experience gained from serving the community with academic knowledge.

The early project objectives were:

1. To mobilize and organize City University students to participate in volunteer work in the community.
2. To serve underprivileged children and youth and other marginalized groups as the project's core mission.

The intended outcomes for university students were:

1. To facilitate students to gain more knowledge of the needs of people faced with social problems, thus enhancing their ability to help effectively.
2. To encourage students to take action toward community building on individual, group, and/or organizational levels.
3. To facilitate students to identify and apply the dynamics between personal and social problems and values, in an ecological perspective.
4. To assist students to develop more understanding of volunteerism as a social, organizational, and community process.
5. To help students align personal values and commitments, to community goals by identification with the project and the serving agencies.

After two years, the project grew from around 150 volunteers to around 300 volunteers and the model was found to be facilitative for retaining volunteers and receiving on-going feedback from local NGOs. Volunteers were also found to be participating enthusiastically, and there were overwhelming requests for those who were not hall residents to join. In 2007, a meeting was held with the head of SS department, Vice-President (Student Affairs) and myself to discuss the future development of the CYEP. It was agreed that the project would become a departmental project, funded jointly by the Teaching and Learning Fund of our university and the SS Department. Since then, it became an official departmental project, and it was opened to participants from all departments, and not just the hall residents. During the following six years (2008–2014) we were funded only by the Teaching and Learning Fund from CityU until 2011, when we received our first donation. From 2014 to 2018, the project slowly evolved to be almost totally funded by community donations in 2017. So, incrementally, we grew in numbers. From initially being only staffed by two project officers, we gradually expanded to five, then six, and to 2016–17 to having six project officers and one project supervisor. In the last eight years, we have worked closely with the Development Office and the Alumni Relations Office in our University to involve community leaders, donors, and alumni. We also learned in this process, that CYEP has become a popular choice for groups of potential donors who want to contribute to the community through a university platform serving the community. By donating to CYEP, they also indirectly contributed back to the community.

2006: Implementing the second International Conference on Youth Empowerment: Volunteerism

One year after the formal implementation of the CYEP, I applied for another round of funding from the Maximizing Student Learning Fund to organize another international conference on youth empowerment. The second one (in 2006), was called 2nd International Conference on Youth Empowerment: Empowering Youth through Volunteerism. At that time, I chose to focus on volunteerism because of CYEP, which was just evolving. The conference was very successful, with more than 400 delegates from overseas and Hong Kong. More than 100 students were recruited to help prepare and organize the conference. I wanted to expose students and staff in CityU to more international concepts on volunteerism. A book called the *Youth Empowerment and Volunteerism: Principles, Policies and Practices* (2009) was edited after the conference, with myself as the first of the three editors (Liu, Holosko & Lo, 2009). The book laid some cornerstone concepts for CYEP, as noted in its preface:

> Snyder and Omoto use empirical studies mainly from their own extensive body of research and present a three stage Volunteer Process Model (VPM), comprised of antecedents of volunteerism, experiences of volunteerism, and consequences of volunteerism. They clearly address the underpinning psychology of volunteerism and empirically answer the important question-who gets involved in volunteerism and why? ...Omoto and Snyder extend their model to illustrate and justify the role of community context, linkages and connections to their volunteer model. ...they clearly argue the case that any model purporting to understand volunteering that is devoid of community context, is seriously remiss.
>
> *(p.xii)*

> Risler and Holosko present the core elements, distilled from the literature, of a youth empowerment model...a blueprint for implementation....a series of examples and open-ended process questions for others to address, in planning and applying this approach.
>
> *(p.xii)*

The above are just brief glimpses of numerous concepts covered in the book, and they are really important guideposts for CYEP to find its direction and to set its future goals. Holistically for the project, we see volunteerism as an ecological process with individuals being the youth volunteers and the NGOs, with the community as the context, and we paid attention to "who gets what and why?" which is an important motivational issue of volunteerism especially for young volunteers; we then adopted the Volunteer Process Model to see youth volunteering as a sustaining and nurturing process for youth development and empowerment, with three sets of process questions (Risler & Holosko, 2009; Liu, Ye, & Yeung, 2015):

a **Process questions for building a supportive environmental context for the volunteer project**:

1. What are the cultural norms and attitudes toward youth in the community?
2. What organizations provide opportunities and supports for youth to volunteer?
3. Are there mechanisms to promote group identity, inclusion, and affiliation in the volunteer experience?
4. What resources are available to provide supports for youth volunteer initiatives?
5. Are adult mentors available and accessible for the volunteer initiatives?

b **Process questions for creating a meaningful interactive context for the volunteer project:**

1. What is the purpose, nature, and duration of involvement of youth in this volunteer initiative?
2. Can youth become involved in active decision-making to plan their volunteer participation?
3. How welcoming and supportive is the host organization/community to the volunteer initiative?
4. Can different skills of different youth be accommodated in the learning process?
5. What processes are available to help youth commit to the programme?

c **Process questions for enhancing the knowledge-based outcomes for the volunteer project:**

1. What projects and accomplishments were achieved by the group?
2. What were some of the individual accomplishments achieved by the youth in this experience?
3. What challenges were overcome by members through the volunteer experience?
4. What community resources were mobilized, procured, and/or leveraged to achieve the desired objectives of the volunteer initiative?
5. How satisfied were the individuals, groups, organizations, and/or communities with the experience?

As such, the above three key processes formed the guiding principles for CYEP to grow and develop its future. Based on these meaningful process questions, we will describe our chosen values, our structure and delivery models, and other human connection networks.

Creating a supportive environment and culture for CYEP

CYEP in our university environment was a new model of how to organize university students and mobilize university resources to serve the community's needs. As any other new youth project, it needed a very structured process with well-defined goals and clear vision for it to develop, grow, and sustain. The creation of the CYEP was a new challenge within our university, because there was no preceding example. Volunteering and community service before were mainly confined to social work students only, as students and staff from other disciplines were quite unfamiliar with such ideas. So, in order to build a new culture and to amend some old beliefs, we needed to facilitate all levels of individuals, including students and staff, to become involved in the project via a very personalized journey. To put it more simply, we invite all parties to have new and involved experiences in the project, so that they own part of the project and are proud of themselves for being part of it.

Anchoring assumptions of CYEP

1 **It starts with a youth-centred empowering approach:** for any social programme to be created, it is always important for it to be anchored on a clear focus. Our main goal is to create a person-centred approach to see the needs of university students, which is to see them as young people (instead of just being students), and on how to return power to youth (shifting the paradigm that education might be a disempowering process for students) to enhancing their life development.

2 **CYEP started serving mainly children**: when the project was started, it was engaged with six projects for children, including serving a group of children living with Asperger's syndrome, children from single-parent families, children from

newly arrived families, children from families receiving CSSA (Comprehensive Social Security Assistance Scheme), children who were low-achievers in schools, etc. We offered mainly mentoring and learning tuition services to young children of different background in this stage. Also, serving children was also supported by evidence-based literature which has a positive impact on the growth of the serving young people (Haski-Leventhal, Ronel, York, & Ben-David, 2008). Over time, the project gradually added more target groups when it expanded its services and with more staff in the following years. However, children are still our biggest group of service recipients up to today. Our follow-up studies on the impact of youth while serving children also proved to be supportive of our design (Liu, 2014).

3 **We had joint partnerships with NGOs for service delivery and for volunteer training**: since our inception, we always jointly partnered with NGOs to deliver services, instead of directly offering our community service without the mediation and partnership with an NGO. The rationale for our choice of method (and we share this with volunteers too) is that we should be aware of our responsibility for service recipients. If we do not think we can offer after office hour services to the service recipients, or our services for them are only partial, and we do not have a physical location, where we could provide service recipients a community support location? Under all these circumstances, we therefore should not and could not offer our service. Ultimately, NGOs take the primary responsibilities for all the service recipients we served. On the other hand, and as time evolved in our partnership, NGOs shared more in the later stages the responsibility of training volunteers and enhancing the CYEP learning goals for our student volunteers.

4 **Implementing a coaching system**: for the majority of youth, we have to be aware that they might need extra support to go through a volunteering process and be successful in that process. We thus created a coaching system for all student volunteers, comprising two major parts. Firstly, we do not match volunteers individually to NGOs; instead, we structure all our services using a "group approach", meaning that the volunteers will be formed as volunteer groups first. Secondly, our service recipients are also served on a group base. Thirdly, all volunteer groups and then all service target groups are headed by one project officer. The whole team for one service target group will be called a project and will be given a name. For example, Project EM would mean Project for Ethnic Minority Group. Project CY1 would mean Project for Children and Youth Team ONE. Each project officer would oversee the whole process from recruitment, training, managing service schedules, de-briefing, team building etc., with basically all individual and group development work will be taken up by one trained member of staff. In normal times, one project staff member would take up three to four projects. Overall, such simple and direct coaching system is found to be effective in helping the volunteers to identify with the agency, feeling safe from being rejected and assessed by the NGOs who do not really understand them, and focussing on serving the service recipients and feeling supported by their own team mates.

Conclusively this chapter has outlined the conceptual journey that CYEP, as a case study of volunteer project, went through before it was actualized. These conceptual inputs form the foundation structure and value guidelines for CYEP to grow and develop as evidenced in the following chapters. Without a clear set of conceptual guidelines, a young volunteer project will lose direction of its goal for the community, values for people, and its programmes on how to facilitate people to interact meaningfully with the social environment.

References

Haski-Leventhal, D., Ronel, N., York, A. S., & Ben-David, B. M. (2008). "Youth volunteering for youth: Who are they serving? How are they being served?" *Children and Youth Services Review*, 30(7), 834–846.

Liu, E. S. C. (2014). "Youth's perception on the impact and meaning of working with children." *Journal of Psychology and Psychotherapy*, 5(2), 177–182.

Liu, E. S. C., Ye, C. J., & Yeung, D. Y. (2015). "Effects of Approach to Learning and Self-perceived Overall Competence of University Students." *Learning and Individual Differences*, 39, 199–204.

Liu, E. S. C., Holosko, M. & Lo, T. W. (Eds.) (2009). *Youth Empowerment and Volunteerism: Principles, Policies and Practices*. Hong Kong: City University of Hong Kong Press.

Risler, E. A. & Holosko, M. J. (2009). "Blueprint for a Youth Empowerment Model (YEM) through volunteerism." In E. S. C. Liu, M. J. Holosko and T. W. Lo (Eds.), *Youth empowerment and volunteerism: Principles, policies and practices* (pp. 57–81). Hong Kong: City University of HK Press.

5

THE EVOLUTION AND MATURATION OF CYEP

Building a CYEP coaching model for volunteering

CYEP offers a unique and supportive learning framework for its volunteers with a strong emphasis placed on training and coaching elements. The volunteers are trained by experienced project officers, who are frequently registered social workers possessing skills in problem-solving, relationships, communication, effective community development, and personal development. Student volunteers are taught to identify underlying social problems, so as to effectively provide support in their specific service. The volunteers' personal growth is reflected in the services they deliver to those in need, and in their own learning. As indicated in Figure 5.1, the coaching model consists of seven stages of engaging volunteers, the ultimate goal is to empower youth from recruitment to becoming life-long sustainable volunteers.

Creating a meaningful interactive context for CYEP to evolve and mature

Service modes: we started the project with only one service mode, which was to deliver regular service to the NGO projects we were engaged with, since we thought frequent meetings with volunteers would facilitate relationship building among all those who previously were not connected. At the start, we defined regular service as having the frequency of service, number and duration of sessions, estimated number of service recipients, and number of volunteers per academic semester being agreed upon between CYEP and the engaged NGO projects before the academic semester started. This was to ensure that the commitment and expectation of services were clear to both parties so that each side was able to gather service recipients and recruit enough volunteers in a planned manner. One

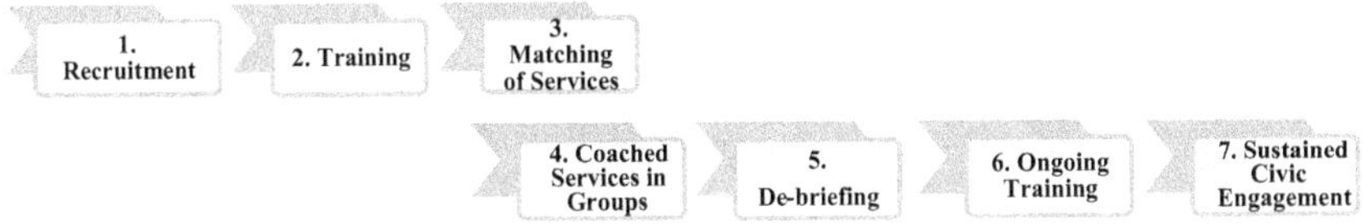

FIGURE 5.1 CYEP coaching model for volunteering

example of a regular service is a "Mentoring group for the children with Asperger's Syndrome" which is scheduled usually to have eight sessions in eight weeks (from week 4–10 of a semester with 13–14 weeks, all dates pre-arranged before volunteer recruitment and service recipients enrolment exercises start) x three hours per session x eight children living with Asperger's syndrome x 16 volunteers. However, real implementation experiences informed us that students on campus are often challenged and limited with their study commitment to courses, ending up with many potentially enrolled volunteers not being able to commit any regular services.

So, in order to meet the needs of students who could not join regular services, we started to organize one-off services. One-off services could happen in a regular mode, but not as regular as weekly. One-off services could also be a child development programme that is carried out once per semester or even once per year. One example of such one-off programmes is the "Outdoor Adventure Ship programme for children and youth", in which a group of 25 volunteers accompany 25 children or youth to experience all types of sea adventure games on board the adventure ship run by an NGO. Our project arranges the necessary programme procedures and invites one of our partnership agencies to arrange their service recipients to participate. Nowadays, such kinds of short and usually one-day programmes could be launched around 20 times a year, and they are usually very popular. By developing and diversifying programmes through the line of regular or one-off programmes, we in fact have made our service opportunities more dynamic and flexible and able to meet the needs and schedules of more student volunteers. Some of our one-off services include a day visit to CityU campus so as to enhance secondary students' understanding of university life; an exhibition of art work by a group of women recovering from abusive relationships; an adventure ship for various target groups; the promotion of gender equality with NGO Rain Lily (an NGO focusing on women's protection and right) in campus; a fund raising campaign for the Guide Dog Association; supporting a kindergarten to offer outdoor activities for children; street soccer games with the marginal groups (e.g. homeless); photo exhibition on the life of the ex-prisoners in campus etc.

In sum, we learned during the process that university students are a quite homogeneous group that ensures the project will have certain expected levels of knowledge and language skills and have much volunteer potential. However, they could also be a very heterogeneous group who come from many different backgrounds and have challenging time schedules. To accommodate their schedules and needs, volunteer projects have to be as flexible as possible, and it is not wise to judge them by just how much time and how regularly volunteers could join the services. We should send a message to our volunteers that they should try their best to fit in a regular service, if not, one-off service or a minimal participation is better than not participating at all.

Design effective recruitment and matching strategies: most organizations in Hong Kong do not devote enough time to the recruitment and matching process or those processes are often not on their priority list when using volunteers; they simply accept new volunteers depending on their manpower needs, particularly during periods when their staff are busy. It is called a process of "selection" of volunteers, but in CYEP we have challenged this prevailing notion. In fact, the term selection indicates an agency-centred perspective, as if volunteers were there to match the agency needs. This is the same type of logic in the job-market, and in fact we have agencies that select only those persons who have certain skills, but not others. However, this logic contradicts the nature of volunteering, so we try to follow a somewhat different approach. In CYEP we see each volunteer as an asset and we try to offer each person the opportunity to volunteer. We do not "select" volunteers, meaning that we do not reject anyone. Instead, we try to offer the motivated ones the opportunity to become a volunteer. Then we try to match each person to the service that is potentially best for them (Liu, Wu, Lo, & Hui, 2012). When we need to respond to a crisis and larger community events we may recruit volunteers for only the purpose of helping the victims, and/or completing the event. In this case, the focus may be on the service users. However, when serving target groups who are suffering from long-term deprivation, we aim at nurturing a group of committed volunteers who will in the process, develop their own identity with the problems and needs of the target group, gain the knowledge on how best to help, and will have more potential for sustaining their commitments for a longer time.

We believe that volunteers should be matched to the service not only depending on the needs of the moment, but also on their unique preferences and abilities. Volunteers always have some reasons for joining a service, and these are as important as the organizations' needs, so they should be equally taken into consideration. Literature shows that volunteers may quit earlier, if they are assigned to something that they do not perceive as sufficiently challenging, stimulating, and/or meaningful (Mjelde-Mossey, Chi, & Chow, 2002). At times, volunteers also are not completely aware of the motives that drive them to volunteering. Young persons in particular, may join an organization or a project with a very vague idea about what they really want to do. Even in such cases, it is still important for the organization to have some discussion with them, individually or in group, and assess if their interests and expectations are being met or not, in the services they are offered. If not, they should be welcome to share their experiences and see what can be done to fill the gap, if possible. An attitude of open communication is always the best way, even when the actual problem cannot be solved. Giving room for open communication may still give volunteers hope that they can find a different role/project in the same organization. It will show them that they can trust the organization, and that they can build something. This is particularly important in the initial phases of volunteering, when new volunteers have not yet developed a strong volunteer identity. In fact, if their initial experiences are disappointing, they may quit volunteering and never come back. What we learned in CYEP is: if volunteer's expectations and programme needs do not match, discuss it with the volunteer – do not avoid it.

Originally, the stage of volunteer recruitment (Step 1 of the CYEP coaching model for volunteering, see Figure 5.3) takes place during the first month of each semester. After recruitment, the enrolled volunteers are invited to an orientation day, in which they are introduced to a brief history of CYEP; goals and definitions of volunteering; the impact of volunteerism on service recipients and society; the relationships between volunteering and social capital building; the projects supported by CYEP and the collaborating agencies. At that stage, these students do not yet formulate any service preferences, and only at the end of the orientation day were they asked to fill a form and express their preferences. After collecting these forms, and in light of the students' preferences, skills, as well as the places available in each service, the match-making (Step 3 of the CYEP coaching model for volunteering, see Figure 5.1) was conducted. However, we noted that this system soon became unsustainable. Year after year, the number of applications significantly increased, reaching over 1,000 or more volunteers yearly since 2012. Only a few years after CYEP was launched, it was no longer possible to personally handle all the volunteer applications by hand, neither was it possible to conduct all of the interviews by one individual, or gather 2,000 students together (for the orientation day) to present each of the 30 services promoted by CYEP. Then, an internet-based application system was implemented, so that applications are now submitted only online. Additionally, we created information booklets with detailed descriptions of the various services, so that students can express their service preferences from the moment they apply to join CYEP.

Today, candidates are invited to go through the list of services (available online), and indicate their preferences according to their availability (i.e., they are asked to assign 1 to indicate the highest priority, and 19 to indicate the lowest priority). They are asked to express a preference for each service, and if they could not/do not want to join some specific service, they are asked to clearly state "Not available". With this system, students not only can indicate a list of preferences, but they can say if they are available and want to join more than one service. Students can apply at the beginning of each semester; normally, the deadline is before the "kick-off" day (e.g., 15 September for the autumn semester). Once the form is completed and submitted, CYEP staff will go through the applications and match candidates who may best fit that project. If possible, the staff will try to assign volunteers into their first option services. However, as each service has limited number of available spots, students may be matched to work in other services, depending on various considerations by the staff members. Each CYEP staff member is responsible for two to three projects, on average, so they will directly contact only the candidates for those specific projects. This way, each staff member will only deal with a portion of the totality of candidates.

Emphasis on training and debriefing: from day one when the project was started, we have emphasised on-going training and debriefing (Steps 2 and 5 of the CYEP coaching model for volunteering, see Figure 5.1). However, in the early days, we offered our training programme in three areas. First, we had offered overall training for all registered volunteers on the general concepts, definitions, rationales, impacts, management, etc., of volunteers and volunteering projects. Second, we offered one session for training volunteers' skills to better communicate with service recipients. Third, since most of our service recipients are children, we also offered training on how to play and design programmes for children. However, as we developed and as we are enrolled with more volunteers and we are already serving 30 projects (instead of six), we find this initial training package can no longer meet the needs of our volunteers. We then diversified our training by the nature of individual services, be it either children and youth services, elderly services, mental health services, etc. We give project supervisors the freedom to structure the content and the schedules for the training packages designed for certain target groups. In addition, there is a culture that we will invite volunteers who have graduated or experienced volunteers in the same nature of service, to participate and share past experiences on all kind of skills and knowledge for serving. Concerning the overall training on definition, concepts, values and ethics, impacts, etc. on general volunteering work, we work with Volunteer Ambassadors (VA, to be discussed in the next section) to run training sessions for those who are interested. Otherwise, most of the skills and knowledge training is done on a small-group basis and by individual officers. In the later stages, we also succeed in involving all our partnering NGOs to take up some training tasks which greatly benefits the volunteers' knowledge and understanding of the agencies' historical background, value base for their service model, and their difficulties and service gaps for a particular target group.

As noted in Figure 5.1, de-briefing is an essential element of follow up on-the-service training, for these volunteers. In the early days when we started to implement de-briefing for volunteers, we did it on an ad-hoc basis, after the service was finished and it was carried out on campus. However, upon receiving positive feedback from both the project officers and volunteers on the usefulness of de-briefing for future services, we started to implement it in a more systematic way. First, we carried out de-briefing right after each session of service and on spot of where the service is carried out. The latest development of de-briefing is that we invite social workers or service managers to run part of the de-briefing right after services, together with our project officers. Genuine feedback from professional staff is found to be highly encouraging for volunteers. On top of these, and in most services, we also implement a service logbook for each volunteer. This is done in the way that an individual volunteer engaged in regular services will have to write certain reflections on what they have done and learned in the process. De-briefing for the international services is most challenging, because the international services nowadays last for four weeks. We have structured all the teams working on the same site to have a de-briefing almost every evening after services and to write in their service logbook each day, and to discuss an agreed-upon plan with partners for the services for the next day. All seem time consuming, but it is very encouraging that most teams have been accomplishing this in an excellent way, and have positive feedback that they can enjoy and reflect upon from the process.

Volunteer Ambassador Scheme: seven years after we implemented CYEP, we started to feel that many volunteers were ready to be leaders. However, there was no clear structure which could nurture them, or to allow them to fit in comfortably. In 2012, with an idea of identifying leaders, we implemented the Volunteer Ambassador Scheme (VAS). We openly announced this exercise to all volunteers with information on their roles. In 2012, only around ten applied and were interviewed. We finally selected six and started to involve them in some project tasks similar to the volunteer recruitment exercise. Two years after we implemented it, it grew to a bigger scheme and had around 18–25 VAs each year. In 2014, we changed the structure and divided the whole group into four sub-groups and each carry different project tasks for the CYEP. The four sub-groups are: Training Team, Networking Team, Community Engagement Team, and Promotion Team. Our experience has confirmed that all established volunteer projects need to find a way to nurture and sustain the devoted members in the project. Otherwise, the project might fail to meet the aspiration of some volunteers who want to do more for the project they identified with and finally, this elite group of volunteers will lose interest in the project and leave. Among all tasks, we find the VA group is most effective in doing recruitment work for the project. Each year when a semester starts, the VA group will set up a recruitment counter and are ready to meet new potential volunteers individually for explaining and sharing CYEP to them. Most of our recruited volunteers are in fact recruited through friendship networks, a method which is also well-supported by literature (Clary et al., 1998).

Another positive contribution of the VAs is that they represent a bridge between the project officers and the regular volunteers. The role of the VAs is to "shadow" project officers to carry out their duties, as if they were also officers in service. In this role, the VAs are contributing to: 1) establishing and maintaining a network of volunteers within the project; 2) supporting and providing training for volunteers; 3) assisting and coordinating volunteer services and activities; 4) designing service programmes; 5) hosting part of service programmes; 6) facilitating volunteers' reflection; 7) networking among volunteers group; and, 8) providing feedback to officers and social workers about service arrangement, and situation as they arise, etc.

Levels of services: when the project started, it was mainly run on a group-work basis. Through small group works, a group of volunteers would meet a group of service recipients, for a more structured group work basis. For example, a mentoring group for a group of ex-mentally ill patients who are in the process of rehabilitating but need social support before they go back to school or get a job, or some who are unable to have a clear direction for a few years, but definitely need some social supports from the community. For such kinds of group, we usually arrange with the NGO on a clearly targeted schedule for one semester. However, during such group meetings and whenever the service recipients are accomplishing some specific tasks, for example, drawing or doing exercises, we will match individual mentoring supports for the service recipients one by one. From such arrangements, volunteers will quite often have a chance to meet with individual service recipients. Usually, student volunteers are more capable with group activities, but they find it more challenging if they have to meet and help an individual service recipient. However, all these individual levels of interaction between volunteers and service recipients are still carried out within group sessions. There is never one individual volunteer being matched or arranged to any organization on an individual base and never without a project officer being the coaching staff to groups of volunteers.

About six years after implementing such groups, the project tried to mobilize some interested volunteers to become engaged with some comparatively community based or macro based of work. Thus volunteers need to understand the needs/problems of our service recipients from a structural perspective, and not confine their thinking to only individual problems. Our first attempt was to prepare a group of volunteers to host a press and community conference to understand the needs and problems of the children that we were serving. We named the conference "CityU Cares for Children". At that time, we served around 300 children in CYEP. At the press conference, we summarized the background, problems, and our services to let the community know about the general problems/needs of children from the vulnerable sector, namely, children with learning problems, emotional problems, and family problems, etc. We then also introduced to the public what and how we design programmes for them. We found volunteers learned a lot from such differing perspectives of work. Since then, we created a line of work for "community scale" of work or "advocacy work". Examples of these works include a press conference on the language barriers of the ethnic minority groups, raising money for the Guide Dog Association, and the phenomenal Homeless Outreach and Population Estimation (H.O.P.E.) project done in two years, 2013 and 2015, for carrying out a city-count on the number of homeless by more than 300 student volunteers in one night.

Internationalization of CYEP since 2011: to globally motivate volunteers and to sustain their interest in the project, we are always challenged with what and how to input new concepts and endeavours to the project so as to attract the diversified interest and needs of the volunteers. In 2011, we decided to follow the new wave of service learning activities among some local universities attempting international services in Hong Kong. Our first international volunteering programme was organizing a group of volunteers to work in Cambodia. At that time we did not have a good international contact for service learning and we also faced many constraints, financially. Against all odds, we finally were able to obtain some programme money and were engaged with the "International Volunteer Headquarters" (IVHQ) and started to do international volunteer service in collaboration with IVH's sub-office in Cambodia. During the first year, the program lasted only ten days, and we were only able to afford seven volunteers.

It turned out to be a good experience among volunteers and staff, and our volunteers participated enthusiastically with many transformational stories noted among our volunteers. This motivated us to continue to pursue this and we also applied different sources of student activity money and donations to sustain our international services. Today, our international and cross-border services have covered several countries including Cambodia, Nepal, and Myanmar and mainland China. In 2014, a student-initiated donation group was formed after service to help a school purchase desks and chairs for a village school in Cambodia. A part-time teacher was also paid by this student group so that this village school could be supplied with at least some teaching support instead of none. We also gradually expanded the length of our international services to two weeks, then three, then finally four weeks from 2017, so as to align with the funding requirements of the internship programmes from CityU. We also merged the international service learning with an internship goal and submitted funding proposals to the internship source every year. In 2014, we noted significant development for our international service learning. In the summer of 2014, we sent out four international service teams to Nepal, to Cambodia, and two to Myanmar. Since 2017, we have limited our number of international service to two groups, one to Myanmar and one to Cambodia, each with 10–12 volunteers for four weeks.

Organizing regular or yearly ceremonial functions: from the beginning, CYEP organized two yearly functions, the kick-off ceremony, mainly for new volunteers, donors, and all offices and departments in CityU which have been assisting us, in September when the autumn semester starts; and the Happy Carnival for all serving volunteers, all service recipients, agency workers, and their senior management, donors, and all offices and departments in CityU who have been assisting us, at the end of April, when the spring semester ends. These two functions become our project rituals, as we have come to learn that a mass event/gathering is important for any volunteer project. We contend that organizers of volunteer projects should make ways to help all stakeholders have a chance to visualize the impact of a volunteer project, and to identify and own its mission and vision by having a chance to meet as a massive group in the format of a celebration type of event. For the CYEP, the Happy Carnival became our flagship programme each year to celebrate the concerted efforts for the year. Besides the ceremonial issues that might include presentations of prizes and awards to volunteers, we also arranged some performances by our service recipients (e.g., singing by the elderly) and volunteers (e.g., volunteers dancing with the youth from the minority groups), and exhibit some art-work generated from the service sessions, etc. To make the main funders and supporters feel a sense of belonging to the project, we also invite guests and donors to come and meet with the volunteers and the service recipients. For the Happy Carnival of CYEP, usually after the ceremonial part, a nice but simple lunch is offered. After lunch, all service recipients will be entertained by many game booths, DIY booths, photograph booths etc. All of these are well designed and delivered by the volunteers for hundreds of our service recipients to spend the afternoon on the university campus. The whole programme runs for eight hours at the weekend and this is a very popular carnival for the deprived and low-income families participating. We received very positive feedback that they see the project as well as the university as being very accommodating and caring to them, because it is free of charge to join and it is organized on the university campus. Although it requires a lot of planning to implement the Happy Carnival, it does have a noticeable impact on the volunteers, especially for the newcomers who witness the scale of the event, and the efforts of the experienced volunteers. For those who had participated in it for the second and third time, they usually act as leaders for part of the whole event, and they just enjoy it because they know it is a moment for the others to understand their competence in organizing it. Through such kinds of mass programme organization, we help the volunteers to realize its overall impact on the community. It has also inspired many younger volunteers to gain more confidence in delivering a large-scale organized task.

Connecting volunteers through multi-media: from face-to-face to virtual interaction: when we started, we use mainly paper enrolment forms, phone calls and face-to-face interactions to recruit and connect with our volunteers. We changed to online enrolment and service selection methods from 2012. From 2012 to today, the social media online platform that we are using to enhance our volunteer project includes Qualtrics, Facebook, YouTube, WhatsApp, Instagram, Online video call, and website. In 2016, we were invited by the European University for Volunteer (a virtual university for promotion of volunteering) to make an online presentation on the topic "Multi-media Youth Connection: From face-to-face volunteer work, to virtual interaction" and to present the impact of adopting multi-media methods on the volunteer recruitment and sustainment. We found that from 2006 to 2011, our mean yearly enrolment of volunteers was 360. However, after the adoption of the online enrolment method, the mean yearly enrolment of volunteers jumped to 1,346 for four years. The mean service hours for the first period was 6,622 and the second period was 25,441. Because of the jump of the enrolled volunteers, CYEP also increased its partnering projects with NGOs from 17 projects to 48. Although there are multiple factors, rather than only one factor that could boost the statistics of the project, we feel that without the facilitation of the multi-media connections, we would struggle to handle the management of over 1,000 volunteers and 40 community projects (including both regular and one-off services) with a team of only seven staff for direct coaching and management of volunteers. So, for a volunteer programme to grow and develop, and especially for a youth volunteer project, it is a must to develop its multi-media platforms and its skills to manoeuvre the platforms.

Implementing specially designed scholarship scheme for outstanding volunteers: after running CYEP for a few years, we were convinced that some awards offered to outstanding volunteer might help to boost the spirit of the project. In 2011, we wrote a proposal to a donor for an award scheme and we were able to start this initiative. However, we also noted that most awards and scholarship schemes were given to individual volunteers which lacked follow-up coaching on how the reward recipients could further enhance the project development. With all these considerations, we implemented our unique Outstanding Volunteer Award Scheme called the Mustard Seed Foundation Outstanding City-Youth Awards (as it was sponsored by the Mustard Seed Foundation). A total of HK$30,000 is for five awards each year since 2011. Each award recipient will receive HK$ 6,000, but awarded volunteers are then required to use HK$2,000 for implementing self-initiated community projects (e.g., a camp for the youth), with the support of CYEP staff members. Or, they could use this money to attend a conference or other training related to volunteerism. The spirit of these scholarships was to recognize the effort of volunteers, yet coaching them how to use it for giving back part of it to the community. Over the years, volunteers made different use of this money. Some used it to create their own musical instruments for the service recipients. Some used it to run a summer programme for children, others to join international service programmes, whereas others went to international conferences. The five awards are named:

a Leadership Award: for outstanding service and demonstration of leadership skills: in taking initiatives, mobilizing peers, advocating for service recipients, and contributing to the empowerment of the project as a whole.
b Dedication Award: for outstanding service and dedication: who sets an example in the excellent quality of service, as demonstrated in the longevity and continuation of participation, punctuality, attendance, and investment of efforts and energy into the cause(s).
c Innovation Award: for outstanding service and demonstration of innovative ideas: utilization of creative solutions and methods in volunteer services, and generation of new and "out-of-the-box" perspectives and suggestions that are effective.
d Potential for High Achievement Award: for demonstrating potential to achieve excellence in volunteer services.
e Highest number of volunteer hours awards: for a volunteer who is the highest achiever in that academic year in number of volunteer hours with CYEP.

Enhancing the knowledge-based outcomes for the volunteer project

Two years after CYEP was implemented, we started to systematically collect empirical data to understand more about our volunteers. In 2009, the research team created in the project published an article "Psychometric Properties of the Volunteer Function Inventory with Chinese Students" (Wu, Lo, & Liu, 2009). Two hundred seventy-nine CYEP volunteers participated and the findings of the research has given us much insight on the motivational issues of our volunteers. We also published the articles we collected from the International Conference on Youth Empowerment: Empowering Youth through Volunteerism in a book: *Youth Empowerment and Volunteerism: Principles, Policies and Practices* (Liu, Holosko, & Lo, 2009). Examples of our other publications by different research groups from our department on youth volunteerism are Cheung & Liu, 2017; Liu, Ching, & Wu, 2017; Cheung, Lo, & Liu, 2012, 2015, 2016; Liu, 2014; Liu, Wu, Lo, & Hui, 2012.)

Besides mobilizing our project staff to systematically collect data on youth volunteering, we also applied to other research and programme funding sources to facilitate implementing new services and measuring our impact on our volunteers and service recipients. From 2013 to 2018, we were funded by the UGC Knowledge Transfer Earmarked Fund for five consecutive years for these goals. Our last proposal for the Knowledge Transfer Fund in 2017–18 was entitled: "Reciprocity as Empowerment – A Bi-directional Knowledge Transfer Project to Enhance Students' and Service Recipients' Development through Examining Perceived and Experienced Mutual Benefits." From our knowledge transfer funding, we received two awards for its excellent impact on volunteering work, and for serving different service recipients; the first was the Excellence in Knowledge Transfer Award in 2014, and the second was the Certificate of Merit in Knowledge Transfer in 2013.

Since 2010, CYEP has become active in enhancing both the staff and volunteers' exposure to international exchanges through participating in international conferences. Volunteer groups participated in the International Association of Volunteer Effort (IAVE) conferences and other international service learning conferences at least six times since 2010. The project convener participated in 11 international conferences in the last eight years. Two recent examples of those conference presentations are:

1. 33rd FICE Congress and 2nd CYC World Conference, Vienna, Austria, 22–25 August, 2016. The presentation topic was "Youth Development: Impact on Youth While Mentoring and Caring Children."
2. 25th IAVE World Conference in Augsburg, Germany in October 2018. The topic was "Social Indicators of youth volunteering in Hong Kong", basing on the findings of our latest research on youth volunteerism in Hong Kong, funded by the Public Policy Research Funding Scheme / Strategic Public Policy Research Funding Scheme from the Policy Innovation and Co-ordination Office of The Government of the HKSAR.

Since 2013, CYEP has issued its own newsletter and publicizes its work with the assistance from VAs in the publicity team. CYEP had its own dedicated internet link attached to the SS department, and has its own Facebook link to facilitate volunteer recruitment, publicity of new one-off services, and to publicize all the service requests from different NGOs (recruitment of individual volunteers on behalf of the community's NGOs). All social media work, research activities, academic conferences participation, and publications in books and journals are important on-going work for us to maintain our ongoing community linkages and networks so as to make sure that we do not just offer a volunteer project, but also maintain a conceptual flow to and from our project. The goal of this knowledge-based work is important for us to both examine and measure our work, and to monitor our impact on volunteers and service recipients. This volunteer project within the university arena is rather distinct from other community-based volunteer projects.

Selected highlights of some other facts and impacts of CYEP over the years

1. Officially branding the project with its mission via a logo

We started with delivering volunteer service to six local services and one of the services is supporting one of the NGOs in Hong Kong to deliver their writing counselling project called the "Uncle Long Legs" project. In this project, volunteers received training from the agency on how to answer letters collected by the agency from primary school pupils so that they feel that they were listened to and supported. A student, Chris Cheung, from the School of Creative Media of CityU was in this early stage of CYEP invited by us to design a project logo for CYEP. Among all current projects, he was inspired by the "Uncle Long Leg" project and came up to the our project log as shown in Figure 5.2. Actually, by rotating the CYEP logo (see Figure 5.2), it resembles a person, with the heart as a head, the enveloped as the body, and the arm. The drawing itself resembles the way we write "heart" in Chinese (心). So, this logo has multiple meanings, and Chris was very creative in capturing the essence of our project. We always noted that we wanted the volunteers to use the heart, meaning to be real, to be respectful, and genuine, which is also what is encouraged by our Chinese culture.

FIGURE 5.2 The City-Youth Empowerment Project logo

2. The collaborations of services to NGOs by the CYEP are many and various as indicated in Tables 5.1 and 5.2.

Through various collaborations with community-based organizations, the project provides an array of services listed below:

TABLE 5.1 Various Collaborative Projects, Partners, and Activities of CYEP's Regular Services (2005–2018)

Regular Services [only those collaborations lasted for 3 Years or above are listed)	
Mental Heath/Rehabilitation work	
Working with Children and Youth with Disabilities (Special Education Needs)	Hong Kong Red Cross Princess Alexandra School

(Continued)

TABLE 5.1 (Cont.)

Regular Services [only those collaborations lasted for 3 Years or above are listed)	
"Walk with body and mind!" - Social Support Group with Adults recovering from mental illness	Alliance of Ex-Mentally Ill of Hong Kong
Working with severely mentally-challenged children and youth (Special Education Needs)	The Mental Health Association of Hong Kong - Cornwall School
Developmental projects for Children and Youth	
Tutoring services to primary students from single-parent families living in Hong Kong	Caritas Integrated Family Service Centre, Sham Shui Po
Tutoring services to secondary students from single-parent and new-arrival families in Hong Kong	Caritas Integrated Family Service Centre, Sham Shui Po
Working with Children with Asperger's Syndrome	The Boys' & Girls' Clubs Association of Hong Kong
English Interview workshops with primary school students from low-income families in Hong Kong	ELCHK Hung Hom Lutheran Primary School
"Uncle Long Leg Letterbox" Letter Counselling Project for children	ELCHK Social Service
Tutoring & mentoring youth under the Police Superintendent's Discretion Scheme (youth who have committed minor crimes)	The Boys' & Girls' Clubs Association of Hong Kong
Tutoring service to primary students from deprived families in Hong Kong	Caritas Community Centre - Tsuen Wan Yi Pei Square Coummunity Service Centre
Tutoring for Primary and Secondary School Students from low-income families in Hong Kong	Society for Community Organization
Tutoring for children and youth from low-income families and new-arrival families in Hong Kong	Hong Kong Christian Service Shumshuipo Central Happy Teens Club
"Personal Finance Mentoring Scheme" with youth from ethnic-minority, single-parent, and low-income families in Hong Kong	Yan Oi Tong
Tutoring for primary and secondary school children and youth from low-income and new-arrival families in Hong Kong	Society for Community Organization
Tutoring for primary school students who suffer from various types of personal/family difficulties: "You seem like fun!" Project	St Francis of Assisi's Caritas School
Parental Supporting Groups (enhancing parenting skills for parents whose children are joining the CYEP's children and youth developmental programs)	Society for Community Organization

(Continued)

TABLE 5.1 (Cont.)

Regular Services [only those collaborations lasted for 3 Years or above are listed)	
Elderly Service	
Elderly Home Visiting Programs	The Neighborhood Advice-Action Council
Services for the Minority Groups	
"Chin Change" – Chinese Changes Your Life, Chinese Language Workshop for Ethnic Minority Youth, and "Walk with our dream" Mentoring Scheme for Ethnic Minority Youths	Caritas Youth & Community Service Caritas Community Centre - Ngau Tau Kok
"Chin Change" – Chinese Changes Your Life, Chinese Language Workshop for Ethnic Minority Youth, and "We all live under the same sky!" Mentoring Scheme for Ethnic Minority and Newly Arrived Youths	Hong Kong Christian Service Kwun Tong Happy Teens Club
"Fight Against Public Exam! - Special Tutorial Group for Ethnic Minority Youths, and "I plan, I do!" Future planning Mentorship Group for Ethic Minority Youths	Hong Kong Christian Service Kwun Tong Happy Teens Club
International Services	
See Globally, Serve Locally: International Service-Learning Program to Cambodia	2012-2016: National Borei for Infants and Children (NBIC); Save Children and Community Development Organization (SCCDO) 2017 until now: National Borei for Infants and Children (NBIC); People Improvement Organization (PIO);
See Globally, Serve Locally: International Service-Learning Program to Myanmar	2014 until now: myME(Myanmar Mobile Education Project)

TABLE 5.2 Various Collaborative Projects, Partners and Activities of CYEP's One-off Services (2010–2018)

One-off Services (only those collaborations lasted for 3 Years or above are listed)	
Developmental Services for Children and Youth	
One-day CityU tours for secondary school students in the P.A.T.H.S. program	Hong Kong Federation of Youth Groups
Adventure-Ship programs for children from deprived families	The Boys' and Girls' Clubs Association of Hong Kong
CityU tours for Secondary School Students from low-income families	Hong Kong Family Welfare Society ATAA JC TKO Youth Square
Mock Interview workshops for primary students	The Hong Kong Federation of Youth Groups Lee Shau Kee Primary School
CityU tours for Secondary School Students	Po Kok Secodary School
Elderly Services	
Winter Elderly Home Visits	The Neighbourhood Advice-Action Council

(Continued)

TABLE 5.2 (Cont.)

One-off Services (only those collaborations lasted for 3 Years or above are listed)	
Dragon Boat Festival Elderly Household Visits	The Neighbourhood Advice-Action Council
Services for the Minority Groups	
"Care in Tai Lam" in Tai Lam Correctional Institution	Society for Community Organization
PEME Project EM [Ethnic Minority] Empowerment	Hong Kong Christian Service Centre and its "Harmony and Enhancement of Ethnic Minority Residents" Project (CHEERS)
Homeless Outreach and Population Estimation H.O.P.E. HK (2013 and 2015, territory-wide homeless population city-counts)	The Salvation Army Society of Community Organization St. James' Settlement Christian Concern For The Homeless Association
SoCO Homeless football team - 'City-Younited' and Football Friendly Match with ex-homeless persons	Society for Community Organization Street Soccer HK

3. Data on the number of CYEP volunteers, service recipients, and service hours (2006–2018)

As indicated in the below table, the accumulative statistics on volunteers, service recipients and service hours over the last 12 years have been gradually increasing. In 2012–13, there was a jump of statistics when compared with the previous years. This was due to the fact that CYEP started to receive some outside donations and therefore was able to employ more staff and extend its service scope. We lost count of the statistics from 2005–06 because we were quite unprepared for such a long list to count statistics.

TABLE 5.3 Number of volunteers, service recipients, and service hours

Year	*No. of volunteers*	*No. of Service Recipients*	*Service Hours*
2006-07	196	278	4,815
2007-08	312	480	4,502
2008-09	213	422	4,896
2009-10	477	708	7,573
2010-11	545	697	8,141
2011-12	418	570	9,803
2012-13	1,436	1,139	19,758
2013-14	1,762	2,312	22,078
2014-15	1,977	2,415	27,217
2015-16	2,019	2,549	36,098
2016-17	1,630	2,095	28,335
2017-18	1,110	2,096	23,447
Total	12,095	15,761	196,663

4. Milestones in CYEP's development

- *2005* CYEP started in a City University of Hong Kong Student Residence, where we organized an opening ceremony in August with Dr. Philemon Choi, Chairman of the previous Commission on Youth, Professor Wing Lo from SS Department, Miss Rebecca Chan, former Director of Student Residence Office, and Miss Peggy Wong, former Residence Master of Hall 4 as our guests for its opening. Subsequently, each year, we adopted the routine of organizing an opening "CYEP Kick-off ceremony" for the new volunteers, donors, and invited staff from CityU to meet and to greet.
- *2006* CYEP launched its first "Closing Ceremony", at the end of the academic year for all volunteers and service recipients to meet and share. This ceremony was later re-named "Happy Carnival", and is still delivered yearly.
- *2008* CYEP was endorsed and enlarged by CityU, and made available to all enrolled students.
- *2009* CYEP staff doubled, with four members.
- *2010* CYEP staff increased to five members.
- *2010* CYEP organized its first press conference on "CityU Cares for Children" reporting on the local statistics and needs of the deprived children we were serving together with our volunteers.
- *2011* CYEP received its first donation from volunteer community members (from the Mustard Seeds Foundation).
- *2011* first international volunteering programme in Cambodia (this programme continued to be delivered yearly, until 2018).
- *2012* with the grant received from the "Mustard Seeds Foundation", CYEP started awarding outstanding volunteers with various annual scholarships.
- *2012* CYEP implemented the Volunteer Ambassador Scheme (VAS), in order to identify and support volunteer leaders.
- *2012* CYEP was awarded with the local UGC Knowledge Transfer Earmarked Fund, for the research project "Serve, learn, and change – Enhancing Knowledge Transfer Process to Promote Social Changes".
- *2013* CYEP developed new "Community Projects". The *Homeless Outreach and Population Estimation (H.O.P.E.)* project was launched for the first time in Hong Kong, in collaboration with Christian Concern for the Homeless Association, The Salvation Army, Society for Community Organization, and St James Settlement, with 300 student volunteers from CityU.
- *2013* CYEP was awarded with the Hong Kong Community Volunteers 2017 (Non-profit Organisation) Highest Service Hour Bronze Award, presented by Agency for Volunteer Service in recognition of its contributions to volunteer work.
- *2013* CYEP was awarded with the UGC Knowledge Transfer Earmarked Fund, for the project "The Carbon Trade Game project" – Bringing participatory learning experiences on environment and sustainability to local schools and communities.

- *2014* CYEP hosted the Joint-symposium with the Silberman School of Social Work at Hunter College – The City University of New York, about project H.O.P.E., in New York.
- *2014* CYEP received its largest donation from community members.
- *2014* CYEP organized international volunteer service in Nepal (one year) and Myanmar (2014–2018).
- *2014* Dr. Elaine LIU, Associate Professor of Department of Social and Behavioural Sciences and founder of the CYEP, was awarded with the UGC Teaching Award, (granted by the University Grants Committee), in recognition for her dedication to CYEP.
- *2014* As the number of VAs has grown, the group was divided into four sub-groups, each of them focusing on specific tasks. The four sub-groups are: Training Team, Networking Team, Community Engagement Team, and Promotion Team.
- *2014* CYEP was awarded with the UGC Knowledge Transfer Earmarked Fund, for the research project "Serve, Learn, and Change" – Knowledge Transfer to Promote Social Changes.
- *2015* CYEP for the first time was re-located to an office of its own (it was in a shared office in SS Department before) to accommodate its ten staff.
- *2015* project H.O.P.E. was expanded and run for the second time. It involved five local universities (Lingnan University, The Chinese University of Hong Kong, The Hong Kong Polytechnic University, The University of Hong Kong, and City University of Hong Kong), a few NGOs (Christian Concern for the Homeless Association, The Salvation Army, Society for Community Organization, and St James' Settlement), and over 300 student volunteers.
- *2015* CYEP was awarded with the Hong Kong Community Volunteers (Non-profit Organisation) Highest Service Hour Bronze Award presented by Agency for Volunteer Service in recognition of its contributions to volunteer work.
- *2015* CYEP was awarded with the UGC Knowledge Transfer Earmarked Fund, for the research project "Empowering Student, Empowering Community" – Bi-directional Knowledge Transfer to Promote the Understanding on Social Issues.
- *2016* CYEP was awarded with the Hong Kong Community Volunteers (Non-profit Organisation) Highest Service Hour Bronze Award presented by Agency for Volunteer Service in recognition of its contributions to volunteer work.
- *2016* CYEP was awarded with the UGC Knowledge Transfer Earmarked Fund, for the research project "Achieving Mutual Empowerment" – Bi-directional Knowledge Transfer to Enhance Students' Development through Community Participation.
- *2017* CYEP was awarded with the Hong Kong Community Volunteers (Non-profit Organisation) Highest Service Hour Silver Award presented by Agency for Volunteer Service in recognition of its contributions to volunteer work.
- *2017* CYEP was awarded with the UGC Knowledge Transfer Earmarked Fund, for the research project "Reciprocity as Empowerment" – A Bi-directional Knowledge Transfer Project to Enhance Students' and Service

Recipients' Development through Examining Perceived and Experienced Mutual Benefits.

- *2017* Dr. Elaine LIU, Convener and founder of CYEP was funded by the Public Policy Research Funding Scheme / Strategic Public Policy Research Funding Scheme from the Policy Innovation and Co-ordination Office of The Government of the HKSAR to carry out the research on "Demographic and Social Indicators of Youth Volunteering in Hong Kong".
- *2018* CYEP was awarded with the Hong Kong Community Volunteers (Non-profit Organisation) Highest Service Hour Bronze Award presented by Agency for Volunteer Service in recognition of its contributions to volunteer work.

This chapter has described how CYEP as a whole created its coaching model for volunteers and designed its programme framework in order to actualize its goals and values. From conceptual to practice, the account of these steps and procedures will serve as good references when planning and constructing a new volunteer project for young people. The next five chapters will detail how the Reciprocal Volunteer Process Model is implemented in the community, as partnered with different NGOs for five different groups of clients: local children and youth with developmental needs, local children and youth with rehabilitation needs, children and youth in our international services, children and youth from local ethnic minorities groups, and the elderly in Hong Kong.

References

Cheung, C. K. & Liu, E. S. C. (2017). "Enhancing the Contribution of volunteering to career commitment with friendship among university students." *Career Development International*, 22(7), 754–771.

Cheung, C. K., Lo, T. W. & Liu, E. S. C. (2015). "Relationships between Volunteerism and Social Responsibility in Young Volunteers." *Voluntas: International Journal of Voluntary and Nonprofit Organizations*, 26(3), 872–889.

Cheung, C. K., Lo, T. W. & Liu, E. S. C. (2016). "Sustaining Social Trust and Volunteer Role Identity Reciprocally Over Time in Pre-adult, Adult, and Older volunteers." *Journal of Social Service Research*, 42(1), 70–83.

Cheung, C. K., Lo, T. W. & Liu, E. S. C. (2012). "Measuring Volunteering Empowerment and Competence in Shanghai." *Administration in Social Work*, 36(2), 149–174.

Clary, E. G., Snyder, M., Ridge, R. D., Copeland, J., Stukas, A. A., Haugen, J., & Miene, P. (1998). "Understanding and assessing the motivations of volunteers: A functional approach. "*Journal of Personality & Social Psychology*, 74, 1516–1530.

Liu, E. S. C. (2014). "Youth's Perception on the Impact and Meaning of Working with Children." *Journal of Psychology and Psychotherapy*, 5(2), 177–182.

Liu, E. S. C., Holosko, M., & Lo, T. W. (Eds.) (2009). *Youth Empowerment and Volunteerism: Principles, Policies and Practices*. Hong Kong: City University of Hong Kong Press.

Liu, E. S. C., Wu, J., Lo, T. W., & Hui, N. N. A. (2012). "Implementing volunteer program to university students in Hong Kong: Enhancing volunteer participation through service matching and organizational support." In B. C. Eng (Ed.), *A Chinese perspective on teaching and learning* (pp. 165–178). New York, NY: Routledge.

Liu, E. S. C., Ching, C., & Wu, J. (2017) "Who is a Volunteer? A Cultural & Temporal Exploration of Volunteerism." *Journal of Human Behaviour and Social Environment*, 27(6), 530–545.

Mjelde-Mossey, L. A., Chi, I. R. I. S., & Chow, N. (2002). "Volunteering in the social services: Preferences, expectations, barriers, and motivation of aging Chinese professionals in Hong Kong." *Hallym International Journal of Aging*, 4(1), 31–44.

Wu, J. K. F., Lo, T. W., & Liu, E. S. C. (2009). "Psychometric properties of the volunteer functions inventory with Chinese students." *Journal of Community Psychology*, 37(6), 769–780.

6

USING THE RECIPROCAL VOLUNTEER PROCESS MODEL (RVPM) TO IMPLEMENT DEVELOPMENTAL SERVICES FOR LOCAL CHILDREN AND YOUTH

Part A

The context

Since its inception, CYEP has chosen to partner with six projects from local NGOs to help children and youth from various deprived backgrounds. The first project was in a number of arranged classrooms on the campus of City University of Hong Kong, we offered different groups of children the opportunity after-school tuition and mentoring services. These services were much appreciated by families who lived in the same city district where we are located, as the parents felt grateful that their children could have a chance to receive free of charge study assistance, in a university just a few blocks from their homes. For most of these families, it was a welcome change to have their children get to know the environment of a university and be offered services. The NGOs who directed their child clients to come to us also welcomed this model of service, because it was a safe space and trained manpower organized and supplied by CYEP. All they had to do was just escort these children to our campus. Since then, children from such deprived families and with needs for developmental opportunities, remain the largest population served by CYEP volunteers.

Using the RVPM model in building a supportive environment

After the project set its goal of focussing on developing children in its early period, we also studied the needs and problems of children's services in Hong Kong for the team to have a better understanding of the issues and to assist our work. Focussing on such work has helped staff to learn skills to manage, and for the volunteers to gain more competence to serve and to reflect on their own development.

Recognizing the developmental needs of children from local deprived families

From a very young age, children in Hong Kong are expected and encouraged to compete academically to be better than their peers, and to engage in many extra-curricular activities, so as to gain a sense of achievement and their place in society. We recognized that this overt emphasis on academic achievements pushes students from deprived families, including single-parent families, newly-arrived families (mainly from mainland China), and the families on CSSA (Comprehensive Social Security Assistance Scheme) to face even more pressure. For example, for the newly-arrived families, Zhang and Ting (2011) found that Chinese immigrant students in Hong Kong face several academic and/or social challenges. Further, their family financial difficulties may affect their self-esteem and limit their chances of obtaining additional resources to study (Pong, 2009). In addition, relying solely on welfare may help these families economically, but it often contributes to disharmony in society, and increases the growing divide between local immigrants and "locals" (Phillion, 2008).

The impact on volunteer youth while mentoring for children

The above discussion has justified the needs and service gaps for children from deprived family background. CYEP therefore had various programmes for assisting children with developmental needs in Hong Kong. However, by focussing on serving children, we also promoted goals for our young volunteers, which increased awareness among university students about the difficulties and needs of children and youth growing up in deprived families, and/or with different types of disabilities in Hong Kong. When this project started, it was only connected with six children-focussed projects. This primary focus (besides recognizing the needs of such children) also carries a unique mission both for the development of the project and for the development of our young volunteers. For these volunteers, we hypothesised that young people would be more competent in helping such children as compared with other groups, since young people are a group which has just passed their own childhood. So, facilitating them to work with children would be an effective way to help them succeed in volunteering in such volunteer projects. For their personal growth, it is proved later on by research carried out in CYEP on our volunteers that working with children is a very meaningful reflective and learning process for the young volunteers (Liu, 2014).

Part B

Using the RVPM model in building interactional relationships

Designing programmes for children with developmental needs

To these volunteers, one aim of these projects was for them to learn practice-based helping skills to better relate to these children, and help motivate them to learn. Over time, these programmes attracted both local and international volunteers, and most of these revealed the deep bonds that they developed with these children, as well as with other volunteers. Often, the relationships they developed and the manifestations of affections they received, were unexpectedly rewarding. In turn, this motivated many volunteers to continue their service for longer time periods and some became group leaders to help new participants. Currently, these local CYEP programmes involve annually about 250 volunteers and over 300 children in Hong Kong. Most of these mentoring programmes were carried out within the campus of CityU classrooms. This became a major part of our regular programmes, and it was also the most popular service all year round for the CYEP. Children and parents gave very positive feedback to such mentorship because they saw the mobilization of people and resources from the university which has substantially helped children's development academically and socially. Our major regular children's developmental projects include:

a *Tutoring & Mentoring for Youth under the Police Superintendent's Discretion Scheme, for The Boys' and Girls' Clubs Association of Hong Kong Jockey Club Cheung Sha Wan Children and Youth Integrated Service Centre*: this service provided academic and developmental support for youth under the Police Superintendent's Discretion Scheme (youths who have committed minor crimes). The role of CYEP volunteers was to provide mentorship, and peer support to care with youth and develop positive relationships with them.

b *Tutoring for children and youth from low-income families and "new arrival" families, for Hong Kong Christian Service, Shamshuipo Central Happy Teens Club*: here, newly arrived students who faced adjustment issues and academic challenges were offered off-site tutoring in English and mathematics on a weekly basis. Volunteers acted as mentors and role models for young students, giving them advice or sharing about their life experiences.

c *SoCO Academic Support Scheme, in CityU Campus*: this service provided on-going academic assistance to children from low-income, and/or new arrivals families. Besides being teachers, volunteers also served as mentors to share about their own life experiences, to be role models and shape positive learning attitudes for these children.

d *Interview workshops with primary school students from local low-income families*: this initiative provided interview workshops to a local group of underprivileged P.5–6 primary school students, who were applying to secondary school. Here, trained volunteers organized, designed, and facilitated a series of interactive interview workshops in English, to prepare these young students for interviews. Most parts of the actual interviews these young students had to go through are carried out in English and are very stressful and challenging for them.

e *English Fun Group for primary school students who suffer from difficulties caused either by inadequate family resources or support*: these local students had inadequate family support, with their parents facing many difficulties, and had limited resources to help their children with academic assistance. This initiative aimed at motivating and supporting these primary school students to learn English, in more facilitative ways.

f *Parents' support group*: in one of the local agencies we collaborated for children services, and after a few years of service delivery, we found that there were always a group of parents (mostly women) who would escort their children to walk to the campus, and most of them would wait until their children finished with the service, and then would escort children home again. Observing that this was happening and inspired by one remark given by a volunteer: "I talked to one of the mothers and found out that she could not help her child because she received very little education herself. She said she should be in the tuition class too!" This in turn inspired staff of CYEP and this agency to discuss the issue and to decide to run a new service for parents. To start with, we recruited those parents who wanted to join, and to learn what their children were learning. This evolved to the addition of computer skills, arts, and drawing, and parenting skills were added on occasion. Presently, our project goal is: "We target a group of children's parents who are from low-income or new arrival families. Volunteers will organize and facilitate a support group with parents ultimately to build up a mutual help network and interpersonal relationship." Of the nine sessions in a semester, around 20 parents will be recruited and also 20 volunteers will be involved in the group sessions which are scheduled to cover parenting and self-care issues, relaxation exercises, problem-solving skills, computer skills, etc. With such a platform for facilitating parents to talk freely and share experiences, many positive changes were noted and many useful networks were formed among group members.

Adopting the Group Matching Model

Research on volunteerism predominantly relies on western literature and little has been done to understand how the local context influences implementing a volunteer project. From western literature, matching of the interest and goals of volunteers to a project is proved to be important in further motivating volunteering behaviour (Bang & Ross, 2009). By implementing CYEP in the early stage by choosing "working with children" as our larger target groups, we created a Group Matching Model. This meant that not just individuals should be matched to a project in order to sustain their interest, but a project within a unique social context should benefit from choosing a certain target group, or even a certain thematic service should also increase the sustainability of the project. This was deemed the

Group Matching Model or organizational matching (Liu, Wu, Lo, & Hui, 2012). Soon after we implemented CYEP, we focused on working with children, based on the belief that young adults who had just experienced childhood and adolescence themselves, young university students would be in a good developmental position that made them an ideal fit to work with children and youth. CYEP carried out a qualitative study to monitor the impact of working with children from N=35 participants on this experience. These results revealed three thematic clusters that illustrated their reflection on their own childhood and increased self-awareness. These included: 1) increased reflection on their own roles, 2) increased reflection on their own development, and 3) enhanced development on their life philosophy (Liu, et al., 2012). A follow-up study with a larger sample of N=120 participants was subsequently carried out about the experiences of helping children. Here, volunteer respondents gained experience on: 1) gaining an understanding about the nature of children; 2) uncovering some pre-conceptions about children; 3) enhancement of values toward children; 4) gaining new skills to relate better to such children; 5) arriving at some sceptical ideas about helping children. About the impact on the volunteer respondents themselves, it was reported that helping such children helped them to: 1) reflect on their own relationships; 2) reflect on and understand their own development; 3) develop their own life growth (Liu, 2014). These research findings have assisted us to see better how working with such children was mutually beneficial for our service recipients and for our young volunteers.

Infusing for multi-level and multi-disciplinary approach

As mentioned earlier in this book, CYEP adopted a multi-level approach toward volunteering: group, individual, and community levels, with everything beginning at the group level. We noticed student volunteers were a homogenous group, sharing similar developmental backgrounds and having common learning needs. Soon after they were recruited and joined a project, they were all trained with practical skills on how to think and work as a team. When engaged in service delivery, they are also guided to see the needs their service recipients as a group, in this case, groups of children. Group settings facilitate the encounters among individuals (not the other way around), and groups can represent individuals at all community levels. As such, group-work thinking has always represented (for us) the bridge between individuals and their communities. From groups to persons, and from persons to groups, we promote a group concept which facilitates a less threatening and more supportive environment for volunteers to practice. This working structure is the skeleton of most of our programmes. Thus, various programmes can have different goals and outcomes. However, promoting a group-work structure implies that all participants (e.g., student volunteers and children) can be at the same time recipients as well as beneficiaries of the program. For the staff, we do not clearly distinguish between "care givers" and "care recipients", in fact we hope that all participants can see one another in a reciprocal positive relationship.

This multi-level multi-disciplinary approach has become a basic programming guideline when CYEP is designing in each services its interactional relationship among the staff, volunteers and service recipients.

Mentoring children to experience creativity together

In 2010, five years after serving the children in different projects, we implemented several new programmes in order to re-focus our projects to advocating a more holistic developmental work for all children, and thinking out-of-the-box creatively to achieve positive outcomes. We experimented implementing some "Creative Learning Workshops" for children aged six to 14 . We focussed this workshop on *The 5 C's Module (Critical Thinking, Communication, Creativity, Collaboration, and Community)* – a modified model from the 4C model of creativity by adding the exploration of raising the self-esteem and community-esteem of children aged from six to 14 (Kaufman & Beghetto, 2009). This workshop focussed on elements that we deemed essential to developing values crucial to personal and interpersonal development, and building an integrated sense of community. The guiding values of this workshop were:

i to value the parallel and dynamic learning process between the volunteers and children,
ii to understand, promote, and appreciate the participants' (children and volunteers) authentic worldview, and
iii to promote a well-rounded sense of personal and community development.

We believe that personal and community development is an integrated process, and often they go hand-in-hand. Through the previously stated 5Cs theme – this workshop highlights these core elements utilizing various interactive activities to facilitate participants – volunteers from CityU, and children (service recipients) from NGOs to explore the overarching theme of "community", within the framework of the goals of CYEP to: 1) learn about the needs of people faced with social problems; 2) experience how the individual and group processes can be combined to form a community building process; 3) facilitate the continuity of the volunteering "life cycle" to a community level; 4) develop the student volunteers' abilities to understand the connection between personal and societal issues.

This type of creative workshop is structured with some sequences of activities and activity details as lay out in Appendix 1 (below). When applied, CYEP officers will adjust the length and content of it according to the real circumstances.

Achieving the macro perspective

In 2010, our enrolled volunteers had already grown from 150 in 2005 to over 500 in 2010 serving almost over 500 service recipients, who were mainly children. In 2010, we worked together with a group of volunteers to carry out a small survey on the background with N=255 children that we were currently serving and found out the following:

- Close to 30% of these children's families are reportedly receiving CSSA
- Almost one out of four had a reported diagnosis of a disabling condition (including: Aspergers' Syndrome, ADHD, Cerebral Palsy, other Learning Disabilities, etc.)
- Almost one out of three (30%) were from single-parent households
- Almost 46% were from new-arrival families
- Almost one out of five (22.5%) of them have reported family issues, e.g., divorced families, low-income families

At the same time, the working group (staff and volunteers) also interviewed a group of volunteers about their experiences working with children and their suggestions for better support for children we served. This formed the mentors' perspectives of children's needs:

- The children need support from the community as well as from their families
- Children's problems can easily be labelled and judged without regard to their background and environment
- Many children are limited in their social exposure
- Many children are restricted
- Children are responsive to good relationships and especially to "play"
- Children's past bad experiences can limit their subsequent development in learning

We then mobilized a group of volunteers to host a press conference on 28 October 2010 to release the research findings. We named it "City-Youth Cares about Children". In a press conference, besides advocating for this care for children, we encouraged our volunteers to have dialogues with the media, and the public on our future development. Here is our coverage for the press conference:

> City-youth Empowerment Project as organized by City University of Hong Kong was implemented for all our students since 2005 and is now enrolled with over 500 volunteers and serving also around 500 service recipients. We have focused on our volunteer work mainly for children because we recognize the importance of providing holistic services to underprivileged children - as a prevention, and/or intervention of self-esteem issues, and to ensure that their psychological, physical, and social development is not undermined as a result of their limited resources. In addressing the alarming social phenomenon of children living in poverty or living with limited resources, and the belief that young people are more responsive to serving children– we designed our program's services to embrace a wide range of work with children/youth. Capitalizing on our access to university students as volunteers, the volunteers continue to engage children in the community through various services: regular tutoring, mentoring, adventure-based activities, cultural exchange workshops, etc. Going forward, some of the project's services will include the participation and engagement of parents, as a pathway to empower an integral

part of the children's supportive network and environment. In addition, the project will also expand the scope of services to include different populations who are in need, e.g. homeless adults, elderly, etc., and encourage more volunteer-led services.

Advocating for children's rights

In 2015, we had another opportunity for our volunteers to engage at community level. In this year, we partnered with the Committee for Promotion of Children's Right to carry out a "Survey on the Child Participation Environment in Hong Kong", with more than 20 volunteers form CYEP being trained and involved in data collection and in the process of disseminating data to the public. Here is the brief summary of the results of that study (Liu et. al., 2017):

> The study aimed to understand the awareness and perception of child participation in schools and NGOs serving children and to identify best promising practices and models of meaningful child participation in schools and NGOs. It used both a quantitative and qualitative research design. Participants included N=331 teachers (77%) and N=99 registered social workers (23%) by using convenience sampling and received N=430 completed questionnaires. Nine focus group interviews were then conducted with a total of N=37 participants: 10 teachers (seven from primary schools and three from secondary schools), seven social workers or children-related workers from NGOs, and 20 students (12 from primary schools and eight from secondary schools). A significant difference was found between social workers and teachers as the former group were able to correctly indicate the origin of the concept coming from "The Convention on the Rights of the Child". Further, 81.9% of respondents had not received any professional training in terms of the implementation of children's participation rights. Social workers reported having significantly higher confidence and knowledge levels, in helping children to implement participation rights in their community participation, religious belief, and political participation compared with teachers. Over 70% of respondents further elaborated that the provision of professional training to adults, such as parents, teachers and social workers was the most important element in helping implement children's participation rights. Social workers accepted significantly more children's advice when participating in the design and implementation of services and activities compared with teachers. Social workers agreed significantly more with the capability of children compared with teachers. The qualitative findings were consistent with the quantitative ones in the view that social workers were familiar with the concept of "children's right to participate" and they knew that it was a pillar of "The Convention on the Rights of the Child". Social workers expressly operated for informing children (and communities) of their rights and teaching them how to exercise, teachers showed a rather different attitude (e.g., they prefer not to use the term rights when speaking with the parents, as they perceive Chinese parents may not like it).

Part C

Using the RVPM model in achieving accountability and transparency: voices of student volunteers and staff

We interviewed one staff member and six student volunteers who had been volunteered for children's developmental services in order to record from their own experience on how this type of service has been delivered. The following represent the results of face-to-face interviews conducted in 2018 with one staff member (S1) and six on-site volunteers (V1, V2, V3, V4, V5, V6) carried out either by the book author and/or a Research Fellow of CYEP, as represented by "I".

Interview with the CYEP staff (S1)

I: What projects are you currently involved with in children's developmental work?

S1: I am involved in three programmes, the first one being the "Tutoring & Mentoring for Youth under the Police Superintendent's Discretion Scheme" which is a semester-based (13–14 weeks) programme comprised of three parts. This project focusses on tutoring and providing academic support to groups of young adolescents' who have committed minor crimes. With special discretion granted by the Police Force, they are referred to a special project under an NGO for a period of time and for monitoring their pro-social behaviour development. We worked with one of these projects in Hong Kong and the services from CYEP represented one major part of their rehabilitation programme, which was to accomplish the planned activities together with a group of volunteers delivered on the campus of City University of Hong Kong. Planned activities include:

a A welcoming party: in the first three weeks of a semester, we recruited and trained 30 volunteers and the NGO also recruited 30 participants from their project. After all the recruitments had finished, a socialization party was arranged for the volunteers and the service recipients to meet and to go through some ice-breaking games and to meet their mentors/mentees.

b Regular tutoring and mentoring programme: as the major and regular programme, service recipients come to our service on campus once a week (a fixed day for an entire semester) starting at 6:00 pm, lasted for around 1.5 hours, and for eight or nine weeks. When service recipients arrive, they are split into five or six groups and each group is placed in a different classroom. One mentor will then be matched with one service recipient and so we must recruit and train 30 volunteers for it. The matching of volunteers and service recipients is a fixed match among two volunteers and two service recipients. This is to guarantee that if one volunteer is missing on a service day because of other commitment, or vice versa, a service recipient is missing a service day, the matching will be changed to either 1 volunteer taking care of two service recipients, or two volunteers taking care of one service recipient. So, it is a workable fixed but flexible way to manage the matching and manpower issues for the programme. In reality, we found that volunteers are very committed to delivering services and are seldom found skipping a service day. Alternatively, it is the service recipients who are found missing service days more often, especially during their unstable or earlier periods of adjusting to a structured pattern of normal and pro-social behavioural routines. If this is the case, we will discuss issues with the volunteers and invite them to do a bit more next time, to encourage the service recipient to attend more regularly to benefit from the service.

c One-outing activity: usually at the middle of the semester, an outing is be organized for the service recipient and volunteers to enjoy a relaxing time together. Over the years, the outings organized could take the form of a BBQ party on campus, a bicycle day, a war-game day, a hiking day, an adventure ship tour, etc. We found both of these groups enjoyed those events very much.

d End of semester party: to celebrate the finishing of one group after one semester, a celebration party will be organized for encouraging service recipients to go through the whole process of learning and socializing with others.

e The second program under my supervision is the interview workshops offered to a group of primary school students from one local primary school with the children's families coming from low-income families. This project involves about 50 volunteers and an equal number of receivers, with one mentor matched to helping one primary school student. This is a comparatively shorter programme as it only lasts normally for four or five sessions, only in one semester, whereas other programmes normally last nine sessions. However, this is a very intensive program with each session lasting for three hours. Instead of the children coming to our campus for service here, we go to the primary school for delivering service. This programme focusses on teaching children practical skills about how to prepare for a good interview and to prepare them to face the interviews for entering their secondary schools. Contents of the training include how to greet the interviewers, how to give a self-introduction, how to answer and be familiarized with current social issues, etc. Above all, the most needed help for service recipients is how to face their difficulties in communicating in English, during the interview. Because of the nature of this service, exchange students from Western cultures with English as their mother tongues, are especially welcome to serve as volunteers in this service. We usually managed to recruit half of them being expatriate students.

f The third service that I am supervising is tutoring children and youth from low-income families and "new arrival" families from one NGO. This programme is delivered at the agency site, and it involves about 30 volunteers and 30 recipients, split into five groups and lasts for eight sessions for one semester, and each time two hours. Same for the first service I mentioned, there is one outing in the middle of the semester, and one farewell party at the end. We did not arrange the welcoming party because this group of children are easier to get warmed up for participation and so we just saved time for other activities. Most service recipients are children who migrated to Hong Kong from mainland China. The most difficult group is those who have just arrived a few months ago, and they are in great need of both academic and social supports. These children also frequently experience problems with their local classmates, and have difficulties being accepted in schools and communities. So volunteers are trained and socialized by the experienced volunteers to be very accepting and respectful to children because children are very sensitive to how others treat them. In addition, being newcomers, they are also challenged with speaking the local language, i.e., Cantonese. This language barrier may also cause difficulties in their academic learning, as they need some time to adapt to their new environments, and to navigate this challenging process. How they experience a caring attitude from a volunteer therefore, becomes very essential to their future adjustment. For those who have already handled their language, and are already here for some time, we will speed up with their academic work and raise our expectations on them, for catching up. Anyhow, for all those who can speed up with their work with less time, the reward is that the volunteers could spend time to play with them for any creative work in drawing, card games and other games agreed upon between the volunteer and the child.

I: What are your goals for the volunteers?

S1: We hope that all volunteers learn more about the backgrounds of their service recipients, and the difficulties they face and to show respect for all children. Furthermore, especially during training and de-briefing, we will discuss and encourage them to learn about the available resources for these groups of children, and what are environmental constraints coming from the discrimination from the community, the peer pressure or bullying, and even the school policies or government policies which are impacting the welfare and well-being of these vulnerable groups. Finally here, we help volunteers acquire the skills for planning suitable activities for these children. We will even discuss how conflicts between local Hong Kong people and newcomers from mainland China affect the volunteers' acceptance toward these children. We of course, advocate for all newcomers, to learn more about Hong Kong, but we also set a goal for the local volunteers to become sensitive of their own attitudes and deep biases on these newcomers and risky young adolescents. Volunteers should be reminded that young students did not choose to come to Hong Kong from mainland China, but they came because their parents chose to come here. Some children are rather passive, and do not engage with others. In addition, because of the language barrier they cannot develop meaningful friendships in Hong Kong. Some find it difficult to adapt to the crowded environment of Hong Kong. Yet others are hosted by relatives like grandparents, and live without their parents who remained behind. Learning Cantonese is not a main obstacle, because they can learn it by speaking constantly with their new friends. All these have become our common understanding (between staff and volunteers) on why helping our serving children with their academic work, and helping the children to meet other children in group settings are essential. For example, we will facilitate them to have opportunities to meet students who arrived in Hong Kong five years ago, who understand their difficulties very well and how to face them, and can share their own experiences with them. This is what we expected from our volunteers, to be accepting and to be as facilitative as possible, and at last, to be able to spell out the structural causes for the children's behaviour.

I: How do you do recruitment and training?

S1: We offer this programme on a first-come-first-serve basis. Volunteers must attend the briefing sessions before they serve. In all trainings, we explain the challenges faced by this unique population, and then we teach them necessary communication skills, such as how to initiate a conversation with quiet and/or shy children etc. We also emphasise training the volunteers to become acquainted with each other for the same service. A good team work is very essential, as later they will have to work as a team. At the beginning of the service, we group volunteers and service recipients in order to do the necessary matching. During training, I have to observe and understand the new volunteers (old volunteers are easier for me) and I will do the matching with the social worker from the agency, as s/he is the one who knows the service recipients well. Before service, we will meet and discuss who matches better with whom, according to their personalities. We take into consideration that one is more active or passive when engaging in activities, and who speaks more fluently with one language than others for either volunteers/recipients (i.e., English, Cantonese, and/or Mandarin), their previous experiences, etc. Normally, we are able to keep some experienced volunteers, about ten each semester, who continue from the previous semester, and are already familiar with some recipients. They will become the leaders for the service and will serve as the role models to the new ones. Their sharing of their past experiences during training is also very helpful.

I: This is a non-credit bearing project, what do you think of the commitment of the volunteers?

S1: This is a voluntary project that participants join because they really want to do it, and not for any other reason or personal benefit. We make it clear from the onset that we expect all recruited volunteers to attend each meeting, including training and other events. We also explain to the volunteers that if they do not come to attend a session, their matched service recipient will then have no one to take care of them. I found it most effective if I relate their commitment to the benefit and welfare of children, and not really just to CYEP or to the NGOs. We are really glad that most volunteers do live up to our expectations.

I: What are the strengths of this child development programme by CYEP?

S1: This service has been running for many years already, and we are still able to recruit volunteers and have maintained a good relationship with the NGOs. I think the first strength is that we have done a very good matching and coaching work for volunteers. Second, the volunteers know well that if children from lower income families have no support from us, their families can hardly pay for commercial expensive services and get senior and competent university students to give their children such needed free of charge services. Besides tuition services, these families also feel that our students are really sincere to them, as you can see how grateful they are when they attend the year end function (the Happy Carnival) on campus. Wrapping up our services with such meaningful activities, we do feel that our volunteers are very sincere to perform their social responsibilities, and to define their acts of helping are regaining some social justice for the deprived.

I: How do you see the volunteers changing from the beginning to the end of the project?

S1: Some volunteers are very young and are first-time volunteers or new to CYEP. Some are rather passive, in the sense that they do not know how/or what they can do, and have no idea on how to engage with such children. However, after a few sessions, they start to acquire some basic skills of talking and playing with children, and they will become more proactive rather than passive in engaging children. For some more senior volunteers, you can see that they are preparing themselves to become leaders. For example, if some participants are focusing on their phones, senior volunteers often approach them, talk with them and divert their attention, and try to involve them in activities. This means that they are already a role model for inexperienced volunteers, by showing their leadership through behaving and achieving goals. Furthermore, senior volunteers play important roles in the de-briefings and are leading others to be more reflective. I witness that the young volunteers often share in superficial ways when they first join the de-briefings, as they simply respond with simple sentences like "it is ok", or "all is good", when they were being asked to give feedback. But after a few sessions, and especially toward the end of the programme, they are already becoming elaborative and open when sharing their thoughts, and deepening their sharing by telling some funny stories about their interactions with children. At this junction, we will frequently guide them to make some concluding remarks on their common problems and experiences, and instead of lingering on some minute personal experience. This de-briefing skill is also important to further enhance the team approach and to meet the CYEP goal of searching for structural causes for the deprived population for the volunteers. This means that at this stage, volunteers may start thinking more on macro levels, and not just about a single service recipient. For example, they may reflect on what kinds of social resources are available today in Hong Kong. Further, they may reflect on discrimination in our society; and, how this situation may evolve in the future. So, in the initial sessions, volunteers seem to be focussed mostly at the individual level, i.e., their own characteristics, and the characteristics of the service recipients. After a few sessions, they seem to be more concerned about interactions between themselves and recipients, and/or how to get closer to them, and/or how to better engage them, etc. Finally, in the latter sessions, normally the discussion shifts to a more social level, as we may talk about social resources, i.e., are there enough for this target group? What else can be done? Why many others are not helping but discriminating etc.

I: How did this project evolve over the years?

S1: I think the project started with an initial emphasis on academic needs, and later we put more focus on other needs of the participants, and it has become more sensitive about the relationships between volunteers and service recipients. At the beginning, we had fewer structured activities for volunteers, but we noticed that making the volunteers become engaged and responsible for organizing some activities contributed to increase commitment to the service. Our changes made to the training and debriefing methods are also essential. For instance, in the beginning we did not invite social workers to participate in training our volunteers, as we had been focussing on generic skills for volunteering. Later on, we got social workers involved and shifted the training goal to more on understanding the service and service recipients. This has been a very good move. This is because social workers can provide more timely information about these service recipients, their challenges and difficulties, and what engagements skills can be applied, so that the volunteers are more prepared before they actually start the service. I do want to share the difficulties of checking and improving the attendance of the volunteers. For example, for the project of mentoring the young children who had committed with minor crimes, this year, I decided to change the venue of the outing this year to a war-game site, and immediately we improved the attendance to 90%. I think that volunteers also need new excitement and new activities. As a project officer, I have to take care of the feedback from many angles, not just from the service recipients, but also from our volunteers.

Interviews with six student volunteers (V1, V2, V3, V4, V5, V6)

I: Why did you join CYEP?

V3: Initially, I was attracted by the fact that CYEP offered both regular and international services, and I was really stressed dealing with my school work at that time, so I decided to join CYEP and do some volunteering. Interacting with these children taught me a lot about my own mental and emotional state during that time, and it really helped me to calm down.

V4: When I was in year 2, I passed by the CYEP recruitment booth, and someone gave me a leaflet to read. I have always been interested in volunteering, and I had joined some volunteering activities while in high school. Since then, I always thought that if I have some spare time, I would spend it doing more volunteering work and to help others, and I decided that would make me happier too.

I: What do you do in the service, and how is it structured?

V4: Normally, we start with a series of trainings first. In each service, we start with a briefing session. The group leader who is usually a student who had joined the service before, or was a volunteer ambassador before, would be among us and would do some ice-breaking games with us before the real de-briefing by the officer.

I: Why is it important?

V6: I think the briefing session is very important, as not just the schedule for services is important before we start the services. It is important to know more about the group of people that we are working with, what attitudes, emotions, behaviours, thoughts and mood they have, and how to prepare themselves better, etc.

V5: In addition to what one can learn about the services during briefings, I think that a briefing is a great chance for us to learn more about one another. Everyone may have different thoughts about the service, and since we have to work together, it is better to have some shared ideas. After knowing more about others, it is often easier to work as a group.

V3: After briefing, we have a logbook in which everyone has to write their reflections. We often share about what expectations we have, and what do we hope to gain during the semester. Sometimes we might forget what we said or did after a week, but our team leaders can read our log books and give us feedback. Since team leaders have more experience than us, they offer some important suggestions, which may help us adjust our expectations to the recipients more effectively.

I: What were your expectations at the beginning and what have you realized during the project?

V1: I met a lot of friends in CYEP, which is something that I did not expect. As I started to bond with my fellow volunteers, my sense of belonging to City University and CYEP gradually increased, and this is why I continued volunteering. I also found many experienced people who gave me good advice and guidance during the de-briefing sessions.

V4: I joined this service alone, not knowing anyone, but after three semesters, I feel the group is like a family for me. After joining the programme, I feel that I am more capable and familiar with communicating to secondary school students, and building relationships with them. I feel happy when I see that these service recipients continue to join the service in the following semester, because it means they valued what we are doing, and they are willing to maintain these relationships with us.

V2: I wanted to join because I never volunteered in the past. I decided to join a programme that supports children from new arrival families in Hong Kong because as I come from mainland China also, so I thought that we shared some similarities. However, I soon realized that they planned to stay much longer than I do, and we face very different situations. Initially, I thought that I could only help them with their homework, but then they started telling me things about their lives, family, school life, etc. In the following semester, I was not able to join due to my class schedule, and I heard from other volunteer colleagues that some of my recipients asked why I was no longer there, and I was really touched, because that was really beyond my expectations. So,

I realized that it was not just me helping them, but also them giving me and teaching me a lot.

V5: I remember a volunteer once telling me that she would never join the program again, because she could not see any improvements in the service recipients. I have also questioned the meaning of my participation in this service, but I learned that there are some improvements and changes that we would not be able to observe right away, and I believe so.

I: What is the most impressive moment you have experienced?

V6: It is really not one particular moment, but the overall changes that I observed, over time. I joined a programme where service recipients were all girls, and the volunteers were all boys. I could tell there were some gender issues, as we performed drama and played games with them, and we always think of ways to facilitate mutual interaction. During outing activities, we observed that they were starting to get less anxious with us. At the end, I felt that some even became more attached to us. I think that these kinds of changes were really impressive.

V1: I remembered a child who only joined the service for one semester. At the beginning, he was very quiet, he would just stay in his corner, never asking for anything, never talking, even if he was asked with something. But then, one time he was particularly unhappy, and he sat aside me with tears in his eyes. At that time, I was teaching other students, but I noticed him. After some talking, he opened up and told me that he had a fight with his family. I felt that there was nothing I could really do, apart from telling the social worker, and then the social worker had a talk with him. In the following session, he seemed much happier and somehow displayed more openness and trust toward the volunteers. He then became very willing to chat with us.

V4: There was a child in my group, she was always very busy with her homework, and would rarely have interactions with others. I used to sit beside her and see what she was doing. After several sessions, we built a relationship where she would always ask me about her homework. I was a group leader and one time, after the service ended, all of the group members had left, but this child still had questions for me. I stayed until 9:30 that night to teach her English, and we left together. She was not the kind of person who opened up about herself very easily. But when we left, she would tell me about many obstacles she faced at school, some issues she had with her friends, and she asked me for advice. I saw this as a major breakthrough with her, which made me feel much more connected to her. I am not sure if this made her happier, but I really appreciated that she would open up to tell me these things about herself. I really liked the fact that we can share with each other things about ourselves, not simply me just teaching her.

I: What have you learned by doing this project?

V1: After joining, my knowledge about children and youth services increased a lot. When I now see children in some difficult situations, I often think about how I would deal with them. I have also reflected about how to eventually become a parent in the future. I think my experiences here provided me with perspectives on how to take care and teach a child, and to not simply use an authoritative approach.

V4: For the past two semesters, I have been serving secondary school children. Over time, I learned to see things from their perspectives, e.g., why sometimes they cannot sit still to complete their tasks. I would try to plan some activities that they might be interested in. This helped in my relationships with them, and also increased the cohesiveness of the overall group. For instance, if the members in our group were not so familiar with each other, we had to think of ways to help them to build better relationships.

V3: I want to add that now I know much more about Hong Kong in terms of our society. These service recipients truly showed me openly about the problems they faced in life, and I am very grateful to them.

I: You volunteered with other projects and organizations as well. In your opinion, what is the strength of this project, in comparison to others?

V3: CYEP is better than other volunteering services because it offers important de-briefing sessions. CYEP treats de-briefing very seriously, unlike other organizations. In CYEP, de-briefing is well-structured and is delivered in the same format across various services. This is definitely the most unique feature of CYEP, and I believe it to be the most useful component of the entire service.

V2: I think CYEP targets many vulnerable groups in our society, whereas other organizations may focus only on other populations, which are not necessarily suitable for me.

V1: I think de-briefing allows us to better reflect, which definitely consolidates volunteer learning and emotions. It is really easy to forget one's thoughts after a week, and after a whole semester. The logbooks distributed to volunteers, to read it back after some time, were a really unforgettable experience. It reminded us about this unique experience that we had, and it may inspire recipients to make more meaningful changes to themselves, in our society. This is indeed a positive thing for the volunteers, recipients, the University, agencies, the families of the recipients, and our community overall.

Appendix I

Creativity programme for children

Activities Plan

Week 1: Developing creativity of volunteers

- Activity 1: Student volunteers will be utilizing various art media (visual images from newspaper and magazines, objects, painting, drawing, etc.) to construct a collage illustrating their life goals. Free-form association will be utilized and guided questions will be asked when working with students to visualize and verbalize their dreams and life goals.

- Activity 2: Student volunteers will come up with a guided imagery using music and various art media, and create an art project based on that image. Suggested topics can be: dream, an incident/event that is memorable (creating new possibilities), or free association.

Week 2: Collaboration of student volunteers with children

Children and student volunteers will work together to create a pamphlet introducing the community of their community in the following steps:

- Data and information collection
- Meaningful and thoughtful selection of information
- Constructing an informative pamphlet including the following aspects of their community according to the students' understanding and perception:
    - Historical background
    - Residing population / social composition
    - What makes their communities special?
    - What are the areas that need improvement?
    - What are the potential solutions for a sustainable community development?

Week 3: Engaging in a community project

Children and student volunteers are to conduct a community-guided tour as hosts to introduce their community to visitors from another community (collaboration with another community-based agency), utilizing the pamphlet that they have created as a tool. The purpose is to:

- Cultivate a sense of pride/esteem in one's own community
- Experience the connection between self-esteem and "community esteem"
- Identify strengths and opportunities about their own community
- Address limitations and immanent risks in the community
- Develop solutions for sustainable community development

Week 4: Achieving critical thinking and communication

The partnering children and their volunteer mentors will be given some materials on a current/social affairs topic. They will also be guided with questions that prompt critical examination of the topic, and be encouraged to "think out of the box" for suggesting their "authentic" answers. The partnering groups will gather together to share of their experience and to come up with a discussion guide, the groups will then engage in a lively debate on the topic, drawing upon their critical thinking and communication skills.

Outcome

What was unique about this workshop was that volunteers first received four sessions of training before working with the children. The purpose was to foster an opportunity for volunteers to experience their own sense of the 5Cs (Critical

Thinking, Communication, Creativity, Collaboration, and Community), thus enabling them to bring forth and integrate their own experience into this collaborative learning process. Volunteers later shared that they enjoyed the "Creativity" session most, as they were rarely encouraged to pursue that quality of thinking; and not until they experienced the creative process personally, they did not believe in the transformative effect of the creative process.

This creative force was then integrated into the volunteers' interaction with children, for example, before the activity of "Community" started, volunteers utilized images/logos that symbolize the concept of "community" to engage in free associations with children about their perception, thoughts, and concept of community, and how they make sense of community – using visualization and free association. The children worked together to create a pamphlet on their own community and then presenting their pamphlets with their parents as audience – learning about one's community and the importance of sustaining one's community thus became a collaborative and fun/creative process. Being able to take ownership of their projects, and to present their own research in front of their parents, has given the children a chance to experience a sense of empowerment, and has also given the parents a chance to view their children in a different light – instead of children, they have also become agents who carry with them the knowledge of some very important qualities for personal and societal development.

References

Bang, H. & Ross, S. D. (2009). "Volunteer motivation and satisfaction." *Journal of Venue and Event Management*, 1(1), 61–77.

Kaufman, J. C. & Beghetto, R. A. (2009). "Beyond big and little: The four C model of creativity. "*Review of General Psychology*, 13, 1–12.

Liu, E. S. C. (2014). "Youth's perception on the impact and meaning of working with children." *Journal of Psychology and Psychotherapy*, 5(2), 177–182.

Liu, E. S. C., Wu, J., Lo, T. W., & Hui, N. N. A. (2012). "Implementing volunteer program to university students in Hong Kong: Enhancing volunteer participation through service matching and organizational support." In B. C. Eng (Ed.), *A Chinese perspective on teaching and learning* (pp. 165–178). New York, NY: Routledge.

Liu, E. S. C., Hui A. N. N., Lam, S. H. P., Busiol, D.Fung, A. H. Y., & Suk, S. T. (2017). *Awareness and implementation of children's participation rights: An experience in Hong Kong for research and practice*. Hong Kong: City University of Hong Kong, & Hong Kong Committee on Children's Rights.

Phillion, J. (2008). "Multicultural and cross-cultural narrative inquiry into understanding immigrant students' educational experience in Hong Kong." *Compare*, 38(3), 281–293.

Pong, S. L. (2009). "Grade level and achievement of immigrants' children: Academic redshirting in Hong Kong. "*Educational Research and Evaluation*, 15(4), 405–425.

Zhang, K. C. & Ting, C. L. M. (2011). "The education of new Chinese immigrant children in Hong Kong: Challenges and opportunities. "*Support for Learning*, 26(2), 49–55.

7

USING THE RECIPROCAL VOLUNTEER PROCESS MODEL (RVPM) TO IMPLEMENT REHABILITATION SERVICES FOR LOCAL CHILDREN AND YOUTH WITH SPECIAL NEEDS

Part A

The context

According to the Census and Statistical Department of Hong Kong (2014), 578,600 persons (or 8.1% of the total population of Hong Kong) have one or more disabilities with impairments, including: restriction in body movement (320,500 persons, corresponding to 4.5% of the total population); vision (174,800 persons, or 2.4%), hearing (155,200 persons, or 2.2%), and/or speech difficulty (49,300 persons, or 0.7%); mental illness (147,300 persons, or 2.1%); autism spectrum disorder (10,200 persons, or 0.1%); specific learning difficulties (17,700 persons, or 0.2%); and/or attention deficit/hyperactivity disorder (ADHD) (12,800 persons, or 0.2%). About 67% have only one type of disability, and the remaining 37% present multiple disabilities. Overall, these data represent a significant increase compared to the 361,300 persons (5.2% of the total population) in 2007. This survey also indicated that the total number of persons with intellectual disabilities in Hong Kong was likely to be about 101,000, representing a prevalence rate 1.4%.

In a work setting for young adults with disabilities, Li (2004) examined their self-perceived employment opportunities and working conditions among a group of young adults with mild intellectual disabilities. Whereas all participants described having jobs deemed important to them, the majority described difficulties in finding a job, due to their abilities. Furthermore, at least half reported feeling discriminated against in the workplace, due to all kinds of difficulties. Overall, the majority of respondents from this research experienced poor relationships with colleagues and employers and felt they lacked social acceptance.

In schools, a large portion of children with special needs are receiving education in inclusive schools. However, for the students with most severe or multiple disabilities, their families are either not available or unable to take care of them, and many of them are thus sent to residential schools. However, Pearson and colleagues (Pearson, Lo, Chui, & Wong, 2003) found that teachers who received special training to interact with special needs children show more favourable and accepting attitudes toward integrating them in mainstream schools than their untrained colleagues. Nevertheless, the effects of teacher training are nullified if the environment is not ready to receive special needs children. This means that the schools as a whole (i.e., all teaching teams and the students) need to be more proactive in creating a more accepting environment for the disabled students. On the other hand, this may imply the need for extra funding for training as well as for additional counsellors and specialists support. Li (2004) suggested that integrating people with disabilities in society require promoting education on disability and equal opportunities among citizens, in both education and work contexts.

In the Hong Kong Mental Health Conference 2017, a group of world-renowned speakers and different professionals gathered to discuss on mental health problem in Hong Kong (South China Morning Post, 2017). Dr. Lucy Lord, Conference Co-Chair, stated that the support for individuals with mental problems in Hong Kong is quite insufficient, making the burden of taking care of family members with mental problems usually falling on the family members or social service agencies, and mental health stigma is a consequence. Additionally, mental health rehabilitation is another aspect that must be addressed when responding to local mental health issues.

According to a recent survey (South China Morning Post, 2017), due to long waiting lists for basic services, a lack of financial assistance, and schools that seem unable or unwilling to help, parents of children with special needs have to pay expensive private assessments and specialist therapies if they want to secure early assessment and intervention for their children. The average waiting time for the sub-vented pre-school rehabilitation services in the 2014/15 school year was just over 19.5 months, compared to 10.5 months in 2009/10. After kindergarten, the waiting time increases. Community groups asked the Hong Kong government to extend subsidies for therapy from pre-school to primary school pupils, as some low-income parents use the bulk of their funds for private sessions. Among them, non-Chinese speaking children with special needs are even more vulnerable, as their chances of receiving support are even smaller (South China Morning Post, 2018). Also, existing services to assist the disabled groups with special needs in Hong Kong are often criticised for being "impersonalized", "fragmented", and/or not promoting social inclusion. Actually, some posit that these services also are not completely free from stigma and contribute to marginalizing children with "special" needs.

The above account serves only to provide a brief contextual background of rehabilitation service in Hong Kong. It is beyond doubt that rehabilitation services for all age groups in Hong Kong are on the rise, and existing services could hardly meet all needs and demands. On the other hand, there is also a long history of volunteer work in Hong Kong being sufficiently flexible and versatile to play a very important role in identifying service gaps and designing programmes to cater for their unique needs.

Using the RVPM model in building a supportive environment

The project started with services focussing on children and youth, and for both developmental and rehabilitation work with different groups of service recipients as described below. We made efforts to study the needs and problems of children and youth with different types of disability in Hong Kong together with volunteers, and encouraged these volunteers to learn how to understand the impact of disability on the lives of our service recipients, and ultimately to become more accepting and inclusive of the disabled.

Recognizing the needs of disabled children and youth in Hong Kong

In the past 13 years, CYEP has served different groups of disabled individuals, mainly 1) children living with Asperger's syndrome; 2) young people with both physical and mental disabilities living in residential schools; and 3) young adults from self-help groups who are undergoing rehabilitation from mental illness; and 4) young children suffering from severe disability in residential home. For all such groups, CYEP adopts a mentoring one-to-one, and person-centred approach. Through these programmes, our service recipients are given quality personalized time in a respectful environment to experience a healthy social life in small group activities. Volunteer students also have the opportunity to develop the necessary skills about how to interact with different groups of disabled individuals, from children to adults, and learn about the challenges of living with disabilities. Four local projects under CYEP were established and have already gained a reputation for how to deliver mentoring groups. The four existing projects together involve each year, about 200 local volunteers and 100 local children, youth, and adults with various physical, and/or mental difficulties. We also learned in this process that while serving these three projects, the three target groups (children living with Asperger's syndrome in NGOs, disabled youth in residential schools, and adults recovering from mental illness from self-help groups) had never received such intensive and persistent long-term services from anywhere before. Our services for the children living with Asperger syndrome has already been implemented for 13 years (one of our very first projects), our services for the disabled youth has lasted for 11 years, and our service for the self-help groups for young adults recovering from mental illness has lasted for 8 years.

Promoting volunteers' acceptance through mutual knowledge

Besides working with children and youth holistically, CYEP also aims at offering student volunteers opportunities to interact with children and youth who have various unique special needs. Such first-hand experiences are effective in promoting respect and social acceptance among our volunteers, and refining their micro skills on how to deliver respect and acceptance to groups of vulnerable children and youth, and/or children and youth with disabilities. With dual goals for filling the service gaps and promoting volunteers' acceptance of the disabled, unique programs are designed as shown in Part B.

Part B

Using the RVPM model in building interactional relationships

1 Designing programmes for children and youth with disabilities

a *Mentoring Schemes for Children living with Asperger's syndrome* – This mentoring scheme aims to create a platform for children to develop more positive social experiences to enhance their sociability, and discover their positive strengths. Volunteers' roles are to improve the children's socialization skills and academic performance. Volunteers and mentees meet a total of eight times in one semester on-site in the agency. Besides normal group work, we also arrange service recipients to participate other activities, like BBQ in CityU, summer day camp, and other community outdoor activities.

b *Working with Children and Youth in Residential Schools* – This service provides opportunities for volunteers to work with youth living with physical, and/or mental disability through academic tutoring and other meaningful and fun activities in local residential settings. Offered in association with the agency and a residential home attached to a school, this project helps enhance academic performance, social skills, and self-efficacy. Frequent outing activities during the service period are organized in order to gain further understandings of a "barrier-free" society with our service users. For this service there are two service sessions per week with different group of volunteers, serving the same group of service recipients. This service is offered twice a year (Semester A and B). During each semester there are 14/15 sessions. Besides regular group work, we also organize one-off community projects for them, locally and across the border to Macau and Taiwan in the last three years.

c *"The CC" – Cornwall Caregiver – Working with Severely Mentally-Challenged Children and Youth at Residential Schools.* The Cornwall School provides a "barrier-free" learning environment and quality care for local mentally-challenged primary and secondary students, who have severe to profound ranges of intellectual disability. Here, trained volunteers support students' mental, physical, and social development. Usually, a group of around 10 to 12 volunteers will be recruited to serve on one-to-one bases for 10 to 12 children to help children in taking meals, reading in the library, playing with toys etc. All activities are indoors only and within the residential school.

d "*Walk with Body and Mind*" – *Social support groups for adults rehabilitating from mental problems.* Here, we offer regular group "Walk with Body and Mind" with Alliance of Ex-mentally Ill of Hong Kong for individuals who are recovering from mental illness. This type of social support group is organized by CYEP two times in a year with 10 to 15 members and eight sessions each time. The main goals of groups are to provide meaningful interactions among the volunteers and the service recipients in CityU campus, so as to accompany the member to get in touch with the community by engaging in outdoor activities, and to be involved in some small-scale advocacy work within campus. We involve some disabled groups (e.g. the ex-mentally ill patients) to run advocacy work in campus in order to facilitate them to be more "outgoing" for a "community contact".

Infusing for multi-level and multi-disciplinary approach

As mentioned earlier (in this book), CYEP adopts a tripartite approach to volunteering: at group, individual, and community level. However, the portal for our work occurs at the group level. We have found that group settings facilitate the relationship encounters among individuals (not the other way around), and groups represent individuals at community levels. We implement a similar working structure to the programmes for children and youth with special needs also. Basing on this, such examples of programs are offered:

a) Implementing the "Documentary of a Barrier-free city – From Hong Kong to Macau" in 2014:

> After serving the same group of youth from a local residential school for the disabled, many volunteers were touched by the wish and dream of a group of disabled youth who have never been travelling outside of Hong Kong before. So, a group of volunteers decided to write a proposal to apply for the Community Services and Engagement Projects (CSEP) in commemorative of the 30th Anniversary for City University of Hong Kong. This involved an out of town tour to Macau (another Special Administrative Region of China and a city which is close to Hong Kong) with a small group of disabled youth. Shown below is part of the proposal written by students with the assistance of a staff when applying the CSEP fund:
>
> "To have a travel opportunity is the dream of the disabled youth. This application is going to make our dreams come true. We dream of equality, everyone should have equal opportunities to travel and to broaden their

horizon. We dream of diversity, everyone should have rights to access the community and live together. We dream of barrier-free community, it is the first step of social inclusion. To empower volunteers and a group of disabled youth, we want to make a change to the society to become better together! Volunteers and disabled youth are going to raise the public awareness on the importance of barrier-free facilities in a society. Our service recipients will be the facilitators to lead us in understanding and comparing Hong Kong and Macau's barrier-free environment…The target groups are a group of disabled youth and a group of CityU students. The university students will take a role more in assisting the disabled youth and work in an equal relationship. The students will learn in the process on how to work with people who have different abilities. This is important in creating a social inclusion atmosphere and to achieve integrated education. As well, disabled people are used to be disempowered."

This proposal and subsequent planning efforts lead to a four-day tour after six months of careful preparation and planning. This trip proved to be a unique success for all stakeholders and parties involved. It was truly life changing for many of these disabled youth.

b) The "Documentary of a Barrier-free city – From Hong Kong to Taiwan" 2016:

Two years after the successful Macau trip, we received a donation from a donor who himself is also a wheel-chaired person, for us to implement a similar trip to Taiwan by plane (the Macau trip was by boat). Similarly, we followed the best practices learned from last trip, and have involved some hall mates from the residential school who had previous experience with Macau trip to participate. When members from the residential school were interviewed and selected, they met with CYEP volunteers to discuss on their goals of the trip and divided up their work. All the final participants were formed into three groups. All together, they drafted the theme and itinerary of the trip while the responsibilities of contacting the organizations and planning the details of each visit were shared among the groups. The donor was also arranged to meet with the group and to brief the hall mates his experiences of visiting overseas countries on wheelchair. Participants also got in touch with Taiwanese students with disabilities and social workers from educational institutions and related NGOs for arranging the exchange activities. As the volunteers and students collected information, they learned more about the similarities and differences regarding barrier-free practices and facilities in the two places. Once again, the trip to Taiwan proved to be another resounding success for all parties involved and was also a once-in-a-lifetime experience for these disabled students.

c) Partnering with service recipients to deliver community education and campus advocacy:

For both the physically disabled hall mates from the residential school and the previously mentally ill service recipient from the self-help groups, we made several attempts for some of them to work with the volunteers to deliver community education exhibitions, dialogues with university partners in small-scale seminars, and collecting opinions concerning university students' attitude towards disability, etc. De-briefing sessions were offered and found the university campus a very meaningful and convenient venue for us to nurture both volunteers and service recipients for advocacy skills for "speaking for the minority groups".

Part C

Using the RVPM model in achieving accountability and transparency: Voices of student volunteers and staff

We interviewed one staff member and four student volunteers who had volunteered for disabled children and youth in order to record from their own real experience on how this type of service has been delivered. The following represent the results of face-to-face interviews conducted in 2018 with 1 staff member (S1) and 4 on-site volunteers (V1, V2, V3, V4) carried out either by the book author and/or a Research Fellow of CYEP, as represented by "I".

Interview with the CYEP staff (S1)

I: *How are your programmes structured?*

S1: : Each session of direct service lasts for three hours only but we have to prepare extra time for travelling and de-briefing. We meet on campus and travel together to sites. After each session, we also need time to conduct the de-briefing sessions on-site. Altogether, it lasts about four to six hours, overall. When the semester starts, I prepare the topics for training and further discuss these with the Volunteer Ambassadors (VAs) who are going to assist me with the project, before I finalize the training content. Usually, in the first two to three weeks, we focus on relationship building between these young students in residential school and our volunteers; then, in the next four to five week period, we may discuss other macro issue, for example, how to enhance the welfare of the disabled, how to implement sex education for the disabled, the career goals for the disabled, etc. Gradually, in the last two sessions for de-briefing, we are usually ready to discuss on some community-level topics, like local policies that are affecting the disabled and current issues. Our service recipients may suffer from various types of disability, and these volunteers have to learn patience, in order to be able to effectively communicate with them. They also have to learn the unique features and needs of different groups of service recipients. For example, if they are working with a group of youth in wheelchairs, the first thing they have to learn is to know how to use a wheelchair.

For each service, we only have one member of staff, so I arrange to have two VAs to help me; they are like “my hands”. Without their help, I think I could not be effective at all. I also try to identify some potential volunteer leaders from the new volunteer groups. The VAs usually help me a lot with de-briefing, and also with data collection. We conduct research on different issues, and then they will do the research and design the flow of the de-briefing, and learn how to table these results and issues. We need to have more ideas about how to discuss topics, and to be prepared about what questions volunteers will raise, or what materials, maybe a video, a newspaper clip, or maybe some policy document, that they think is helpful for the de-briefing. Finally, I also design the required logbooks with VAs. The logbook is a reflective booklet that we use in services for helping volunteers re-think about what s/he has done in their service. In the de-briefing, some students are very reluctant to speak in front of others, so the logbook is another channel for us to understand more about them. We will give the logbooks back to the volunteers before each de-briefing session. Both the VAs and I will look at the logbooks and give our feedback. The logbook is a way to personalize some feedback, and de-briefing will remain a group-based sharing.

I: *How do you do the matching?*

S1: Every programme has its own matching system. In the residential school (for the disabled), we normally have 30 service recipients matched with 30 volunteers. I will try to understand/assess the language proficiency of our volunteers; I know the hall mates quite well, and in time, I will match a service recipient to a volunteer with parallel language ability. In the first session, I will divide them into two or three groups, and with the help of the VAs, we will facilitate them to engage in some ice-breaking games. In this setting, we have younger residents who are only six or seven years old, and are in primary schools. We also have some older secondary school students who might have stayed in the residential school for more than ten years, and are in their early twenties. So the matching then results in discussions with the social worker, about how to best utilize the volunteer manpower and for the best outcomes on the students, some who need language skills, some who demand physical exercise, some who are emotional, etc. After some time, the matching will be settled, and honestly, that it is not an easy task. We usually will keep this matching going for the entire semester. After matching, it is basically a one-to-one mentoring project that the activities flexibly arranged basically in three areas. Volunteers could accompany the hall mates to go through their dinner time (some volunteers even bring in their own small dinners and eat with the hall mates), then homework and reading time, and if time still permits, and with the permission from social workers, the volunteers can accompany some older hall mates to go out for a walk to the nearby shopping mall, and/or its supermarket to have a tour or to buy some daily necessities, or even to have a hamburger for a treat. The direct service time is around three hours overall, and then we will say goodbye to the hall mates and all leave the site together.

I: *How do you provide the training?*

S1: Most of our services start in early October so in September, we spend two to three weeks recruiting volunteers. Then, we spend one additional week for volunteer training. Finally, we are ready to start services. We require all volunteers to attend all training sessions before they could start service. The training normally lasts two to three hours. There, I will introduce myself, then cover the basic background of CYEP, as well as the basic background for a particular project. The second major part is to help volunteers to explore their hidden values and pre-occupations on people with disabilities. What follows will be having the volunteers openly define the meaning of "providing service" to the disabled. I also show them some videos, and I use different methods to promote their participation awareness, and then table more ideas about disabilities. I will try my best to reserve at least the last hour to talk about the real routines of work, in one service day. Of course, we also cover the divisions of labour, the matching of mentees, their schedules and other logistics, and so on. At this stage I do not talk too much about policy, or welfare; as I just want them to focus on the people they are going to serve. It is CYEP's agreed upon goal that we want volunteers to believe that we are serving the disabled population, and we believe that by serving in the right way, we are also changing people's perceptions. We invite volunteers to avoid thinking they are "God" or "Angels" who can save people from disability. Their disability will still have to be faced by them personally, we are here just to support and accept them through their developmental time. Personally, I myself try to do the same thing each day. After joining CYEP, this angle of doing service was the most impressive point for my learning. We are not only serving the disabled, but we are also learning from them. I spend much time helping our volunteers understand that they are not just here to serve others, but to contribute, so they are also getting something personally from this experience. I keep on re-inforcing to them the right attitude by saying that "Put yourself at the same levels of your service recipients, you are not superior, you are not just here to give a helping hand, or to save anyone. Instead, you are here to learn how to serve, and how to communicate with the people with special needs".

I: *What is the most challenging part working with volunteers?*

S1:: Dealing with volunteers is fun, but it is also time consuming and challenging because I need to provide them with some structure for learning. At the same time, I need to take into consideration how the volunteers are affecting the learning of the children and youth service recipients. We run non-credit bearing programs, so there is no consequence if volunteers do not attend. However, if they do not show up, or if one does not notify us in advance that she/he is not coming, the service recipient will be left with no one to take care of them. However, I do recognize some volunteers will face some unexpected hurdles in their own lives, from families or studies. I also have to be understanding of them, besides respecting the service recipients. So, if I need 40 volunteers to run a project, I will normally recruit 45 volunteers, and get myself ready to manage the project well.

A challenge that many volunteers face is that they are not very familiar with the service target group, even if they have gone through one session of training. I have found that if they don't feel competent, they will just hide away their problems, and refuse to discuss them with me. My role therefore, is to just make them feel challenged, and feel that they have to be better than before. Otherwise, they will lose interest, and will not even participate in the de-briefing sessions. When I see a volunteer sitting in the de-briefing sessions but looking at his/her own phone, I know that she/he is losing interest, and I have to do something more to make them interested. I sometimes will use scaled answers for questions, and use activities to encourage deeper reflection. Dividing volunteers into smaller groups for sharing is often effective, especially if the big group consists of students coming from different backgrounds, I sometimes will allow one group to use Chinese to communicate, and another group using English to share then, a change of language might help increasing their ease in sharing. Another group of volunteers are those who are very dependent, and they will ask me many questions during the service time and need me to be besides them. However, I cannot be everywhere. Some volunteers simply do not know how to answer some sensitive questions, and/or they do not know how to react. For example, some do not know how to say "no" to the request for their personal phone number, Facebook, etc.

I: *This is a non-credit bearing project. What is the commitment of the volunteers?*

S1: Most of our volunteers will complete the programme. Maybe some will miss one or two sessions because of class or assignments, or some other duties. I make it clear from the onset about our expectations for participation. During their training, we will show them the schedule for services, and we invite only those who are all available to join. I do explain that a minor absence is always acceptable, but not a very irresponsible way of being absent and without prior notice. Overall, we are quite satisfied with their attendance.

Interviews with 4 student volunteers (V1, V2, V3, V4) serving with two projects in a residential school for the disabled children and youth

I: *Can you briefly introduce the nature of service you are serving?*

V1: I serve a group of children and youth who are mostly living with physical disabilities. We provide academic support and mentor them with exposure to life experiences and help them to be in touch with the outside world.

V3: I served in the same site and the children there are mostly suffering from physical disabilities, but they possess similar levels of intelligence as normal children. I also serve in another project with children who are mostly suffering from very chronic intellectual disabilities, and their usual intelligence levels are around that of a child at three to four years old. They need help with feeding and might have difficulties with eating, and for instance, they might bite their tongue while eating. So, we have to learn from the workers there about how to offer help during their feeding time. We also help prepare some entertaining and play activities so as to encourage them to engage in some motor movement training, e.g. to encourage them to move their eyes or limes. Apart from that, we also provide some planned exercises to stimulate their brain activity.

I: : *How did you join CYEP, and why did you choose the children and youth with disabilities program to serve in?*

V1: : I joined CYEP during my first year in university, because my friends were also volunteers. Initially, I thought about joining the tutoring service, as tutoring seemed more interesting. Instead, I thought I never had the chance before to interact with children with disabilities, and I decided that I should join, to learn more about them.

V2: : I have always thought of participating in volunteer work. When I was in mainland China, I did some volunteer work where we were supposed to help children with their homework, but seemingly they did not really need our help. So, when I heard about CYEP, I decided to register as a volunteer. I enrolled in the residential school for the physically disabled mainly because it fit my schedule, and that it does accept volunteers who do not speak the local Cantonese, but with me speaking Mandarin is also welcome by the hall mates.

I: *What were your expectations at the beginning and what have you realized while doing the project?*

V3: I joined the service with mentally disabled children and youth and it only accepted around ten volunteers. I thought it was good, because a smaller group would mean that the group mates would be very close and easy to communicate with. Our officer told us in advance that these students are mentally challenged. I thought about that if a volunteer would like to receive verbal appreciation from service recipients, I should be aware that I would not get it. Some older volunteers told that even if you take care of a child for three years, she/he will not be able to recognize us. However, I take this as a challenge. I remember once I helped a little girl who could not grasp things, and after some training, we finally helped her to be able to do it. After achieving this, we were then assigned another task to help her. I was thinking that those tasks will never have an ending or will never be stopped, then, was it still meaningful to spend time doing all these? However, after joining this service, I realized that these children are really innocent and no one can understand why they have to go through all of these hurdles in life. Sometimes when I finish a service day and I leave the school and the sky is already dark, my brain is full of questions of life! Anyhow, I stayed in this service for some time already!

V2: My awareness and knowledge about disability has increased. For example, going to many outdoor activities, I realized that the so-called "no barrier" society is still very inadequate. There are simply not enough local facilities for our disabled.

I: *What have you learned by doing this project?*

V1: My experiences in the residential school for the physically disabled can be divided into three stages. In my first year of service, I partnered with a local student to counsel a service recipient, but my help was minimal. The following year, I was paired up with another service recipient who was known to be needy and dependent on volunteers. Through this experience, I learned how to communicate with volunteers and even service recipients, who had different personalities. I started to question whether I should follow everything these children asked, and let them for example be needy, or should I be harsher and educate them about their behaviours. Finally this year, I started to observe how to assist younger volunteers. The volunteers we have in CYEP are all very caring people, but there are other issues that only an observer notes. For example, some service recipients are really impolite and insist that volunteers do their jobs for them, and do not thank them. Some inexperienced volunteers may think that it is simply because they are children, so they do not pay much attention to it. However, I may bring this issue up as a topic in the de-briefing sessions, and ask volunteers to share their opinions about it. I have been with this service for so long that I have met a lot of volunteers, and there has always been a barrier-free vision. This is why I kept re-joining this service.

V3: I have more perspectives to reflect about, after joining this service. For example, there is a new policy that when a taxi driver encounters people with a disability and requests help, they have to oblige. Years ago, I never heard of such issues. Honestly, I really would not even care before but now, I pay much more attention to such concerns, because I am aware that this actually matters as it does impact a unique and different group of vulnerable people.

V4: I think that the services I provided to the disabled children and youth in the residential school are far less than what I gained from them. The reason why I chose social work as my major was really affected by my volunteering experiences during my first year. I think by joining this service, my personality also change regarding how to be more empathetic. My empathy did not just appear one day, as there are times that I realize that I am more patient in listening to others, when others talk to me about their problems. I am also more likely to think more about understanding their feelings and perspectives. Thanks to volunteering, I re-discovered and confirmed the importance of communication and reciprocal interactions between people.

I: *You volunteered in other projects and organizations as well. In your opinion, what is the strength of CYEP, in comparison with others?*

V3: In the past, I joined some programmes for children with disabilities in mainland China. Although these services were led by social workers, they were only focussed on helping with their physical needs. But here, apart from taking care of their daily lives, we focus on how to communicate with these children, and how to be mindful of their psychological states as well.

V4: Social work is an accredited profession in Hong Kong, whereas in mainland China people generally are still not clear about what social workers actually do. Second, in mainland China, there is little awareness of the needs of disabled persons, because we do not often see them on the streets. So, I think it is a good idea that CYEP includes this group of service recipients. Our volunteers are very compassionate to them, even though they may feel that their impact is minimal. We cannot really measure how much help they have given to our recipients, or the changes and improvements made, but I can tell you that volunteers learn much about life throughout the service program. In the beginning, volunteers do not have much knowledge about this target group, but after serving for a semester, our volunteers are able to acknowledge the difficulties these children face in daily life, and what they really need, etc. Our volunteers surely gain new insights and perspectives, and they certainly know more about how much to communicate with children and youth with disabilities.

References

Census and Statistical Department of Hong Kong (2014). "Special Topics Report No. 62." Retrieved from http://www.statistics.gov.hk/pub/B11301622014XXXXB0100.pdf.

Li, E. P. Y. (2004). "Self-perceived equal opportunities for people with intellectual disability." *International Journal of Rehabilitation Research*, 27, 241–245.

Pearson, V., Lo, E., Chui, E., & Wong, D. (2003). "A heart to learn and care? Teachers' responses toward special needs children in mainstream schools in Hong Kong." *Disability & Society*, 18(4), 489–508.

South China Morning Post (2017, 2 October). "Hong Kong students with special needs not properly supported by government education system." Retrieved from https://www.scmp.com/lifestyle/families/article/2113236/hong-kong-students-special-needs-not-properly-supported.

South China Morning Post (2018, 16 January). "Hong Kong's school system shuts out non-Chinese-speaking special needs children." Retrieved from https://www.scmp.com/comment/insight-opinion/article/2128474/hong-kongs-school-system-shuts-out-non-chinese-speaking.

8

USING THE RECIPROCAL VOLUNTEER PROCESS MODEL (RVPM) TO IMPLEMENT INTERNATIONAL SERVICE FOR CHILDREN AND YOUTH IN CAMBODIA AND MYANMAR

Part A

The context

Global volunteerism in international settings is constantly increasing. These programmes can be short-term, e.g., during volunteers' course of studies, or more long-term, e.g., during a gap year taken by volunteers. In most cases, these experiences are described by volunteers as being very transformational, both for their own personal growth and development, and their careers. In line with these opportunities, CYEP developed various international programmes for helping disadvantaged children, in both Myanmar and Cambodia since 2012.

Using the RVPM model in building a supportive environment to develop and deliver international services to Cambodia and Myanmar

Values and goals for international service

Internationalization and "global mindsets" have become the trend for enhancing student learning among universities globally. In Hong Kong, for example, The University of Hong Kong's vision is that "The continuing globalization of higher education is inevitable", and that "Internationalization is a path to augment the University's core mission", which is "to augment opportunities for everyone in teaching & learning, research, and knowledge exchange. We are committed to diversity, inclusiveness, and dispersing the benefit of internationalization locally and globally. We aspire to be Asia's Global University" (The University of Hong Kong, 2017). City University of Hong Kong has also established a Global Services

Office to help the university globalize, and "enrich students' international and multi-cultural consciousness, exposure and learning experience" (City University of Hong Kong, 2017). International Service Learning (ISL) programmes may represent a viable pedagogical elective conduit for achieving this global evolution. Comparing domestic and ISL groups, Miller and Gonzalez (2010) found that the latter, more so than the former reported more identified and significant impact on one's: 1) personal growth; 2) career preparation; and, 3) awareness of global needs. Additionally, ISL participants often adopt a more affective and enthusiastic tone when reporting their experiences, than do domestic-SL participants. Service learning is a practice that combines both academic learning and social responsibility. When services are provided abroad, it is deemed as ISL. ISL has been defined as "a structured academic experience in another country in which students: a) participate in an organized service activity that addresses identified community needs; b) learn from direct interaction and cross-cultural dialogue with others; and, c) reflect on the experiences ways to gain a deeper understanding of global and intercultural issues, a broader appreciation of the host country and the discipline, and an enhanced sense of their own responsibilities as citizens, locally and globally" (Bringle & Hatcher, 2011, p.19). Many ISL programmes are being increasingly adopted not only by universities but also corporations to develop responsible global leaders, meaning individuals with outstanding cross-cultural relationship skills, responsibility, ethics, with global mindsets, community-building skills, and global organizational expertise (Pless, Maak, & Stahl, 2011).

CYEP anticipated this process of growing internationalization by developing various volunteering programmes abroad in Cambodia (2012–2019), Nepal (2014), and Myanmar (2014–2018). We posited that an international experience could have a new and unique impact on the life of both volunteers and service recipients, which could also bring an exciting new horizon to the whole project too. When we developed these programmes, international volunteer programmes in Hong Kong were still a very novel idea and initiating such programmes was challenging for both staff and volunteers. After much discussion, in 2012 we made a new connection with an international volunteering link in Cambodia. Two years after serving children in Cambodia, we received special funding in 2014, to organize services to three countries, Cambodia, Nepal, and Myanmar in 2014. From 2014 to 2018, we were able to secure funding to continue serving Cambodia and Myanmar, only. International service is still on our agenda for 2019. The scale and coverage of services will depend on the availability of funding. Based on CYEP's history, our extension to international services has also been focused on serving children and youth services too.

Educational needs of children and youth in Myanmar

According to the United Nations Development Programme's Human Development Index, Burma ranks 145th, out of 188 countries, for public expenditure on education (United Nations Development Programme, 2017). There are significant differences between education in the main cities and the most rural areas. In a country where education is officially compulsory for five years, the dropout rate was estimated to be 44.8% in 2000 and 28.5% in 2005 (more recent data are not available). For example, families may not be able to pay the schools' fees, books, uniforms, supplement teachers' salaries, and/or participate in school's renewal works; parents fail to understand the value of education, and/or are not motivated to send their children to school; parents have little expectations on the value of education for making a living, particularly in rural areas; poor health conditions; poor school environment, poor management (Lwin, 2007). There is a general lack of educational facilities, schools, as well as teachers and even textbooks, particularly in the border areas of the country. Often teachers are not sufficiently trained for the profession and are paid poorly. Finally, education in Myanmar is mostly texts-based and exams-oriented, so that students have little chance to develop their creative and critical thinking (Lwin, 2007).

In Myanmar there are also monastic schools that provide basic education. Monastic schools have a longer tradition, dating back a few centuries. In the past, they used to provide education to a wide variety of people, from royalty to the poor. Today, in royalty monastic schools, children from the most needy families (or orphans) can learn language, sciences, history, numeracy, and geography, besides Buddhism. Monastic schools are present in all regions in Myanmar, and it is estimated that today they provide an education to more than 150,000 children. Although these schools are administered through the Ministry of Religious Affairs, they receive almost no government support and mostly rely on donations, which makes staff recruitment and retention difficult for them, as they cannot pay the same salaries as government schools. Most of those monastic schools rely heavily on foreign donations and the assistance from many volunteers from all parts of the world.

The needs of children and youth for education in Cambodia

Cambodia has an incredibly high number of orphans in the population. Many children have lost their parents (i.e., due to HIV), while other parents cannot provide food, accommodation, and education for their children. Our volunteers are expected to gain more understanding on issues faced by orphaned children. Volunteers were placed at various local organizations/NGOs for orphanage work. Orphanage work ranges from cooking, administration, cleaning, painting, singing, and sports to assisting with homework, feeding, caring for children, and teaching. Volunteers may also work in an orphanage or center for HIV infected or disabled children, where the focus is less on teaching and more on childcare, because in Cambodian society disabled individuals are often rejected.

Most orphanages also have fixed weekly activities, focusing on education such as Khmer literacy classes, English classes, or more general teaching. Topics such as morality, hygiene, and Khmer traditions are also discussed with the children. Many orphanages support creative activities like painting, drawing, or Apsara dancing (a

Khmer traditional dance). Some orphanages organize outings such as visits to the beach or villages. The experiences of participating in these activities and services will become beneficial assets to enrich CYEP as children and youth are our primary service.

Since 2012, CYEP has been serving in Phnom Penh Cambodia with orphaned children living with disabilities and HIV/AIDS. Our intention was to build an ongoing working relationship with the partner-organizations and the local communities, to ensure our services were more sustainable. We recognize the importance of providing holistic services to underprivileged children with limited resources. In addressing the alarming global phenomenon of children living in poverty, this service aimed to embrace a wide range of work with children and youth, and to broaden their horizons. Different activities were organized in two settings including: simple games, cleaning days, creating thank you cards for care workers (mama), art activities, watching movies, balloon twisting, drawing, painting, home visits to students' homes, etc.

Core values of international services

Over the years, CYEP has established partnerships with different NGOs and volunteer agencies operating in Myanmar and Cambodia (since we had only organized one international service to Nepal in 2014, the details of the service to Nepal will not be covered) to support our students for overseas service. International volunteers face different and greater challenges from local volunteers. For the duration of our international volunteer programme (up to one month), volunteers live together and they have to adapt to a new culture, with very different living conditions. They also have to find ways to interact with, and teach children who do not speak English. So, international volunteers must be wary, respectful, enthusiastic, kind, and proactive in their participation. When they succeed, the main outcome is often an intrinsic transformational experience for them as a group member, and as individuals, and for the children they help. Through international service learning, we wish to achieve the following learning outcomes for our volunteers:

1. Gain an understanding on the problems and limitations faced by those deprived children.
2. Through interactions with NGO's, learn about ways and perspective of serving underprivileged children.
3. Gain perspectives on the impact of socioeconomic developments and history on local social problems.
4. Learn about and appreciate different cultures, and bring our culture to another country.
5. Draw on our previous experiences working with children with diverse issues and backgrounds to provide support to deprived children in other countries.

6. Provide leadership opportunities for volunteers when planning activities, taking initiatives in problem-solving and identifying resources that will appropriately address children's needs.

Part B

Using the RVPM model in building interactional relationships

Our recent international services included:

a *International Service to Yangon, Myanmar*: empowering local children through education (four weeks, about ten volunteers, and 80 service recipients). Since 2014, CYEP has collaborated with the *Myanmar Mobile Education (myME) Project,* in Yangon. This unique programme provided a classroom-like setting and educational assistance to disadvantaged children who had no access to formal education, including the colloquial "tea-shop children" (children working in local tea shops), children from rural communities, and students in monastic schools. Tea-shop children engage in learning activities for at least two hours per day, and tea-shop owners are compensated for the children's time away from work. This project aimed to offer: 1) academic development (English teaching, life-skills, and vocational training, interactive learning); and, 2) teach them new skills and development (understanding children's psychological and cognitive development, assessing their study levels and needs, designing and implementing activity-based learning);

b *International Service to Mandalay, Myanmar*: (four weeks, about ten volunteers, and 420 service recipients). Here, CYEP works with the Phaung Daw Oo Monastic Integrated Education School to introduce and implement a more child-centred approach in their classrooms. Primarily, our volunteers help with curriculum development and teaching English. This project introduced volunteers to a different and unique understanding of how religious groups in the community level could take lead in helping children.

c *International Service to Phnom Penh, Cambodia*: (four weeks, about 15 volunteers, and 130 service recipients). Since 2012, CYEP has been going to Phnom Penh, Cambodia to serve orphans with disabilities, and/or HIV/AIDS. There, our local community partners are: 1) *National Borey for Infants and Children (NBIC)*, a state-operated orphanage that cares for orphans with HIV/AIDS-positive, and special-needs children below 18 years old. Here, our volunteers help groups of children with severe disabilities; and, 2) *Save Children Community Development Organization* (SCCDO), an organization that provides education for children from poor families. They also have a school in the Samki Village near Phnom Penh, and there our volunteers engage local children in various learning activities in school, and in a wide range of other initiatives outside school, including some maintenance work in the village. The volunteers from CYEP will be split into two groups and each group will serve one of the two connected NGOs for services.

Part C

Using the RVPM model in achieving accountability and transparency: Voices of student volunteers and staff

We interviewed one staff member and four student volunteers who had volunteered for international service in order to record from their own real experience on how this type of service has been delivered. The following represent the results of face-to-face interviews conducted in 2018 with 1 staff member (S1) and four on-site volunteers (V1, V2, V3, V4) carried out either by the book author and/or a Research Fellow of CYEP, as represented by "I".

Interview with the CYEP staff (S1)

I: : *What projects are you currently involved with?*

S1: : I am going to Myanmar for the third time, where we work with the *Myanmar Mobile Education (myMe) Project,* which was started in 2014, with the aim to provide free education to children working in local tea-shops. In Myanmar, tea-shops are small restaurants where people go for tea and snacks. Often times, these shops employ very young children from poor families who live in the countryside but have moved nearer to the cities for work. Those children have to work from early morning to evening, and seven days a week. Tea shops are also their evening shelters. These children are faced with no choice but to work hard to support their families. Thus, they are deprived of school and studying opportunities. Project *myME* was initiated in order to offer these children a chance to receive some basic and non-formal education. The project provides children literacy and numeracy skills, vocational subject skills, and some practical skills that might improve their life quality. Started in 2014, with new donations, myMe expanded rapidly and today it is serving more than 1,000 children from the tea-shops, monastic schools, and the community projects for the underprivileged. Teaching is mainly delivered in special designed buses which are equipped with tables and chairs for the teaching and learning to be carried out. Volunteers from CYEP often teach them some English. The children are also motivated to learn English and be prepared when they got older, hopefully to find a better job working as a waitress/ waiters if they can communicate with overseas travellers.

The community projects for unmanaged underprivileged is another project by *myMe*. It targets children from low-income families in various countryside villages. These poorer villages usually are situated in some unmanaged countryside with streets that are often unpaved and dirty, and so people living in those areas are challenged by many hygienic problems. While working in these villages, besides offering some teaching and learning activities, our volunteers also teach some life-skills and personal care training for these children. Classes are scheduled in advance by *myMe* and so children cannot just enter the arrived and parked buses. It was the rule of *myMe* that children with the assistance of their families have to first apply for joining this project, undergo an interview for assessing their needs, and be finally assigned to a group. Thus, based on their assessed levels, they are told what classes/bus they should join, on what day and time of the week.

Finally, the *myMe* project also serves children in monastic schools, where they are preparing themselves to become monks. In these cases, the teaching is delivered in schools, and a teacher from *myMe*, who is known as a "facilitator". The facilitator goes regularly to the school, e.g., three times a week, and when our volunteers are serving the project, we will accompany the facilitator to visit the school. As we have already established a mutually trusted relationship with the local agency and facilitators, normally our volunteers will also be trusted to design the teaching materials and take the leading role in classes. Another strength of this programme is that when we were there serving, we are the only volunteer group partnering with the local agency hosts. We find this an effective arrangement, so that the agency can concentrate on our partnership, and would not be disturbed by having many volunteer groups serving at the same time, in the same agency. Thus, our volunteers can spend a considerable amount of time with the facilitator, and with his/her assistance, by that our volunteers can learn more about the serving children and their needs, and subsequently they can develop more meaningful, tailor-made programmes.

I: *How did this programme evolve over the years?*

S1: This programme has expanded since the first year I took part in it. In the beginning, *myME* offered students only basic literacy and life-skills classes. Over the years, new classes were implemented, and our volunteers contributed to selecting new subjects and designing new courses. For example, now there are hygiene and environmental classes, as we wanted to teach students how to keep their residential places clean, and how to better protect their living environments. Further, now there are vocational classes, as many children aspire to something more than just being an entry-level waitress/waiter, so they are taught English language, and computer skills.

I: What are your goals for volunteers?

S1: Overall, because we are serving a very unique group of children, we have been focussing on discussions with volunteers to learn and understand the issues of child labour. When they join this service, we normally discuss some of the realities of current policies in Myanmar, as well as in some neighbouring countries. Generally speaking, we want our volunteers to be more aware about what is happening in places outside of Hong Kong. We want them to open their eyes and see what happens in the real world, not just confining their own life perspectives.

I: *How do you do recruitment, is it the same process as for the other local programmes?*

S1: The process is similar, but for international service, we conduct an additional interview. We do not require volunteers to have had any previous experience, but we will ask about their reason for joining international services, and what they really want to achieve. At the onset, we want to learn more about them, individually and personally, so as to evaluate their potential and readiness to be international volunteers. Then, whereas local services are based on a "first-come-first-serve" basis, international services are based on consensual staff assessment on the readiness of the volunteers to go for four weeks for international services. After the recruitment process, we will organise a briefing session for twofold purposes. First, as the volunteers have to work and live together for four intense weeks, we want to create some bonding times, and allow them to get acquainted with one another, before they start off. Second, as we have found, it is more effective if new volunteers learn about the programme directly from former participants (we do accept one or two former participants each time), so we normally have former volunteers share their experiences, and offer advice about how to prepare for this unique learning adventure.

I: *How many service recipients you have, and how do you do the matching?*

S1: This year we had eight volunteers, who operated in four sub-groups of two volunteers each. Each group was in charge of delivering different classes. Normally, the agency shared with us the schedule of the classes, the subjects taught, the ages of the children, their backgrounds, whether they are monastic or tea-shop students, and based on this information the volunteers choose what classes they want to teach.

I: *What is the relationship between CYEP and the agencies?*

S1: Generally speaking, agency support is essential for both the service recipients, and the volunteers. In most of our programmes, CYEP officers may know something about the recipients' backgrounds, but the ones who know more about them, are the on-site agency social workers. Further, the stronger the agency support, the stronger the commitment of volunteers. In turn, if volunteers are highly committed, the programme has more opportunities to become sustainable (other factors are the volunteer's levels of satisfaction with the services, and their relationship with service recipients). This agency support is also very important in such international service, but personally I found that current volunteers benefit more from the guidance and support from our former participants, most of all.

I: *How do you see volunteers changing from the beginning to the end of the project?*

S1: International volunteering requires participants to be both mature and independent. They should be able to take care of themselves, for one month. They need to have some practical, communication, emotional, and interpersonal skills, as during the project, they need to work, cook, live, and do everything with others, 24 hours a day. In these circumstances, it is possible that some conflicts may arise, and when this happens, they cannot simply quit the programme and go home as they have to learn how to face these conflicts. Thus, these experiences can be very formative and enlightening for them.

Furthermore, they need opportunities to improve their own teaching skills. In Myanmar, no matter if you speak Cantonese or English, the children will not understand you. So, how do you teach and keep them engaged in class? This is a major challenge for all volunteers. Some of them at the beginning really do not know how to approach such children. My colleagues and I will talk to them, and help them overcome their difficulties. Additionally, we also encourage them to learn by observing other volunteers. This usually works, and then volunteers improve quite quickly. This whole experience, and the skills they learn here, is something they will bring with them everywhere they go in life.

Another thing that I noticed is that the international volunteers open themselves up more so, than do local volunteers. Normally, students who volunteer in Hong Kong simply follow what they are instructed to do, whereas international volunteers seem to have a greater curiosity, and seem to be more enthusiastic and involved. Maybe, it is because they became more familiar with each other, they also became more willing to express themselves. So, by being overseas and delivering services, they feel they have to seek support, so besides acquiring practical skills, they also grow in various areas, psychologically and emotionally, and interpersonally.

Interviews with 4 student volunteers (V1, V2, V3, V4)

I: *What were your motives for joining this programme, and how did you prepare for the selection interview?*

V1: In the interview, I expressed my interests about this programme. I wanted to show a positive attitude during the interview, so I did a lot of research about the programme and about the country. To me, the location was definitely an attraction, as I heard that Myanmar is a deeply religious place, and I was curious to see how local people live and practice religion. But I think the main reason why I applied, is that I wanted to be of help to others.

V2: I wanted to join because I thought that I was old enough now to go out to explore the world. After being accepted into this programme, I informed my family, and they were a bit worried, because one month was a quite long period of time.

V3: I prepared for the interview by reflecting and asking myself why I wanted to join this programme, and what I wanted to gain from this experience. The interview was quite challenging, as the officers asked me how would I handle some difficult situations, and how would I deal with others.

I: *How was the interaction with your team members?*

V1: In total, we were four boys and four girls, and altogether, we got along quite well. We were divided to smaller groups, and I teamed up with another girl. I ended up doing more work than her, and we had some arguments, but in the end, we learned more about each other. I think this experience has been very useful, as it will help me to adapt better to different working environments in the future. Apart from the organizational skills, I learned more about how to express my emotions more openly. Normally, I tend to withhold my emotions, unless I have a tantrum, but during this service, I realized the importance of expressing my thoughts more thoughtfully and timely. I learned to be honest with myself about what I feel toward others persons, and in particular, I learned to accept that negative emotions that may arise during conflicts.

V4: We did not know each other very well before we went to Myanmar, and we interacted as "colleagues" rather than "classmates". This has been a new and interesting experience for me. I think this has introduced a "work dimension" to me, which in fact has helped the overall functioning of the group, and on how to achieve our common goals.

V3: In Hong Kong, when we encountered any difficulties, we can just go home and feel safe, but in Myanmar, we could not hide. Luckily, I found nice group members, whom I could talk to, and share my feelings. So, I learned how to face some problems alone, but I also learned how to rely on others.

I: *What were your expectations at the beginning and what have you realized while doing the project?*

V3: I could never imagine experiencing communication problems, but as the children cannot understand English, a local teacher always had to translate. This made me think that we were problematic for them, because they could not use their standard teaching materials, their methods, and someone always had to be there to translate. However, at the same time this motivated me to give back, and do my best to develop and try out some new teaching materials that could be useful to them.

V4: I expected Myanmar to be very poor, with no facilities, requiring us to walk several miles to reach our destination, but this was not always the case. I also expected longer teaching hours, but in reality, we have to spare most of the time in the office for preparing lessons, and reviewing the teaching materials. That is the reality of a working environment.

V1: I was impressed by the passion and the kindness of all the teachers. Even though they received a very low salary, they were very committed to what they do, and they were happy to communicate with us and to facilitate our service.

V2: Being raised in Hong Kong, I had a certain image of teachers that was very different than the teachers we have met. The teachers in Myanmar were much kinder than I thought, and from the first moment that we met, they tried to "break the ice" with us, by asking questions, trying to learn more about us, and facilitating pleasant interactions between us. They really made the atmosphere comfortable and welcoming. I was also very surprised by the children's attitudes toward learning. This was definitely something that I should learn from them. For example, when they reached the bus, they were very quick to get ready for their lessons, and even if they were very tired, they still tried hard to keep focussed and ask questions. I can tell that they really wanted to gain more knowledge, and change their lives. I found their attitudes very inspiring. Also, the teachers were very young, some even younger than me, but they looked very mature. Finally, the workload for the preparation of classes was definitely greater than I expected. Before joining this service, I never really considered that preparing a class is so complex. You have to think what topics children may be interested in, what they may be unaware of, and what was important to teach.

I: *What have you learned by doing this project?*

V1: I learned to communicate better and work more efficiently with others. I found the dynamics of our overall group to be very interesting. Initially, we got along really well, and we could share ideas on many topics, but at one point we had an argument, and we did not talk to each other for a while. It took us a few days to overcome this conflict and re-connect. This episode was very meaningful to me, as I learned that some people's working styles might not match yours, or your expectations, and it really requires some effort and maturity to positively deal with diversity and difference.

V2: I think that after the trip, I became slightly more extroverted. I am not a person who easily expresses their own thoughts and feelings in front of others, and I knew that this could be a problem, in this context. However, I found out that when I build a solid relationship with my teammates, I can communicate more easily, and openly to others. So, finally the group became a resource for me.

V3: I learned what it means to be a more responsible person. Providing this kind of service for one month presented some challenges, as you have to be persistent, even though there are times that you think you might give up. But after completing the service, the feeling is very rewarding. Plus, I had the chance to experience something very non-ordinary, for me. At City University I am a student, so I can just sit and listen to the class, but in Myanmar I was the teacher, and I realized how difficult is to be a teacher; as you really need to spend a lot of time, for preparing just one lesson.

V4: I learned to appreciate all of these teachers. I have a lot of admiration for them. These children do not have many chances to receive any formal education, and these teachers are very devoted to help them. This makes me reflect about my own life, and the resources I have in Hong Kong. It makes me think that I really should treasure what I have, and try to get the best out of it, daily.

References

Bringle, R. & Hatcher, J. (2011). "International service-learning." In B. Bringle, J. Hatcher, and S. Jones (Eds.), *International service-learning: Conceptual frameworks and research* (pp. 3–28). Sterling, VA: Stylus.

City University of Hong Kong (2017). "Global Services Office." Retrieved online from http://www.cityu.edu.hk/gso/au_overview.htm.

Lwin, T. (2007). "Education and democracy in Burma: Decentralization and classroom-level educational reform. " In *Forum: International forum for democratic studies*. Retrieved from http://www.thinkingclassroom.org/uploads/4/3/9/0/43900311/8._education_and_democracy_in_burma,_2007.pdf.

Miller, K. K. & Gonzalez, A. M. (2010). "Domestic and international service learning experiences: A comparative study of pre-service teacher outcomes. "*Issues in Educational Research*, 20(1), 29–38.

Pless, N. M., Maak, T., & Stahl, G. K. (2011). "Developing responsible global leaders through international service-learning programs: The Ulysses experience." *Academy of Management Learning & Education*, 10(2), 237–260.

The University of Hong Kong (2017). "Vision Statement." Retrieved online from http://www.global.hku.hk/vision-statement

United Nations Development Programme (UNDP) (2017). "Human Development Data (1990–2017)." Retrieved from http://hdr.undp.org/en/data.

9

USING THE RECIPROCAL VOLUNTEER PROCESS MODEL (RVPM) TO IMPLEMENT SERVICES FOR LOCAL CHILDREN AND YOUTH FROM ETHNIC MINORITIES

Part A

The context

In Hong Kong, ethnic minority youth from South and Southeast Asian countries frequently face discrimination and social exclusion, mainly due to language barriers, and cultural and religious differences. As a result, they normally do not have the same opportunities as local youth. Here is another case example that addressed this local issue.

Using the RVPM model in building a supportive environment

Recognizing the social service needs of children and youth from ethnic minorities

In today's Hong Kong incoming ethnic minority groups from South and Southeast Asian countries, namely Indian, Pakistan, Nepal, Indonesia, the Philippines, and Thailand, they frequently face local discrimination and social exclusion. Such youth often have limited access to education, even though they are the ones most in need of it. In the academic year 2011/12, ethnic minority students from these countries comprised only 14,076, or less than 2% of the entire student population (Census and Statistics Department, 2017). Literature suggests that these non-Chinese students generally come from lower socio-economic backgrounds, have difficulties in learning the Chinese language, face various social adjustment problems, have poorer academic results, and have fewer opportunities than Chinese students, meaning that even though some were born in Hong Kong; they also do not have the same rights, opportunities, and respect of other Chinese individuals (Hue & Kennedy, 2014; Law & Lee, 2012). In Hong Kong, many of these ethnic minorities think they do not have the same educational opportunities as other students, either Chinese or other international students (Ku, Chan, & Sandhu, 2005). Specifically, they feel they have limited options, because even though many public schools claim that they use English as the official language for instruction, actually in most cases Chinese is essential or preferred. Conversely, these youth cannot afford to pay the higher fees of private international schools, as other Western, Japanese, or Korean students do. Moreover, according to this research, such students sometimes feel discriminated against by their Chinese teachers, and/or classmates. In this same study, one out of four reported that their teachers held stereotypical notions about ethnic minority groups, and it was also perceived that they preferred teaching Chinese students rather than other ethnic minority students. Similarly, in some cases, they feel that their Chinese classmates do not like them, as locally ethnic minority groups are often perceived and described as misbehaving, impolite, or dirty. Another discrimination area reported in this study concerned their religious practices. In particular Muslim students mentioned that they are not given a room where they can pray, and they also find it almost impossible to meet their dietary needs in schools (e.g., they are only allowed to eat Halal, meaning "permissible, lawful" food, which is slaughtered according to the Islamic law, as described in the Koran). Ethnic minority youth's perception of being discriminated goes beyond the school; many also have strong feelings that Hong Kong people do not have an equal consideration of different races and nationalities.

Local ethnic minority groups frequently report more health and disability problems than the main population, however they appear to have poorer access to health services. It was noted that services for ethnic minorities do not always undertake comprehensive needs assessments; procedures and assessment methods are normally calibrated on the main population, so that minority needs are often unmet. Specifically, it was observed that services for minority groups should focus on: mental health promotion, primary care, access to care, effective services for people with severe mental illness, caring about carers, and preventing suicide (McKenzie, 2008). Finally here, it was pointed out that people from minority groups often are unaware of their rights and the resources available to them, and that there are frequently disconnections among various agencies, and mistrust between the different service entities (Mirza & Heinemann, 2012). Locally, educational needs are a priority among ethnic minority groups. The Chinese language is the main obstacle for these students. For most of them, difficulties are mainly due to their inability to speak Chinese, while many who can speak it struggle to read and write Chinese. Language barriers may limit their participation in society, and in fact most minority students think they do not have the same educational opportunities as local Chinese students in Hong Kong, due to limited school choices while the chances for further education beyond senior secondary education (also due to familial values, as they are expected to go to work rather than studying) are restricted. Additionally, some students report that not all of their cultural and religious values and practices are allowed, and/or practicable in Hong Kong (Ku et al., 2005).

According to the Population By-Censes in 2016, there were 584,383 ethnic minorities living in Hong Kong, which is 8% of the population of Hong Kong (Census and Statistics Department, 2017). Among the challenges they faced are:

poverty, cultural differences, language barriers, opportunities in education/employment, and social mobility. According to a recent government report, almost one in five are people living below the poverty line. Free half-day programmes are provided by kindergartens in Hong Kong, but one in four has shut its doors to ethnic minorities, while others do not give such pupils any support in learning the Chinese language, which is crucial for their social mobility. Furthermore, as observed by frontline social workers, ethnic minority parents are usually less familiar with Hong Kong's educational structures, competitive environments, or situation at the societal level, as well as policy systems related to it.

Because of the existence of many social barriers, most children and youth from these ethnic minority groups lack accessibilities to study pathways and career resources. This is reflected in their exclusion from several other community environments (e.g., employment opportunities, access to health services, etc.). In turn, most of them remain unmotivated and marginalized, and lacking opportunities for fair chances for education and acceptance by the local community. Our previous experiences of organizing support groups and outreaching to them in centers and in secondary schools was very successful. However, in order to sustain their involvement with our group activities, we needed to provide them with more pro-active stable and long-term relationships. Long lasting and trustful relationships was the key for success for this service. We therefore, were constantly challenged with how to maintain a stable group of volunteers and staff, and how to maintain collaborative relationships with the NGOs. We were also challenged with a lack of resources to provide deeper levels of intervention, both in group and individual levels.

There was very limited support for these parents about how they should nurture or protect their children's welfare and rights, including educational, entertainment, social connections etc. The parents themselves also suffer from insufficient understanding and competence to offer much comprehensive care to their children. It is quite common for such parents to be "invisible" in the child-rearing and development processes. We planned therefore, to implement parental education and home visit services in our service delivery.

Part B

Using the RVPM model in building interactional relationships

Designing programmes for children and youth from ethnic minorities

Over the years, CYEP worked with different NGOs to develop various local initiatives for local ethnic minorities in Hong Kong. Some focussed on learning the Chinese language, whereas others focussed more on academic and personal mentoring. Here are our major works:

a) *Project Ethnic Minority Empowerment (PEME)*: this is a joint university student initiated programme, which aimed at empowering ethnic minorities in various community venues by providing community services, advocacy, and social networking. Its mission is to promote cultural awareness and harmony by bridging the gap between local ethnic minorities and international student cultures. PEME organizes events that provide students from different backgrounds with opportunities to make new Chinese friends, and better understand each other's cultures and their differences, and uniqueness. Team members consist of ethnic minority students from different universities under the coaching of trained CYEP staff. PEME mainly targeted the second or third wave of newer immigrant students, originally from proximal Asian countries like Nepal, Pakistan, India, Bangladesh, Indonesia, and the Philippines. On average, each project PEME service project comprised 15–20 volunteers. The main goal of these projects is both academic and personal development for these service recipients. The process of inclusion in mainstream culture was achieved primarily in groups, and partially through individual mentorship. These projects are possible due primarily to these committed and trained volunteers, who thus were very proactive in developing ongoing new activities and involving participants. These passionate and very committed volunteers often were themselves sons/daughters of immigrant families in Hong Kong and as such, they had empathy and a very good understanding of their service recipients, and had a strong desire to help them.

b) *"Chin Change" – Chinese Changes Your Life Chinese language workshop for ethnic minority youth*: volunteers assist ethnic-minority youths to learn Chinese language (for everyday and academic use) and to help them better integrate and advance in schools.

c) *"Fight Against Public Exam!" – Special tutorial group tutoring service for ethnic minority youth*: this is a project for helping senior secondary ethnic minority students to prepare for their public examinations in various academic subjects (e.g., Mathematics, Business, Accounting, Chinese, Science, Liberal Studies and Information and Communication Technology).

d) *"Face the Challenge Together!" – Mentoring schemes with ethnic minority youth*: here volunteers help youth from various ethnic minorities learn the Chinese language (for academic and everyday use) and other subjects (math, science, business). In addition, they help them plan their careers and personal development. Finally, trained volunteers meet regularly with their parents, so that they can appreciate different perspectives of their daughters/sons.

e) *Tutoring and mentoring group for Centre for Harmony and Enhancement of Ethnic Minority Residents (CHEERS)*: we worked with Kwun Tong Centre, Hong Kong Christina Service to provide tutoring and mentorship group work to primary and secondary school children and youth in the centre group, two groups, seven sessions and 15 members in each semester.

f) *Tutoring and mentoring group for Delia Memorial School (Hip Wo), Caritas*: we offered intensive group interactional activities between secondary school students and student volunteers in a three whole-day mentoring programme, usually delivered during summer.

g) *Tutoring and mentoring group for Ngau Tau Kok Centre, Caritas*: we offered tutoring and mentoring groups in the centre for their members with ethnic minority background, usually two groups, seven sessions and 15 members in each semester.

h) *Non-regular on campus various types of social activities for the ethnic minority youth*: we carried out job interview skills training, Chin-Change programmes, as either initiated by CYEP or agencies irregularly and on demands for different groups of youth on campus for different social activities.

Essential paradigm shift when designing programmes for children and youth from ethnic minorities

There are likely various ways for integrating ethnic minority students, such as improving their educational opportunities, offering language courses, and/or promoting the use of the English language as the official medium and, amending curricula to match their changing students' needs. However, it is first necessary to promote encounters and exchange relationships between local students and different ethnic minority groups, to foster a process of mutual knowledge, appreciation, and respect of cultural differences, so as to offset stereotypes, and prevent cultural and racial resentment. Our aim was not to simply integrate these ethnic minority groups to the local culture; instead, the presence of minority groups offers opportunities for our volunteers to experience diversity and develop more cosmopolitanism, as this cultural inclusion dimension makes people citizens of the world, and prepares them to live more comfortably in various international cities.

Therefore, we perceive serving the minority groups as an opportuniy to promote more cultural responsiveness in our community. These involve all stakeholders: Chinese students, ethnic minority students, youth volunteers, teachers and social workers. For example, some teachers are aware that it is essential to collaborate more proactively with students' parents, as some ethnic minority parents prioritize and value traditional religious practices more so than academic goals. However, this task is not necessarily a teachers' mandate, and furthermore some teachers expressed the feelings that when promoting such relationships, they work against both the examination-oriented cultures and their families' values. We wanted to build an understanding from the perspective of the minority themselves, and not that of the dominant group. This could be achieved if all parties engaged in this process first-hand, so that they could learn more about the other's culture, as well as about their own culture and their own assumptions and ways of thinking. Through various CYEP programmes, we aimed at offering a setting in which all types of students would encounter one another, and learn to better respect and understand the culture and backgrounds of various local ethnic minority groups. In turn, they would reflect more meaningfully on their own backgrounds and beliefs.

Infusing for Multi-level and multi-disciplinary approach for ethnic minorities

Our service experiences taught us that long-established and trustful relationships with ethnic minority youths are of utmost importance in promoting change. For many, their problems are also deep-rooted, mainly due to the language barrier and lack of information, and many are not confident, and/or hopeful about their futures. Most of those whom we contacted were on the edge of learned-helplessness, unmotivated, and mentally troubled. However, we also observed that NGOs also lacked the manpower to improve their services in this area, not because they were entirely lacking of resources but because they lacked a long-term plan and the experience to address this population. CYEP's approach offsets this local service gap by offering the following assumptions and initiatives:

- Extending more work in the secondary schools directly, which saves the NGO manpower in all levels of communication work. Normally, our volunteers offer tutoring and socialization opportunities, but we also work on enhancing motivation, confidence, cultural identity, and life and career planning.
- Mobilizing university students from ethnic minority groups to run a self-initiated group and deliver programmes for cultural exchanges.
- Identifying these motivated youth and offering them individual engagement programmes for deeper levels of change, mentorship support, and career planning.
- Working with parents to conduct home visits. In fact, we observed that these youth seriously lack parental supports for their personal development.
- Advocating for more attention for the needs and learning barriers of these ethnic minority students: besides establishing a joint university program, delivering direct services to different groups of these ethnic minority children and youth, in 2014, by a joint effort with the Hong Kong Christian Service and the mobilized university students, we carried out "A Research on Impact of Chinese Education on Academic and Career of Ethnic Minority in Hong Kong". Jointly with the agency, and over the years of providing Chinese learning services to ethnic minority students, we saw a need for deeper investigation on the difficulties of these students in Chinese learning, and how it affects their academic and career prospects. In order to understand how students with an ethnic minority background perceived their Chinese level and their academic prospects, the research has captured the factors affecting their learning and career development. Seven secondary schools participated in this research. A press conference was organized in summer of 2014 to disseminate the research findings to the public and to invite more support to these students.

Part C

Using the RVPM model in achieving accountability and transparency: voices of student volunteers and staff

We interviewed one staff member and four student volunteers who had volunteered for ethnic minorities in Hong Kong in order to record from their own real experience on how this type of service has been delivered. The following represent the results of face-to-face interviews conducted in 2018 with 1 staff member (S1) and 4 on-site volunteers (V1, V2, V3, V4) carried out either by the book author and/or a Research Fellow of CYEP, as represented by "I".

Interview with the CYEP staff (S1)

I: *What projects are you involved with?*

S1: We have four projects with three different organizations. The first is partnered with a secondary school in collaboration with an NGO. There, we offer workshops and mentorship with children and young adolescents from the lower academic forms, for enhancing their spoken Cantonese and written Chinese skills. With the same NGO and the same secondary school, our second service offers mentorship to selected upper form students, and helps them with their homework tuition, career training, and individual mentorship. The third service is with another NGO, in which we offer a project which is specially designed for a group of Pakistani young students, which deemed taken as a marginalized group within a community of mainly ethnic minority students. Our fourth project is with a third local NGO, which jointly created a project called Project CHEERS. This project is rather a large service, because we involve groups of university students from many ethnic minorities, and we work with them to mentor groups of secondary school students also from different ethnic minorities.

I: *What are the main problems faced by these ethnic minorities groups?*

S1: Hong Kong has a long colonial history of recruiting and employing Indian soldiers to work in Hong Kong. So our first generation of ethnic minorities came in this wave of army recruitment and so Indian persons are our largest population among all ethnic minority groups. Second, we now have a number of immigrants coming from Pakistan, Nepal, the Philippines, and Indonesia who looked for stability and employment in Hong Kong, and then finally settled here to work and raise their children. As time evolved, the present younger generations of ethnic minorities in Hong Kong are actually third and fourth generations, mostly born in Hong Kong who are faced with many unique problems from the education system. Some challenges for minorities are quite prevalent nowadays, for example, Chinese has become a core requirement for students to be eligible to enter university, the demand for

Indians to work in the army has ceased, the job market is becoming more competitive, etc. Underneath the surface, because of low achievement in education and poorer results in employment, these immigrants also faced with deep-rooted racial discrimination and are labelled as being weak or lazy. Against these odds, in our programmes, we try to cultivate a more inclusive environment, and to foster acceptance and respect during our mentoring work. We found that the families of the children we met are faced with a sense of learned helplessness after suffering from a long-term poverty. Unique to their own culture, most families from the south-Asian countries are still upholding their cultural belief that their children should go out and get a job at a very young age, and do not want to believe that education is a necessary criteria for facilitating their children to climb the social ladder. Therefore, between CYEP and the local NGOs, we knew that besides working with such children and youth, we also have to work with their families in order to bring more possible changes.

I: *What are your goals, for the recipients and the volunteers?*

S1: First, we were approached by local NGOs for collaboration, mainly because they were in great demand for a large group of volunteers who could support this group of children and youth with their academic and intellectual work, in both Chinese and English languages. Second, because our volunteers were born in Hong Kong and are university students, they already know the rules of performance in Hong Kong for public examinations. So, using university students as mentors for such a large group of underachieving young students seemed to be a "good-fit". I would say that both the academic and personal development of different ethnic minority children and youth in Hong Kong are our main concerns. Indirectly as an approach, we always emphasized that it is a very good thing for both the children and youth from ethnic minority groups and our volunteers to mix, and mutually learn more about their culture and become more open and accepting to differences. We also emphasized that participating in activities carried out on the university campus is also inspiring to those who have not yet joined the university, for socialization and acculturalization to the university environment. So we highly valued the cultural learning activities being carried out on campus. I still remember how a girl noted to me that she was impressed by the round-shaped huge lecture halls in the university. Thus, CYEP was offering them a platform for meeting with university students, and to observe and get to know the university environment. Racial inclusion and mutual acceptance have been our guiding core values. I truly see the changes in our students in accepting and interacting with the ethnic minorities during activities. During de-briefing, I also found that they become more understanding of the other cultural backgrounds, religions, cultural issues, and how local Hong Kong policy affects the lives of these ethnic minorities. So at all levels, we want our volunteers to be more critical in their thinking about the challenges faced by these ethnic minorities in Hong Kong. We also had good rewarding experiences of mentoring some ethnic minority students and have successfully mentored them to get through public examination and enter our university or other universities. We are very proud of them, indeed, and many of them are now our volunteers.

I: *How do you do recruitment?*

S1: On average for each project, we aim to recruit about 15–20 volunteers. For Chinese classes, of course knowing how to write and speak Chinese is a recruitment criteria. For other activities there are not many specific criteria, as long as they are available and are willing to take part, they will be accepted. But for the "CHEERS" project, we look specifically for volunteers from ethnic minorities and they have priority to be volunteers.

I: *What is the relationship between CYEP and the agencies?*

S1: It really depends on the capacity of the agency, as we play different roles in different projects. We work closely with the social workers from the schools we are serving because they know very well the students from these ethnic minorities, their class schedules, their backgrounds, their language limitations etc. Usually, for the projects to be offered in the schools, the school social workers will take a more leadership role in suggesting programmes. Alternatively, for the programmes to be carried out in the agencies, we will take more lead and will involve the volunteers to participate more in planning and preparing. Concerning the "CHEERS" project, it is quite important for us to maintain a group of steady and involved university students (who themselves also have ethnic minority backgrounds), who are also very skilful in mentoring ethnic minority children and youth.

I: *What is the training?*

S1: We first introduce CYEP and define service learning, then we talk about the service recipients' backgrounds, the background of the agency, and finally the macro picture of the project, the historical background, the political reasons for migration, and the social policies for discrimination, etc. Finally, we talk about the unique roles and perspectives expected from these volunteers. For the "CHEERS" project, we provide more social and cultural background information. We have developed some structured games, and will introduce the volunteers about how to carry out role-plays, cultural exchanges, etc. Foremost, we want the volunteers to be very sensitive to their cultural differences as well as deep-rooted resistance to their service recipients, who are from ethnic minority groups. The social workers who help us to do training might discuss about the cultural customs of Muslims, their "dos" and "don'ts". Social workers are also very helpful in providing information about how to do career counselling, or how to motivate children and youth from ethnic minorities in learning for us. So, in different projects, we always discuss the content of the training goals with the social workers and get them involved.

I: *How many service recipients do you have, and how do you do the matching?*

S1: In most cases the ratio is one-to-one. We use around 100 volunteers and so it is also roughly 100 service recipients. We usually will use the first two to three weeks for some group programs and we observe the interactions between the volunteers and the service recipients in groups. That gives us many insights on how to match them in mentorship, or how to divide them into smaller groups for some tasks. Normally, each group comprises two volunteers and two recipients, which makes it more dynamic for their communication. In general, for teaching classes, the matching depends mostly by which subjects the volunteers chose to teach, and what the recipients are interested in learning. Again, groups are normally two-on-two, or three-on-three.

I: *This is a non-credit bearing project. What is the commitment of the volunteers?*

S1: Ethnic minority service is particularly challenging for us, because at times, after the social workers recruit the service recipients, they will try to find excuses to "sneak out" of the project. And if one of them does not join the project, likely their friends will also follow. So, we face this uncertainty, and it directly affects the attendance of our recipients. But in turn, this also affects the attendance of volunteers, because if there are more volunteers than recipients, the volunteers may feel quite disappointed and frustrated. The participation of volunteers is usually good and we can easily maintain 80–90%. However, we do not just want the volunteers to be here because of duties. We want to make them "spiritually" connected to the service. So, my role is important to maintain the attendance of the service recipients, not just the volunteers. If a volunteer came once and twice without the attendance of his/her matched children and youth, they will just feel bored and not needed, and will soon become spiritually disconnected. So, I developed the rule that I will work closely with the social workers on how to encourage more attendance by these children and youth. We found that in between the mentoring programmes, other fun group activities are quite helpful to motivate them to come again.

I: *How do you see the volunteers changing from the beginning to the end of the project?*

S1: Volunteers working with ethnic minorities are usually found to be nervous and shy at the beginning. So, I see that being a volunteer in this service is a big step for a volunteer to open up to different cultures. At the beginning, my role is to remind them, again and again that they have to observe the basic rule of not being so open with girls because girls from ethnic minority backgrounds could be very conservative, or do not comment about anyone's religious issues. But as time passes by, both groups then realize that they are just normal youngsters, and that talking and discussing some sensitive issues would not end up with discrimination or embarrassment issues, etc. That means both groups have already learned a lot, and now they are more relaxed. When we build a certain level of relationship comfort, we can in fact talk about many other topics. And for volunteers, I know they have already achieved seeing others with no notice to skin colour, religious background or language differences. Both groups often then become real friends.

I: *What is the role of the volunteer ambassadors?*

S1: First, they do the initial service shadowing, so they work with their colleagues in service. A staff member will be the person who communicates with the organizations, and also recruits volunteers, but VAs help to network with volunteers, because they are the most experienced volunteers who can best relate with the newer volunteers, and share their experiences with them. Sometimes they may just help out with logistics, like gathering volunteers together, but in other cases they can participate with staff members to write program content together, as they also suggest what activities to do. Second, they can be very handy for assisting us to do the promotional work for this service, arrange training, and do the networking work, etc. So, VAs are very important in being our student leaders.

Interviews with 4 student volunteers (V1, V2, V3, V4)

I: *Why did you choose the ethnic minority programme to serve in?*

V1: Because it was the most suitable for my schedule, and I never had the chance to interact with local ethnic minorities before in Hong Kong.

V2: Partially I joined because I had the time to spare, and partially because I myself am an ethnic minority, so I wanted to help the fellow people like me. I understand well the things ethnic minorities are not getting, such as a quality education, and/or we need more resources that the community is not actually providing. So, I wanted to help more directly with that and try my best to share.

V3: I also wanted to help the ethnic minorities because I myself am half-Philippine, but I did not know how I could do that, until another volunteer told me about the mentorship scheme that PEME had, so I decided to join.

I: *What do you do in the service, and how is it structured?*

V2: There are three things that we do in PEME, namely networking, advocacy, and mentorship. For networking, we have festivals that are designed to show aspects of cultures from different countries (i.e., Nepal, Philippines, Pakistan, India, etc.). There, we present different types of food, and religions customs from these countries, as they are often very different one from another. For advocacy, we planned an event called the Cultural Interactive Workshop, where we simulated our daily life, as an ethnic minority living in Hong Kong. For example, in restaurants they often do not really know what food is appropriate for some cultures, or for people of different religions (e.g., some ethnic minority groups only eat halal or vegetarian dishes and which are not provided in most local restaurants). So, we role-played activities about if we came up with a situation with no common language and different culture, what will be the best way to deal with it?. It was a bit exaggerated role-play and we did it together with our service recipients, but it was really a good visual way for telling them how we sincerely want to understand their real life. At the end, we had a de-briefing session, discussing what we think could have been done better, and what more we can do in the future.

V4: I am a Hong Kong born Bangladeshi, and I think the PEME project is the only one in the university where the ethnic minorities find some sense of belonging, because other projects are designed for Chinese, so there are limitations due to language. I think this unique project provides a platform for ethnic minorities to express themselves; after all, we all need a place for longing and belonging.

I: *CYEP is a non-credit bearing project. You do not get academic credits as a reward for your participation, but nevertheless you committed. Why?*

V2: We all were very interested in helping others, and are passionate about it. This is something you need to consider for everything you do. If you have the ability, passion, and interest – do something. So we decided to help others regardless of academic credit.

V3: I think we do it because of the sense of personal reward that comes from being able to bringing change to other people in Hong Kong. That is what kept me going.

I: *What were your expectations at the beginning and what have you realized while doing the project?*

V4: I think I initially wanted to gain some experience and do local voluntary work, however, alongside being a volunteer, I have realized that there were people who were benefiting from our services, and we were seeing themselves much more positively.

V2: It is like when we plan an event and we think it is very stressful, and we are concerned that participants may not like it or the timing is not right. Then, when the day comes we see that people are actually enjoying it, and many people are actually getting the information that they need. For example, we saw that a person she was mentoring still keeps in touch with her, and tells her "actually I was scared about learning English, but now I feel like it is my best paper so far". When we hear these voices, after all the stress due to the planning and the aftermath of seeing all of this, I would say: "Hey, I should help people, as it feels really good!"

I: *What have you learned by doing this project?*

V4: For us as a team, we learned event planning and contingency-planning.

V3: We also learned how to deal with third parties. For example, we invited some professionals to one of these meetings, and one particular guest was very dominant in a planning meeting. He was the one who was leading the meeting, and even though we invited him, we were supposed to be the ones explaining it to him. He came because we wanted him to talk about minority career paths to our mentees. This became a problem for us, because this was our project, and we wanted to plan it as a team, and not having one who is higher than others, so that was one of our difficulties working with an external source.

V1: As for me, I did not learn too many practical or organizational skills, but more about ethnic minorities and in particular, about Pakistanis, because I never met them before. For example, I did not really know what "halal" meant, and when we wanted to buy some snacks with them, we tried to learn how to read the ingredients so as to understand which one was most suitable for them. Also, I learned why they hold negative perceptions about themselves, as they may be quite noisy and naughty, shouting, but all the way around and this is their culture. We learned a little bit of the Pakistani language, and their costumes, their music, and a little bit about their backgrounds.

I: *You volunteered in other projects and organizations as well. In your opinion, what is the strength of this project, also in comparison with others?*

V4: When you volunteer for NGOs, they focussed mainly on education and employment, whereas we focussed more so on advocacy and networking. Also, the age gap between volunteers and service recipients in our project was not too large, so that it was easier to connect with one another.

V3: I think that we can do more here, because we are the ones planning the events, and the ones who have to take care of issues or stress when something happens. So, we have to plan "A to Z", and we have a back up plan. We have the opportunity to learn, and we are not just people who go to volunteer and can disappear anytime. We put much time and effort into this, so it feels more like it is "ours" as well, and we want to see it grow. It is like when you plant a tree and you keep watering it, and when you see how big it is growing, you are happy and pleased.

References

Census and Statistics Department (2017). "Thematic Report: Ethnic Minorities." Retrieved from https://www.statistics.gov.hk/pub/B11201002016XXXXB0100.pdf.

Hue, M. T., & Kennedy, K. J. (2014). "Creating culturally responsive environments: ethnic minority teachers' constructs of cultural diversity in Hong Kong secondary schools." *Asia Pacific Journal of Education*, 34(3), 273–287.

Ku, H. B., Chan, K. W., & Sandhu, K. K. (2005). *A research report on the education of South Asian ethnic minority groups in Hong Kong*. Hong Kong: Centre for Social Policy Studies, Department of Applied Social Sciences, The Hong Kong Polytechnic University.

Law, K. Y. & Lee, K. M. (2012). "The myth of multiculturalism in 'Asia's world city': Incomprehensive policies for ethnic minorities in Hong Kong." *Journal of Asian Public Policy*, 5(1), 117–134.

McKenzie, K. (2008). "Improving mental healthcare for ethnic minorities." *Advances in Psychiatric Treatment*, 14(4), 285–291.

Mirza, M. & Heinemann, A. W. (2012). "Service needs and service gaps among refugees with disabilities resettled in the United States." *Disability and Rehabilitation*, 34(7), 542–552.

10

USING THE RECIPROCAL VOLUNTEER PROCESS MODEL (RVPM) TO IMPLEMENT SERVICES FOR LOCAL ELDERLY

Part A

The context

In the previous four chapters, we have described different services for groups of children and youth as rendered by CYEP for our regular services, with rationales given on why we have chosen children and youth as our major service target groups. Alongside all these regular services, we had also delivered short term/one-off services for many other different groups, for examples, parents, women, men, elderly, homeless, the blind and deaf, etc. However, it was not until 2013 that CYEP started to extend its regular services to the elderly groups, basing on two reasons. First, from our previous one-off services for the elderly, we observed that volunteers were inspired in unique ways (as different from working with children) and we are convinced we should initiate a new service for elderly. Second, we wrote a funding proposal to implement a new service for regularly visit to a group of single elderly (or "hidden elderly") and we finally got funding from a donor from the community in 2013.

Using the RVPM model in building a supportive environment for CYEP to deliver and serve local elderly

Globally, the elderly are one of the fastest growing groups in many countries of the world, and Hong Kong is no exception. Often, in many countries, health and human services, as well as government policies are found to be inadequate in addressing the pressing issues and problems elderly populations are facing daily (Johri, Beland, & Bergman, 2003). In Hong Kong in July 2017, elderly people had the longest lifespan of any country in the world with men living to 81.32 years and women to 87.34 years (South China Morning Post, 2017). According to the 2018 census statistics of the Hong Kong Government, there are around 1.8 million elderly aged 60 or above, representing a quarter of the entire local population in Hong Kong (Census and Statistics Department, 2018).

Although in Hong Kong society familial values are emphasized, some people may end up being alone in the later stages of their life. Senior citizens who remain living in their apartments and have limited social networks have more chances of becoming secluded, or as we called them "hidden" elderly. These "hidden elderly" defined by the Commission on Poverty (CoP) are those elderly who "are disengaged from the community and disadvantaged yet not helped by the available service and support" (Commission on Poverty, 2006, p.1). Recent studies found that about 10% of the surveyed elder population are unengaged or hidden (Chung & Chung, 2013). A study from the Central Policy Unit of Hong Kong (2008) found that hidden elderly was a group who had minimal contact with other people. Specifically, they had contacts only essential for their survival (e.g., hospitals, grocery stores), but none were related to leisure and/or mutual support. Mostly, they reported feeling useless, neglected, hopeless, and helpless. They were not as much physically isolated, but they felt disconnected from the external world and unable to do anything about it. Not surprisingly, they were often described as passive help-seekers, with limited financial resources, which further increased their sense of self reliance. Besides psychological and social problems, hidden elderly have presented a variety of medical conditions, including hypertension, diabetes, cardiac problems, arthritis, and hyperlipidemia. Likely due to the nature of their living conditions, they show higher rates (about two thirds of the sample surveyed) of drug adherence issues and storage problems (Lee et al., 2013), as well as poor diets, which impacted their vulnerability to malnutrition (Chung & Chung, 2013).

In 2013, CYEP initiated an "Elderly Home Visit" programme for these "hidden" elderly in Hong Kong. This programme was implemented in the city district of Shamshuipo, one of the most densely populated districts in the world. In this community, there is an increasing number of elderly who lack adequate family care and community support. Many often live alone and have difficulties meeting minimal daily needs. Through our partnership with an NGO, CYEP worked with volunteers to serve a group of "hidden" elderly. Since social and leisure activity has been found to be an influential determinant of successful aging, our entry point for this service was to conduct home visitation services. The uniqueness of this home-based visit service is that it allows youth to learn through a conventional "serving" role (providing assistance in daily living). It also provides a platform for the elderly to take on the role of the "well of wisdom" to pass on life experiences, personal narratives, and inspiration for younger generations – instead of assuming a passive role – only to be served and helped. The social interactions in this service promotes feelings of self-esteem while mediating loneliness and isolation for many elderly, and the participatory role, provides a continuity of social role so they can experience competence and recognition. In addition, creative arts elements are offered by volunteers to specifically process their views on overall the aging process, relationship with elderly family members, and issues on death and dying.

Part B

Using the RVPM model in building interactional relationships

Designing programs with elderly

This elderly programme is guided to serve three convergent goals:

Level 1: the elderly benefit from the volunteers through regular home visits to assess their daily living situations and group activities to proactively engage them socially in active partnership roles.

Level 2: social service agencies benefit from the project through their monitoring assessments on each visit about physical mobility, housing condition, socialization, medical and financial support. With these assessments, the agencies can try to minimize or address crisis and provide ways to identify preventative measures, ultimately to lessen the burden of the overloaded social workers.

Level 3: our volunteers have benefitted immeasurably through the project. They gain opportunities to witness and assess living situations of the elderly in Hong Kong, to learn about how social policy, community responses and individual factors combined, impact and affect elderly's access to necessary resources such as housing, healthcare, food, transportation, etc. Volunteers also learn about the history of our city, through the elderly's narrative of their past, which is a valuable form of oral history.

Through regular home visits to elderly persons, we also observed how volunteers could establish better relationships with them, to help them with some daily tasks, accompany them to medical appointments, and support their process of socialization and re-integration within the community. Gradually from this process, we moved our work from individual levels to group and community level of work.

Infusing for multi-level and multi-disciplinary approach

Here, our entry point has been conducting home visits to a group of single elderly. When this had been achieved, we then mobilized resources as well as a large group of volunteers to visit up to 90 single elderly regularly, for 12 individual times in each semester (the number of elderly we can visit regularly depends on the availability of resources and the enrolled volunteers, so far, it ranges from 30–90). On achieving this, we then evolved these to individual home visits to group level of social participation:

1. We group those single elderly from nearby housing estates or locations together, and offered them social activities like having congregate tea and lunch (a very popular breakfast or lunch gathering in Hong Kong in a Chinese

restaurant, also called Yum Cha lunch) together. This was considered as a friendly way to foster relationships and become better socialized. As a result, many of our serving elderly made new friends and formed new social circles through via those activities.

2. We also organized festival-type gatherings and interest groups for example new-year dinners, Christmas lunch party, opera performances etc., with these activities carried out on the nearby CityU campus.
3. From time to time, we also organized some special creative arts and experiential groups for different sub-groups of elderly, e.g., creative circle paintings, mud art, compiling personal life albums or developing personal recipe books, calligraphy writing, etc. Some unique requests and participation from our serving elderly were very inspiring for the volunteers also. For example, we once decorated a classroom to resemble the streets of old Hong Kong and against these backdrops shot photos for these elderly. Another time, we witnessed a very old lady who experienced for the first time in her life to be able to hold a writing brush and she wrote something with the help from a volunteer.
4. For those who are fit enough, we organized various outings, which highly depended on the availability of resources and the suggestions received from either staff or volunteers. We have records of arranging a visit to Disneyland, taking the tram to the peak, going for a BBQ in CityU campus, etc. Many of the elderly did those activities for their first time (and maybe their only time) in their entire life.

Overall, this programme was different from any other CYEP's initiatives; volunteers met only for a short briefing, and then they visited each older person in their own apartment. This was a rather different approach for the service delivery from our other children and youth programmes. Here, volunteers were also delivering services without any social workers from the NGOs and/or CYEP staff on-site. So, training on needed skills, e.g., how to develop relationships with the elderly, how to handle unexpected crisis, etc. were unique and very challenging. Because of this, we teamed up to three volunteers in a small sub-group for the home visits.

Although the staff and social workers did not assist volunteers on-site, they helped them using the agency centre as the monitoring base. Volunteers would first develop relationships with service recipients during the first few visits, then under the supervision and guidance of the project officer, together with the observation and information collected by the volunteers, the agency social worker, the CYEP staff and volunteers collaboratively made adjustments about how to better meet the needs of these elderly, including for the long term goal of improving their well-being and the quality of life. To facilitate better communication between the agency and the volunteers, an assessment form was developed to assist volunteers to observe and assess needs (mainly about the provision of nutrient food, safety of home, the environment, including the function of furniture and electronic appliances, etc.). Taken together, these activities could help the service recipients in bonding with their community, benefiting different stakeholders (the agency, the service recipients, and the volunteers) simultaneously.

Part C

Using the RVPM model in achieving accountability and transparency: voices of student volunteers and staff

We interviewed one staff member and three student volunteers who had been volunteered for elderly service in order to record from their own real experience on how this type of service has been delivered. The following represent the results of face-to-face interviews conducted in 2018 with one staff member (S1) and three on-site volunteers (V1, V2, V3) carried out either by the book author and/or a Research Fellow of CYEP, as represented by "I".

Interview with the CYEP staff (S1)

I: *How is this service structured?*

S1: Most of our programmes follow a similar structure, which comprise recruitment, orientation and briefing, training before service, and then volunteer-service recipients match-making. But with the elderly, this was not possible because they were likely single (or a couple) in one apartment, and they were referred by an agency to receive our service. Our programme randomly assigned volunteers to different homes for visiting, unless a volunteer had already visited some elderly before, and wanted to visit the same person again. In this service we only recruited Cantonese-speaking persons, because most elderly only speak this language. Our volunteer small groups comprised three people on average, so we had to conduct many more de-briefing sessions, than we would in any other CYEP program. On average, these volunteers may spend about two and a half hours for a home visit, then they come back to the center and then write their logbooks, fill in an assessment form, where they are required to report their observations, and then each small group does a de-briefing. So altogether, this service requires much more time, and was implemented in a somewhat different organizational structure.

I: *What are the main problems faced by these older people?*

S1: We called them "hidden" elderly, because they spend most of their time staying home alone, even if they go out, they are only heading for the supermarket. The majority of them have no connection with friends or family. They are either individuals or couples under the service of an elderly center, but are not active community members who will approach the center, or who are motivated to join the activities in the center. Because of this, they are referred to us by this local elderly agency, and we outreached to them through our volunteer home visitation programme.

I: *How many volunteers are involved and how do you organize them?*

S1: It varies each semester but currently, we run this program twice a week. On Wednesday, there are normally around 20 volunteers, but on Saturday there can be 50 to 80. We all gather at a local metro station, and by then, they already know who they are going to visit. Normally each group is made of three people. In the first semester we had groups of two, but it was a nightmare, because when one was absent, sometimes the other volunteer would not feel ready to go by himself. We also do not really want one volunteer to conduct home visits alone, so we usually will organize three together in a small group, which gives us a sense of safety, for both the staff and volunteers.

I: *It seems that in this CYEP programme, it is more difficult to have a stable volunteer commitment and what have you done to ease the difficulties?*

S1: Yes, we do. First, we have to go out to the community to deliver our service, instead of delivering our services at the campus, which makes recruitment somewhat difficult. Second, the major part of our service is delivered on Saturday which makes it even more difficult. In our university, many students have to attend on Saturdays for make-up classes, quizzes, and exams etc. To gather a large group of volunteers (we usually have to mobilize 30–80 volunteers each time) to be able to serve, and in different blocks and streets (although in the same district) is very challenging. Third, our volunteers sometimes have to face the fact that they may go in a small group, without any staff on-site, so for volunteers who are shy, they will not opt for this service. Finally, we can only recruit local volunteers which also makes it difficult to recruit. Even though exchange students or students from mainland China are willing to serve, because of language, we have to turn them down. We do have times that we team mainland students to shadow a local student for this service.

To deal with all sorts of difficulties, we really have to rely on teamwork. The VAs helped me a lot to liaise and contact volunteers, and also to conduct the de-briefings in small groups. I do not directly communicate with these elderly, because this is done by volunteers and the VAs. Fortunately, with the assistance of the social workers from the agency, we have some preliminary information on the individual elderly client already, before we start. I work quite closely with the social workers, and when I meet with the volunteers at the community center, the social worker will usually come and join us to talk to the volunteers. We also communicate via frequent phone calls, or by texts.

I: *How do the social workers perceive the contribution from these volunteers?*

S1: They are very openly happy because we provide resources to particular persons in need and we offer them regular volunteers to help out with their work. The reality of the work of the agency is that it is a social center for the elderly in its district, and we are told that they have roughly 1,000 hidden elderly that they have to take care of under their service network. Our work almost covered 10% of their service. The more active elderly will come by themselves to the center on their own, and spend the day in the center. However, we are helping them with the less active group who seldom or never take the initiative to come to the center. So, they have to pay visits to them, and we help them doing part of their work, so structurally it is very helpful. It is very difficult for these few social workers in the elderly center to manage a regular home visit service themselves. But volunteers can visit local elderly at least five to six times each semester. We have also demonstrated that we can offer more continuous follow-up with these elderly under such a service model. Through these home visits, our volunteers do a very basic assessment, and when they identify some issues or problems that should be addressed, we immediately report them to the agency social worker, who will handle it as soon as possible. In additions, we also organize some outing activities, and bring these elderly to visit Disneyland, the Peak, or to City University to enjoy Cantonese operas, tea gatherings, or to eat together, and all these activities are paid by CYEP's programme fee. So I think the agency social workers really welcome this service.

I: *What exactly is the content of the assessment form that CYEP volunteers will fill in after the home visits?*

S1: They will assess the elderly's emotions, their connections with the family and the community, their ability to walk, to communicate, their ability to do household chores like washing, cooking, etc. Holistically, it is really about assessing their ability to take care of themselves, in activities of daily living.

I: *How do you use the reflective logbooks in this programme?*

S1: Firstly, volunteers will write their logbooks and myself and the VAs read them. Based on various noted issues raised, we use them to do our de-briefing. If we find it appropriate, we will also post some information from the Internet or media to the volunteers, to stimulate them to have deeper discussions on their needs and problems. We try to make their learning and discussions proactively interactive. However, if in the logbook we discover something of concern, specifically about the relationship between volunteers and service recipients, then I will call the volunteer, and ask him/her to have a meeting to discuss about the problem. In most cases, I will try to talk directly with them before or after each service, and try to be as open as possible with them. Accountability and transparency is part of CYEP's overall philosophy.

I: *How do you see the volunteers changing from the beginning to the end of this project?*

S1: I monitor such changes to volunteers very closely. Since we have small subgroups, I can talk to each volunteer, and have close relationship with them, and I can directly observe and identify their changes. I also see changes in the way they talk. Initially, they may not be very open, but after some time they are more sharing. I also see changes in the way they perceive of the elderly, and in the way they handle their issues. I keep a close eye on each participant, and I observe their changes. However, the size of the service has already reached its maximum, and it is almost impossible to apply the same model of work to other projects. It is a very labour-intensive service, and I do think we have done a great job for our community, and elderly.

We also come across some very impressive stories from the volunteers. One time there was a group of volunteers who were faced with an elderly person who initially did not want to open the door for the volunteers to enter his apartment. The volunteers tried to respect this, and stayed outside the iron-gate to talk to the person. In such ways, a relationship was finally built, and they became very good friends, later on. There was another time, an elderly person passed away and the volunteers knew that he had expressed that he wanted a funeral after death. This elderly man died during our service and so the volunteers tried their best to negotiate with the agency to organize a funeral for him. The appeal was finally turned down because he had not instructed the agency to do it for him and he had no close relatives who had the "legal right" to organize a funeral for him. It turned out that we had to spend some time comforting the volunteers who were upset, because they could not carry out this man's final wish.

I: *In your opinion, what are the strengths of CYEP?*

S1: Before CYEP, I was a volunteer in 2011 for another elderly project run by another NGO not related to our University. There, I felt a bit lost, because I did not really have an idea of what I was supposed to do, because I received no training or de-briefing from the social worker. I was just asked to follow instructions and do the various trivial piece-meal things. I got a travel allowance and transportation subsidy, but I was sort of feeling that I am not really contributing or making any real change. I am personally a kind of reflective person so I would say, and was always thinking "what am I doing here?" So, I started to look for other opportunities, and I came across CYEPand became a CYEP volunteer first, before becoming a staff after my graduation. I found out that they were providing organized training before the service, and de-briefings after. I felt that there was a very close relationship between the officers and their volunteers. I particularly appreciated this, because it was different than what happened in other services. Also, I think the close coaching here in CYEP is very valuable, and I did not find anything similar to it in other agencies.

Interviews with three student volunteers (V1, V2, V3)

I: *CYEP is a non-credit bearing project. You do not get academic credits as a reward for your participation, but nevertheless you are committed. Why?*

V2: Because I wanted to meet more people outside of my own social circle, and I did not want my university life to simply be about studying. I wanted to know more about other activities and different groups of people and cultures.

V1: When I volunteered back in primary and secondary school, it was because my parents asked me to do so. But in university, I realized that the more I get in touch with a broader range of people, the more I learn from them, the more my thoughts matured. I think CYEP is a great local platform for me to get in touch with different kinds of people and prepare myself for the real world.

I: *Why did you choose the elderly programme to serve in?*

V2: I think there is a great need to serve our local elderly, because their numbers are increasing. And as our own time passes, and our parents grow older, we have the responsibility to take care of them. So, I thought that by joining this service, I could learn some valuable skills that I may need later in life.

V3: I thought that this service did not require particular, and/or unique knowledge or skills, as it is intended to provide basic supports. Further, this service does not require volunteers to be fluent in English, so I decided to join. I saw that there were other programmes for children, but I was worried that I may say something wrong, that may hurt children. Comparing this to other service groups, I now think the elderly are easier to approach and work with. I also saw this opportunity as a way to get to know them better, and try to bond with a group of people of very different ages and life experiences.

I: *What do you do in the service, and how is it structured?*

V1: This service basically consists of visiting and assessing elderly persons in their homes. It is unlike the normal "one-off" service, as it is more of a regular service. Each small group of students focussed on one elderly person, and hopefully can care for that particular elderly, in long term service. We have to be very careful while assessing elderly persons. We have to respect and observe their surroundings, and little by little, try to build a relationship. I think that with the elderly, it is particularly important not to make promises that you cannot keep, because it might have some negative consequences on giving them a sense of false hope.

V2: In total, there are six home visits, once a week for a semester for the same elderly person. I believe this helps build better quality and longer relationships with the elderly. These elderly generally rely on us a lot, because they do not really have other people who could visit them, and they live alone. So we make efforts to offer care and to sincerely talk with them, we ask about their needs, and actively try to make a difference in their life.

V3: Part of the training also includes learning to chat with them, e.g., how to initiate a conversation, and how to ask more about them, without "pushing" too much. After that, we assess their living environments. We also check if they are taking their medication regularly, if they have regular meals, and how they feel, and then we report these data to the agency social worker. I think personally accompanying them is really important also, as for the elderly people I visited, they did not like socializing that much and seldom leave their homes, but they rarely talk to others. They just go shopping in the wet market, stroll through the park and then return to their home, and for the rest of the day, they just watch TV. So they are basically alone, and have no other ways to express their thoughts or feelings. For us, we are there to provide a channel for them to express themselves.

I: *Who are some of the elderly persons you remember more?*

V2: One I visited was blind, and although being blind, he did want to chat with us, and his attitude was pleasant. We would visit him and ask him about his challenges and difficulties he encountered in daily life. Blind elderly are quite different from other elderly, as the latter can meet others much easier to develop relationships. But for this elderly, he did not feel safe leaving his house, so we tried to accompany him to go to the park, which I think was quite a breakthrough. His only friend would go out for tea and to the wet market with him. I think he really needed our care and help.

V1: An elderly couple we visited were very talkative. When we had the larger elderly gathering, the grandpa promised to attend, but the grandma did not. However they have different personalities, and if one does not want to attend an event, it does not mean that s/he is not sociable. I also remember that there was one time when we discussed some deeper emotional topics with a lady. Most people would advise others to be aware of the things you say during these visits, and that you should not mention their family members or other personal things that might upset them. But I saw this differently, since volunteers are here to build long-term bonds with them, and sometimes I think we can try to talk about some deeper topics, sometimes for a stronger relationship. I think that being unhappy is a normal emotion, and sometimes elderly persons might need a chance to express their negative emotions about this issue.

I: *What were your expectations at the beginning and what have you realized while doing the project?*

V2: As I focused more on my academic learning, I used to think that I did not have much knowledge about the elderly. After participating in this service, I realized that these elderly people really needed our care and attention, because they do not really have anyone else to accompany them, and most feel very lonely.

V1: I realized that many elderly people we visited were not the poorest nor most marginalized in our society, because at least they lived in public estates. This made me think that our society does not adequately care enough about local elderly people. I think and believe that current policies should be improved in our community, so that Hong Kong elderly people can live a more decent and fulfilling life.

V3: Before joining this programme, I expected the whole scenario to be really pessimistic and sad, but this was not the case. Although this is indeed a group of people who needed help, they can live a happy and meaningful life too, as long as they receive some support. Moreover, when they are willing to join some larger structured activities like our Happy Carnival and outing activities, they showed us that our volunteers made a real difference in their lives.

I: *What have you learned by doing this project?*

V2: I learned that a simple home visit can have a huge impact in terms of one's social and emotional support. We did not serve every day, but every week when we visited them, we showed compassion and care in non-materialistic ways. Through these visits, we got to know more about their needs in daily living. Through serving, we brought hope to their lives, and also learned from them, through their personal sharing about life. In my opinion, local elderly mostly need social company from others, and we see the impact on them, when this happens.

V1: It took me some time to learn about the problems they are facing and their actual feelings. Initially, I was able to provide them with some practical help, but later, I also started to see some changes in them. For example, they started to try new things, even smart phones. To me, this meant that they were willing to get in touch with the modern age, and connect with younger generations, and I found this is really beautiful. In this way, these elderly people and their younger generations can support each other through these social media channels.

V3: One time, I brought a Chinese chess with me to the service, without even thinking that it would be too difficult for them to learn, or that they would not be interested. This reminded me to think more empathically from another perspective. So, I started listening more and I tried to prepare some activities based on their expressed interests. Joining this program also helped me to ease some pressure from my studying. I still face pressure but after serving others, it makes me think more positively. I feel like when I am helping others, I am helping myself too.

I: *You volunteered in other projects and organizations as well. In your opinion, what is the strength of this project, also in comparison with others?*

V1: I think that CYEP is a great community platform in Hong Kong. I know that other universities also provide volunteering services, but those are credit-bearing or even compulsory courses, which is completely opposite to CYEP. In CYEP, we can really amass a committed group of students who are genuinely interested in volunteering, without any academic benefit in return. This definitely improves the quality of the services we provide overall, and because our volunteers are so motivated, the whole process is easier and more enjoyable. Although our activities may seem simple, they can bring such a major impact to many people. When I saw this level of participation among our volunteers, I now believe that anything is possible. I think the long-term services were particularly important, because over time, you can see gradual changes in these elderly service recipients. This is what we truly aim for, through our volunteering, to guide a person to change in positive ways.

References

Census and Statistics Department (2018). "Population estimates." Retrieved from https://www.censtatd.gov.hk/hkstat/sub/sp150.jsp?tableID=002&ID=0&productType=8.

Central Policy Unit Hong Kong (2008). "A qualitative study on 'Hidden Elderly' in Hong Kong." Retrieved from file:///C:/Users/Diego/Downloads/Qualitatuve%20Study%20on%20Hidden%20Elderly%20in%20HK_20080902_unlocked.pdf.

Chung, L. M. Y. & Chung, J. W. Y. (2013). "Associations of social participation, demographic, socioeconomic and disease factors with nutritional risk in a group of older Hong Kong adults." *Health*, 5(03), 381–387.

Commission on Poverty (2006). "Ad Hoc Group on the Elderly in Poverty Assisting the 'Hidden Elderly'." Retrieved from https://www.povertyrelief.gov.hk/archive/2007/eng/pdf/EP_Paper4_2006eng.pdf.

Johri, M., Beland, F., & Bergman, H. (2003). "International experiments in integrated care for the elderly: a synthesis of the evidence." *International Journal of Geriatric Psychiatry*, 18(3), 222–235.

Lee, V. W., Pang, K. K., Hui, K. C., Kwok, J. C., Leung, S. L., Yu, D. S. F., & Lee, D. T. F. (2013). "Medication adherence: Is it a hidden drug-related problem in hidden elderly?" *Geriatrics & Gerontology International*, 13(4), 978–985.

South China Morning Post (2017) "Hongkongers top life expectancy rankings worldwide for second year in a row." (July 29). Retrieved from https://www.scmp.com/news/hong-kong/health-environment/article/2104584/hongkongers-top-life-expectancy-rankings-worldwide.

PART III

Conclusions

11

CONCLUSION: EMPOWERING YOUTH THROUGH VOLUNTEERISM

Introduction

From conceptual to practice, this book started by reviewing concepts related to volunteerism, its importance to youth development, the experiences of Asia as well as Hong Kong when pursuing and developing youth volunteerism. Following this, CYEP was used as a frontline example on how to create and manage a youth volunteering project as guided by the Reciprocal Volunteer Process Model (RVPM) developed by this book. Five of the volunteer service programs for five different target groups by CYEP were used to demonstrate the practice of the RVPM. In this concluding chapter, some cases of youth who had participated in these programmes will retrospectively look back to their experience and share how and what CYEP has impacted their life and career goals? From these, we draw the conclusion on how young volunteers are empowered through volunteering.

The voices of past volunteers

Our previous chapters have paid attention to the rationales, structures, interactional patterns, and voices of those participating student volunteers for us to understand how the RVPM is actualized in services. We will now shift to how those actualized volunteer processes and experiences impact young volunteers. To this end, we have carried out a qualitative study by asking five volunteers who had participated in CYEP for at least three years, and have graduated and left the project for one to two years ago to write an in-depth reflection in around 500 words. It is hoped that their long commitment to volunteering in CYEP and the length of time since they left the project can provide us with a small sample of volunteers with similar service experiences, and can help us to draw a composite conclusion on the impact of the project on their development after leaving

CYEP. Three open and broad questions were given to the five respondents to guide their reflection but the real purpose of trying to capture how the project has impacted them was not mentioned to them when the invitations were sent out, in order to avoid their reflections being too focused on meeting our goals. Instead, we only mentioned broadly to them that we want to understand from their past experiences in CYEP. The three guiding questions were:

1. How did you engage with CYEP and what have you done?
2. What was most impressive for you in CYEP?
3. What are the linkages of your experiences in CYEP to your life and career development after you graduated and left CYEP?

The data thus collected was analyzed in a qualitative way to enlighten us how the process of volunteering in CYEP has empowered these young people. The general guideline about empowerment for young people as suggested by Payne was used to build a framework to capture the impact of the project in terms of empowerment when analyzing this set of data. Payne (2008, p.144) said:

> Empowerment of young people arises when:
>
> - we believe in and respect their value as human beings who can, individually and collectively, make choices and act upon them. We offer them, on their terms and in way they feel comfortable, opportunities for learning, growth, and development.
> - we encourage them to reflect upon their experiences and beliefs, find their own authentic voice, and hear the voices of others, and
> - we join them in the pursuit of a fairer, more just and more democratic society.

Basing on these three guidelines, and incorporating the uniqueness of this project, the self-reflection from five volunteers would be analyzed by the method of thematic analysis, to conclude how CYEP has empowered young volunteers by the following five themes:

1. Do the respondents feel that they are being believed in and respected as worthy individuals?
2. What did they experience when they were not yet ready to volunteer?
3. Do they have chance to reflect on volunteer experiences and perceive that their voices are being heard?
4. Do they feel they are being included and have chances to form partnership with staff and other experienced volunteers to create new idea on what and how to do more to better serve the society?
5. Are their volunteer experiences and spirits being sustained in their life and career goals?

Below will be the self-reflection of the three respondents. All gave consent for us to show her/his real English name. Original words by the respondents are being kept with very minor edition from the book author, and there is a minimal cut of the length of the original so as to keep the text easy to read.

CASE 1 GODY, FEMALE, A GRADUATE OF BACHELOR OF SOCIAL SCIENCE IN SOCIAL WORK PROGRAM IN 2016

City-Youth Empowerment Project (CYEP) to me is not only a volunteer project, it's a life-transforming journcy. All along this journey, I experienced the gracious moment of human connections, witnessed the magical power of empowerment and have lived up to the truth of social inclusion. Once in CYEP, the blood of CYEP will forever flow inside me.

My journey began with my mysterious curiosity. Back to spring term of 2013, I was a freshman and walked by the I-cafe lounge one day and met a young lady in a blue shirt (CYEP project –shirt) trying to talk to me. She introduced me the background and nature of CYEP and what could be done in CYEP to me passionately. At that moment, I thought CYEP was just one of the recreational social clubs on campus and I didn't take that very seriously. After I listened to her explanations and volunteering stories, they had driven me to become curious on discovering what CYEP can in fact offer me. Looking back now for the past four years, I believe joining CYEP is the best decision in my undergraduate life! I am not questioning anymore what CYEP can offer me now, I began to question what I can offer to CYEP.

I joined my first service at CYEP which was a service that allowed me to work with children and youth with different level of disabilities (Special Education Needs) at the Hong Kong Red Cross Princess Alexandra School. I offered to tutor and mentor services to children and youth with disabilities on regular Thursdays...Despite the busy semester, I was able to work with the children, which had become the most relaxing moment of the week...The gracious and touching memories with this group of children and youth, I thereby decided to choose Social Work as my Major that I wish to make a difference to society. CYEP has further led me to where I belong to now.

Since then, I was actively involved in the services in CYEP. The service targets I have served include children and youth with different level of disabilities (Special Education Needs), elderly services, H.O.P.E Hong Kong (Homeless Outreach and Population Estimation in Hong Kong), and the parent's group locally and I also participated in international service trips, serving orphans and children in Cambodia and Nepal. The more I engaged in services, the more I found the limit of knowledge that I possess, and I am more eager to learn in class. I am satisfied every time with the volunteer process, feeling good with service recipients and the settings, as I observed, all have guided me to think of my own personal values and to reflect on what can I contribute back to our society. Elaine and the officers treasure the potential and talents of volunteers. They always offer tons of freedom and opportunities for us to carry out new elements in the services...As a volunteer, I feel treasured and honored. Their trust and warmth have allowed us to grow, attempt and excel which other service projects couldn't offer. The empowerment process not only takes place within the volunteers and service recipients but also took place within the relationship between volunteers and officers. The person-centered and humanistic way of social services delivery in CYEP has always reminded me to be a social worker with passion, genuineness, and warmth in our life. By doing so, I believe that my life can really influence another life.

What I also gained a lot in CYEP as a volunteer is gaining a perspective in viewing social issues and the way in service delivery. The serving process always brought the social issues and structural things into our concern... We develop a wiser and empathetic view of human suffering. This learning has always reminded me to put on the lens of "critical about the system, avoid blaming the victims" when I am working with my service users...

I am currently working as a school social worker in a kindergarten and the learning of CYEP has enabled me to provide services with a "social" sense. I have implemented an inclusive project that makes me really proud. We invited some elderly people from an elderly center to become mentors to kindergarten students and their parents to do artwork and planting in a small group. The products from the small group will then be sent out to the elderly who are living alone in the neighborhood. The project allows the cross-generations exchanges by emphasizing strengths. We found the elderly are full of life experiences and wisdom, the parents are good at bridging and taking caring of others, while children are energetic and creative. They use their own strengths to contribute and to bring some care and love to the elderly who are alone. By observing and hearing the feedback from them, I see the changes of three parties – the empowerment and recognition of the contribution of the elderly, the confidence of parents and to cultivate the caring character of young children. Through making use of the strengths of different parties, it maximizes the social benefits. Without the experiences in the CYEP, I wouldn't have such strong dedication to social service with a community sense.

I see the power of volunteerism in transforming one's lives and making continuous impacts on the community. My effort in community services may be just a tip of the iceberg in making a change in our society. Yet, I always believe the ripple effects that will move others to join voluntary work. We all could be a "change agent" with a passion and build an inclusive community. It also reminds me that "small acts could make huge differences" which I hope the spirits of volunteerism could pass from one generation to the next. Thank you CYEP, thanks Elaine!

I am and will be on the journey, what about you?

CASE 2 RUBINA, FEMALE, A GRADUATE OF BACHELOR OF SOCIAL SCIENCE (ASIAN AND INTERNATIONAL STUDIES) PROGRAMME IN 2017

My involvement in CYEP dates back to my first year at CityU, when during one of my lectures I met a CYEP Volunteer, who was a student from South Asian background like me, and recommended me to volunteer with the project for the services for Ethnic Minority (EM) youth in Hong Kong. Although I was interested in the service, I didn't have a very good impression of volunteer services to begin with. So in spite of assuring him that I will look into his suggestion, I didn't quite follow up. It was after his repeated reminders that I finally approached the officer in-charge of the services for EM students. However, it wasn't until the international service trip to Nepal that I actually felt a sense of belonging to the project. The trip to Nepal with CYEP was not only a turning point for my attachment to CYEP but also a life-changing experience for me that changed my definition for social service. The experience of working together with other very dedicated volunteers and the sense of ownership of the service we were given by the project officer changed my understanding of the role for volunteers in the society...By the time I came back from Nepal I already knew I want to continue in CYEP as a Volunteer Ambassador for the project.

At CYEP we were always encouraged to have our own opinion about the service and share those opinions with others to further understand the situation of the target group and to maximize the learning outcome from the service through the de-briefing sessions in the service. As a volunteer, I learnt a lot during the debriefing sessions as other volunteers, students from different disciplines and backgrounds, shared their understanding of the service and the target group and their ideas for the betterment of the services. These discussions enhanced my understanding of the social system and enabled me to see the same social phenomenon from several different perspectives. The experiences broadened my vision and facilitated my whole person development. Respectively, when I became a volunteer Ambassador of the project, I had the training and hence the hands-on experience of conducting the debriefing. Although the experience of leading the debriefing was at times stressful, it was also a very significant experience that changed my approach towards my role. Listening to the reflections and ideas of the volunteers, I was convinced of the importance of the independent ideas by the volunteers. I regard it as the root for change in my approach towards my role because through the sense of empowerment and ownership of service I gained from the project officers as the volunteer ambassador, I became more confident and sure of the significance of my role and my ideas.

Therefore, when the project officer discussed the idea of initiating a student-led service with me, I was comfortable and more confident about my ability to initiate such a project. Leading Project Ethnic Minority Empowerment (PEME) started off as a student initiated project, aiming to provide educational and career guidance to the ethnic minority students in the secondary schools of Hong Kong. The project started only a year after I first actively involved in the project, which is a prime example of how CYEP entrusts its volunteers to contribute to the society through their own independent ideas and their efforts. It is also reflective of my learning process with the project.

In a nutshell, I started off with CYEP some four years ago as a poorly committed volunteer with ambiguous and shallow understanding of volunteering but within two years of my involvement in the project, I had gained the experience as a volunteer ambassador of the project and even initiated a student-led project to lead some services with the ethnic minority youth in the city. The service-learning approach of the project, which involves the learning elements like debriefings, reflective discussions, training camps and other opportunities to learn through services have enhanced my personal growth and my ability to think and work independently.

As a student of Asian and International studies, most of the knowledge I gained through the lectures was quite macro level, where I learnt about countries and international organizations. Without a doubt, it is what I enjoy learning and look forward to learning again but it is through my involvement in CYEP that I gained a better understanding of individuals, their thought processes, their motivations and hence the ability to work with people. At CYEP we work with people from different educational fields, social background and people with different personalities. These experiences have helped me to understand others and empathize with them. As mentioned earlier, I was quite a task-oriented person before my involvement in CYEP and my experience helped me to become a well-rounded person with an ability to consider people's motivations and emotions other than just the task. This ability has definitely helped me at both my social and professional life. I am currently a Project Officer in CYEP and my previous experience as a volunteer and volunteer ambassador helps to create a socially positive and friendly atmosphere in my projects.

During my final year at CityU, just like any other student in final year, I was also finding a job that would suit my personality. Thanks to the experience at CYEP, I was much clearer about my preference for a people-oriented career. At my workplace, many tasks and routine job duties that might be difficult for a fresh graduate were made easy because of my prior experience at the project as a volunteer and more importantly because of the sense of ownership and independent working experiences at CYEP.

CASE 3 SCOTT, MALE, A GRADUATE OF BACHELOR OF BUSINESS ADMINISTRATION IN FINANCE IN 2017

As a volunteer in CYEP, the first few months weren't easy for me. Deeming the service as a tutoring service, I tried every effort on acting as a teacher, teaching him on different subjects such as math, Chinese, and English, asking him to finish the homework, and to memorize most of the stuffs taught on the textbooks. However, with the expectation on improving grades, I pushed him hard to study even when he showed the impatience and annoyance, especially when facing his least favorite subject English. The outcome is quite predictable, he was very angry with me and refused to study anymore for the coming few weeks.

Wondering why my efforts would turn me into this situation, I realized that he was just a kid! If I was given so much work and need to study the subject that I hate when I was tired, I would also be mad! Things obviously were different when I chose another strategy – be his friend. Instead of just teaching, I started to step in his position and treated him as my little brother. With games, casual chats, and some jokes, our relationship gradually got better and better. He still hated the subject English, however, with the deal which we mutually agreed beforehand, he was willing to study that few pages or memorize the vocabularies. Day by day, he unexpectedly became my Cantonese (local Hong Kong dialect) teacher, and we started to chat in Cantonese eventually.

The next summer, the service trip to Cambodia totally taught me a new lesson about life. I was working with several fellow volunteers in the physiotherapy room in an orphanage where most of the kids are with moderate to severe disabilities. My daily duty was to help the kids with messages and some rehabilitation works, also eating and cleaning. Without any previous experience, I felt quite shocked about children's health condition, the sordid environment with countless flies and lack of manpower.

"Incapable" was the only word that can describe my first week there. Apart from feeling uncomfortable when changing the diaper, what disappointed me was not able to understanding what the kids are thinking. A kid once held my hand to the swing and what she only did was looking at me. Not knowing what she wanted me to do, I tried grimacing, singing, telling stories and other methods, but a sense of loss appeared on her face and I knew that I failed. Just at the moment I was about to give up, I played the swing so hard so we both were flying, and she, unexpectedly, burst out with laughter. All she wanted to do was playing on the swing, to enjoy the warmth of the wind.

"Observation" was one of the biggest rewards I gained from the trip. From the expressions, gestures, and what she has done, there must be some traces of the feeling, and all I just need to observe and put myself in her shoes.

Another lesson I learned was to admit my own incapability. I still feel sad when seeing something that I really could not help much. But only when knowing my own weakness, I could know better about myself, knowing how I could adjust my attitude and learn to be better, and what I'm good at.

In 2015 I had my exchange study in Mexico. Not like most of the exchange students who used most of the time traveling, I instead joined the choir and helped in three different services. MiniCamp was a service with Down syndrome children held on every weekend. Alexis. A seven-year-old boy was assigned to be my partner. He was a very active, sometimes restless kid who never got tired...Facing difficulties, and after consulting with friends and making self-reflection, I realized that I had forgotten to "observe" again.

Everyone is different, and I should not treat everyone as the same kid. I have to learn again…I deepened my understanding towards Alexis – we became great friends. Till now I would still skype with Alexis sometimes.

Besides previous few experience, innumerable amazing stories have happened since becoming a volunteer. I was the volunteer ambassador for two years in CYEP, helping with debriefing, organizing services, and connecting volunteers. Dancing is my hobby, therefore I also made use of my skill by posting dancing videos on internet to spread the positivity and happiness for raising US$2,000 to help sick kids in China. After graduation, I served my military service as an English teacher in a primary school in a rural village in Taiwan. I am going to create my new project of helping children with their learning in the future by…

As a fresh graduate who is currently looking for the first job, I know that many others would have a better-looking resume with time spent on different interns and jobs. But I don't regret spending the time on doing services. After all, it's the service-learning experience shaped my personality…I truly believe that with learning and growing from serving the society, we can flip the society of "ME," to a society of "WE."

CASE 4 BEN, MALE, A GRADUATE OF ASSOCIATE DEGREE OF SCIENCE, INFORMATION SYSTEMS DEVELOPMENT IN 2015

I joined several services in CYEP, including elderly, parents, children, homeless, and ex-prisoners. I like making contacts with different groups of people. However, when I first became a volunteer, I also realized that I could become fearful of meeting some people. So, I chose volunteering for the elderly when I started, because I feel quite at ease meeting them. After my first several visits to them, I had built a good relationship with them, and was being treated as their friend when they were willing to share with us. Most of those I have visited are single, and maybe because of this reason, they all were very eager to meet us and were expecting us. To most of them, our visits may mean a lot to them and we might be their only friends. In my role as a volunteer, after knowing them better, I have thought of visiting them more often on my own and be helpful in more aspects to them. However, it is our common understanding that we should draw a line between a volunteer and a friend. Besides constantly visiting them, we should not make the elderly "relying" on us as friends. We have to prepare if we cannot offer help to them anymore one day, they might feel hurt that we are abandoning them. This is a dilemma for a volunteer and I did not have a solution for it! I just hope that other community resources are out there to make their life better, including if they do have family support for them for their elderly stage, these elderly people might have less problems. This is just my ideal solution for them!

I then started to have interest to serve a group of parents. Most of them are parents of newly arrived families. Most people will think this is a group of people who are in urgent need of money and other materialistic help. However, after knowing them, they are a group of people who are being pressurized to adapt to a new environment and are facing many sources of social discrimination and exclusion. When we, a group of university students, took the initiation to play and interact with them, they feel that the community is accepting them, and it might carry of meaning which is more important than money. We tried to discuss many issues about parenting experiences from many different angles, and to create chances for them to share and ventilate. Before this, I myself did not really realize that there are so many angles to understand parenting! I benefit a lot when I am serving parents, and on equal position, both volunteers and service recipients are better prepared for our families!

Conclusively, during my entire four years in CYEP, I learn many things I could not find from books, and feel that I truly live in this community! I am not solving all social problems, but I gain the confidence to share with friends about what is happening in the community, and wishing to bring bigger impacts to others. CYEP is created uniquely for young people and I think this is a good focus, because young people have better idea on how to share feelings and be impactful to others! We therefore are not just serving, we are also spreading our beliefs. By doing so, we are giving ourselves power and we are empowering others.

Both as a volunteer and service learning project, CYEP has given us many chances to use our strength and interest in services. In this process, I have many chances to use my interest in music to serve others. When I was in Cambodia, I had created and made some musical instruments to facilitate our services for children. Though the impact at that time was not really outstanding, this paved my road that upon my graduation, I have been doing all kind of music related work for promotion of expressive arts to people. I have also taken some courses in music and expressive arts to better prepare myself. It is my hope through music and expressive art I can help people to achieve a better and healthier life!

CASE 5 RACHEL, FEMALE, A GRADUATE OF BACHELOR OF BUSINESS ADMINISTRATION IN ACCOUNTANCY IN 2017

In September, 2013, a freshman just entered the campus of City University of Hong Kong and was puzzling what to do to get adapted to the new environment...she walked through the purple zone area and was attracted by an exhibition on volunteer work and was approached by a staff from CYEP. Just a few minutes of listening to the staff's introduction, I found what I want to do.

This freshman was myself, Rachel, I was on the way to become a volunteer right from my first year, and a Volunteer Ambassador for my next three years, focusing on promoting and serving children and youth in CYEP. This became my main focus of my entire four years of study in my university education. During my entire study, for several junctions, I was lost and confused for many times. It was my work in the Princess Alexander School which has inspired me to be positive and keep going ahead! It is a residential school for the mentally and physically disabled children and youth. The residents are challenged with tons of life and survival issues, however, their attitude to life was my source of courage that I anchor my dream for life! I went with two groups of these residents to Macau firstly and then Taiwan for a study tour for barrier-free transportation for the disabled; their energy and potential to prepare and to participate in these two programmes were just astonishing to us! There is a quote that "Individually we are one drop. Together we are an ocean!" I see the power of interdependence from this quote...CYEP is seen as just serving the community by different methods, behind it is a platform to promote solidarity, to create, and to share social resources. When people interact, we give out energy, we influence one another and we grow together! This belief of CYEP has become my soulmate, reminding me that life is influencing life!

What I have done in these years is helping myself by helping others, helping others by helping myself! Sincerity is the core value guiding me. When one is standing and another one is sitting, there are always different angles for seeing the world. Only by both individuals being on the same ground can empathy be achieved... CYEP is for service learning. Both service and learning have to be on equal ground. When I serve, learn, and reflect on the relationship between service and learning, I learn deeper!

In the future, I do not just want to promote CYEP model of service learning, I also want to pass my experience and influence to others, hoping more people are willing to do what they truly believe in. I am lucky to have joined CYEP and share common values with my team mates...each of us is unique and powerful, let us all work together to influence more people!

Analysis

Do the respondents feel that they are being believed and respected as worthy individuals?

Most respondents feel quite strong about the person-centered approach and respectful culture in the project. Below are the most representative statements on this kind of experience:

> "*They always offer tons of freedom and opportunities for us to carry out new elements in the services...As a volunteer, I feel treasured and honored. Their trust and warmth have allowed us to grow, attempt and excel which other service projects couldn't offer. The*

empowerment process not only takes place within the volunteers and service recipients but also took place within the relationship between volunteers and officers." (Gody)

"At CYEP we were always encouraged to have our own opinion about the service and share those opinions with others to further understand the situation of the target group and to maximize the learning outcome from the service through the de-briefing sessions in the service." (Rubina)

"Both as a volunteer and service learning project, CYEP has given us many chances to use our strength and interest in services." (Ben)

"When people interact, we give out energy, we influence one another and we grow together! This belief of CYEP has become my soulmate, reminding me that life is influencing life!" (Rachel)

What did they experience when they were not yet ready to volunteer?

Two respondents mentioned the time when they were not yet ready for volunteering. Both of them felt that they being approached and coached in a very caring way, instead of being pressurized to join. Though others do not really share about how they are being coached when they were not ready, Rachel mentioned about how she was being approached by a member of staff who had explained and introduced CYEP to her and from there she was impressed and made a decision to join. Here are the most representative statements on their experiences:

"She introduced me the background and nature of CYEP and what could be done in CYEP to me passionately. At that moment, I thought CYEP was just one of the recreational social clubs on campus and I didn't take that very seriously. After listened to her explanations and volunteering stories, it has driven me to become curious on discovering what CYEP can in fact offer me." (Gody)

"It was after his repeated reminders that I finally approached the officer in-charge of the services for EM students. However, it wasn't until the international service trip to Nepal that I actually felt a sense of belonging to the project. The trip to Nepal with CYEP was not only a turning point for my attachment to CYEP but also a life-changing experience for me that changed my definition for social service." (Rubina)

Do they have chances to reflect on volunteer experiences and perceive that their voices are being heard?

All respondents are seemingly very pleased with the CYEP coaching model of training and debriefing, and the involvement in the discussion for a structural cause of the social problem, instead of just delivering services without learning. Here are the most representative statements:

"The more I engaged in services, the more I found the limit of knowledge that I possess, and I am more eager to learn in class. I am satisfied every time with the volunteer process, feeling

good with service recipients and the settings, as I observed, all have guided me to think of my own personal values and to reflect on what can I contribute back to our society." (Gody)

"As a volunteer, I learnt a lot during the debriefing sessions as other volunteers, students from different disciplines and backgrounds, shared their understanding of the service and the target group and their ideas for the betterment of the services. These discussions enhanced my understanding of the social system and enabled me to see the same social phenomenon from several different perspectives." (Rubina)

"Besides previous few experience, innumerable amazing stories have happened since becoming a volunteer. I was the volunteer ambassador for two years in CYEP, helping with debriefing, organizing services and connecting volunteers." (Scott)

"However, it is our common understanding that we should draw a line between a volunteer and a friend…This is a dilemma for a volunteer and I did not have a solution for it! This is just my ideal solution for them!" (Ben)

"I see the power of interdependence from this quote…CYEP is seen as just serving the community by different methods, behind it is a platform to promote solidarity, to create, and to share social resources. When people interact, we give out energy, we influence one another and we grow together! This belief of CYEP has become my soulmate, reminding me that life is influencing life!" (Rachel)

Do they feel they are being included and have chances to form partnerships with staff and other experienced volunteers to create new idea on what and how to do more to better serve the society?

A strong sense of partnership with staff and other volunteers could be found in the reflections by the past volunteers. It seems learning rather than just serving is essential for this group of volunteers. Learning has enabled them to see the macro picture of the social problem, and by that, they are found to be even more eager to contribute. Here are the most representative statements:

"What I also gained a lot in CYEP as a volunteer are a perspective in viewing social issues and the way in service delivery. The serving process always brought the social issues and structural things into our concern… We develop a wiser and empathetic view of human suffering. This learning has always reminded me to put on the lens of 'critical about the system, avoid blaming the victims" when I am working with my service users…'" (Gody)

"The project started only a year after I first actively involved in the project, which is a prime example of how CYEP entrusts its volunteers to contribute to the society through their own independent ideas and their efforts." (Rubina)

"Dancing is my hobby, therefore I also made use of my skill by posting dancing videos on internet to spread the positivity and happiness for raising US$2000 to help sick kids in China. After graduation, I served my military service as an English in a primary school in a rural village in Taiwan. I am going to create my new project of helping children with their learning in the future by…" (Scott)

"Conclusively, during my entire four years in CYEP, I learn many things I could not find from books, and feel that I truly live in this community! I am not solving all social problems, but I gain the confidence to share with friends about what is happening in the community, and wishing to bring bigger impacts to others. CYEP is created uniquely for young people and I think this is a good focus, because young people have better idea on how to share feelings and be impactful to others! We therefore are not just serving, we are also spreading our beliefs. By doing so, we are giving ourselves power and we are empowering others." (Ben)

"I went with two groups of these residents to Macau firstly and then Taiwan for a study tour for barrier-free transportation for the disabled; their energy and potential to prepare and to participate in these two programs were just astonishing to us!" (Rachel)

Are their volunteer experience and spirit sustaining to their life and career goals?

In different ways, all of them are continuing with the spirit of volunteerism in CYEP to either their life or career goals. Gody is implementing a volunteer project in her role as a School Social Worker, making use of a group of elderly people to mentor a group of parents and their young children. Rubina is pursuing a people-oriented career. Scott is planning to do more children's learning and has his goal for a better inclusive society. Ben has decided to use music and arts to help people. Rachel will continue to spread humanistic values to others. Here are the most representative statements:

"I am currently working as a school social worker in a kindergarten and the learning of CYEP enables me to provide services with 'social' sense. One project that makes me really proud is... We invited some elderly to be our mentors and teach the kindergarten students and parents some artwork and plants. They will send out the products to the elderly who are living alone in the neighborhood. The project allows the cross-generations exchanges, for instance, the elderly have full of life experiences and wisdom, the parents are good at bridging and taking caring of different parties as well as the energy and creativity from the young children." (Gody)

"Thanks to the experience at CYEP, I was much clearer about my preference for a people-oriented career. At my workplace, many tasks and routine job duties that might be difficult for a fresh graduate were made easy because of my prior experience at the project as a volunteer and more importantly because of the sense of ownership and independent working experiences at CYEP." (Rubina)

"After all, it's the service-learning experience shaped my personality...I truly believe that with learning and growing from serving the society, we can flip the society of 'ME,' to a society of 'WE.'" (Scott)

"...this paved my road that upon my graduation, I have been doing all kind of music related work for promotion of expressive arts to people. I have also taken some courses in music and expressive arts to better prepare myself. It is my hope through music and expressive art, I can help people to achieve a better and healthier life!" (Ben)

> *"I do not just want to promote CYEP model of service learning, I also want to pass my experience and influence others, hoping more people are willing to do what they really believe in. I am lucky to have joined CYEP and share common values with my team mates...each of us is unique and powerful, let us all work together to influence more lives!" (Rachel)*

Though this qualitative research has adopted a case study method and its sampling method is also limiting its ability to generalize its result, however, these first-hand data collected from real life experiences have informed us that there is a unique and positive linkage between youth volunteering and youth empowerment. More studies in the future should be devoted to further confirm the model empirically.

Implications of the analysis on youth volunteerism and youth empowerment

As noted in the concluding remarks in Chapter One, there are three important processes for volunteerism: the individual process, the organizational process, and the community process, and they mutually interact in a chemical way to unveil the succeeding mysterious social phenomenon of volunteerism. With CYEP as a life example and from what we have revealed, volunteers are truly the keys for making CYEP a successful case. However, when CYEP was implemented, young people in our institution were found to be loosely organized for serving the community. It is hard to imagine if they were on their own, if they would be able to achieve what they have now by joining CYEP, as confirmed by the above qualitative data? At this junction, we are inspired to think of what are the characteristics of young people in their endeavor to volunteer? Young people might appear to be confident, yet they need someone to coach them to be fully and truly confident to become and to remain volunteer. They may appear rebellious, but deep inside, from how young people reflect, they aspire to be connected to the community and are committed to building the community. They are highly sensitive to others' rejection and criticism when becoming a volunteer and when volunteering, and could easily give up in those situations. What they need is someone who could understand and accept their "weaknesses" and to believe in their "strength", and who are also willing to spend more time with them and walk with them in this journey. In volunteering, a lone young person may succeed in this adventurous process and become a successful volunteer, but many are being ruled out because of a small fault in such a complicated chemical process. So, when many volunteer projects are puzzling how to recruit and sustain volunteers, we have to understand that young volunteers are also frustrated by where to go and what to do. I argue here that a good volunteer project with a dual balanced focus on both the welfare of the service recipients, as well as the empowering goal for the involving young people should be our solution! Volunteering is said to be one of the most effective processes in nurturing pro-social behavior among young people, however, the process is not yet being used in a successful manner for more and most youth. It still remains a mysterious social phenomenon that some youth can benefit from it, and some could not. The "could not" group is often being judged for not being as motivated and capable as the "could" group, which is purely a judgmental statement in most cases. On the contrary, as evidenced by this book, young people are very forward oriented towards a goal of community building. Aligning with this conclusion, I want to supplement this qualitative finding with another concluding remark on youth volunteering in a recently submitted report by the author of this book to the PICO (Policy Innovation Co-ordination Office) of Hong Kong SAR Government on "Demographic and Social Indicators of Youth Volunteering in Hong Kong" (Liu, 2018), in which over 1,300 young volunteers were interviewed to empirically evidence on different issues about young people's motivation, values, involvement, sustainment, etc., in terms of volunteering. In this report, the concluding remark has drawn on the section for various motivational issues of youth volunteers in Hong Kong [as one example of the various findings] said:

> It is very important to underline that youth engage longer in volunteering when they feel that they can improve on a personal level, and when they believe in what they do. Youth do not join volunteering because it looks good on their CV (a purely self-centered reason), or because they have nothing to do, or for "spirit of sacrifice". Quite on the contrary, youth who volunteered longer did so because they found the volunteer experience valuable for them, because they felt empowered and recognized. Unfortunately, as reflected by respondents, many agencies fail to recognize this and treat volunteers just as cheap labor, expecting youth to simply follow the rules and be content with some meaningless occupation. As emerged in this research, youth expect much more. They expect to be given some guidance (training and supervision), they expect to be involved in some meaningful activities and to grow as individuals. At these conditions, we generated an insight from both the quantitative data and qualitative interaction with youths in the process of research that youths are in fact willing to commit for longer time and give their best to the community.
>
> *(Liu, 2018)*

Synthesizing on a humanistic-empowerment model for youth volunteering

From creation to implementation, CYEP has gone through many processes and stages of development, and has input many concepts to sustain its goal and direction, as shown in different chapters. Basing on the above discussion, a synthesized "Humanistic-Empowerment Model" has been developed to guide future youth volunteering work. The core value of this model is that youth volunteering implementation work should be guided by the Humanistic view on young people. We should see each of our young people as worthy of receiving an enriching transformational journey in their developmental and learning experience. They should also be respected for their individuality and uniqueness, and be accepted for

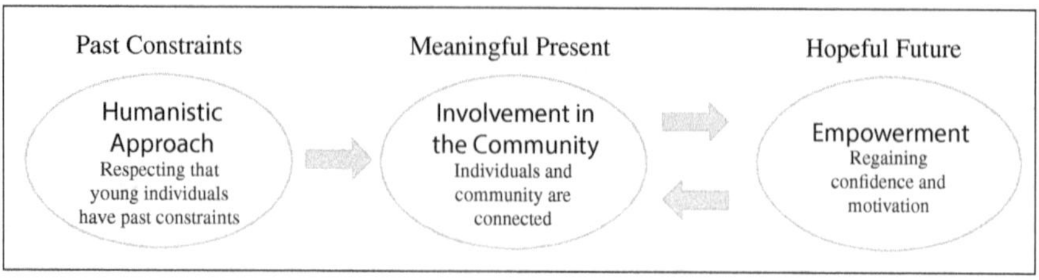

FIGURE 11.1 Humanistic-empowerment model

having constraints connected to their past developmental experiences. It should also be understood that environmental forces such as a fast-growing economy and technological advances influence their upbringing. In contrast, our brief encounters with young people in any youth work context including volunteering work are easily found to be impersonal and structural. It challenges us with what can be done additionally for young people. We advocate that policy-makers and agencies for youth developmental work should openly recognize that volunteering is a meaningful process by interconnecting young people with others within the community, and the community should strive to create opportunities for them to take action in the community through helping, serving, and involving them in social causes they feel strongly about, thus facilitating a process of transformation of their past constraints into present strength. The resulting emerging sense of empowerment will then lead to a positively rewarding reinforcement cycle, which provides young people with a sense of motivation and confidence to involve themselves more and better in the community.

Reference

Liu, E. S. C. (2018). "Completed report on Demographic and Social Indicators of Youth Volunteering in Hong Kong." A research project (Project Number: 2017.A1.058.17C) funded by the Public Policy Research Funding Scheme from the Policy Innovation and Co-ordination Office (PICO) of The Government of the Hong Kong Special Administrative Region, 2017–2018. Unpublished report.

INDEX

Page numbers in italics refer to figures.

For Product Safety Concerns and Information please contact our EU representative GPSR@taylorandfrancis.com
Taylor & Francis Verlag GmbH, Kaufingerstraße 24, 80331 München, Germany

www.ingramcontent.com/pod-product-compliance
Lightning Source LLC
Chambersburg PA
CBHW050447051126
54379CB00004B/129
9781138106437